VOLUME 564

JULY 1999

THE ANNALS

of The American Academy *of* Political
and Social Science

ALAN W. HESTON, *Editor*
NEIL A. WEINER, *Assistant Editor*

WILL THE JUVENILE COURT SYSTEM SURVIVE?

Special Editor of this Volume

IRA M. SCHWARTZ
*University of Pennsylvania
Philadelphia*

 SAGE Periodicals Press *THOUSAND OAKS LONDON NEW DELHI*

Origin and Purpose. The Academy was organized December 14, 1889, to promote the progress of political and social science, especially through publications and meetings. The Academy does not take sides in controverted questions, but seeks to gather and present reliable information to assist the public in forming an intelligent and accurate judgment.

Meetings. The Academy occasionally holds a meeting in the spring extending over two days.

Publications. THE ANNALS of the American Academy of Political and Social Science is the bimonthly publication of The Academy. Each issue contains articles on some prominent social or political problem, written at the invitation of the editors. Also, monographs are published from time to time, numbers of which are distributed to pertinent professional organizations. These volumes constitute important reference works on the topics with which they deal, and they are extensively cited by authorities throughout the United States and abroad. The papers presented at the meetings of The Academy are included in THE ANNALS.

Membership. Each member of The Academy receives THE ANNALS and may attend the meetings of The Academy. Membership is open only to individuals. Annual dues: $59.00 for the regular paperbound edition (clothbound, $86.00). Add $12.00 per year for membership outside the U.S.A. Members may also purchase single issues of THE ANNALS for $12.00 each (clothbound, $16.00). Add $2.00 for shipping and handling on all pre-paid orders.

Subscriptions. THE ANNALS of the American Academy of Political and Social Science (ISSN 0002-7162) is published six times annually—in January, March, May, July, September, and November. Institutions may subscribe to THE ANNALS at the annual rate: $281.00 (clothbound, $332.00). Add $12.00 per year for subscriptions outside the U.S.A. Institutional rates for single issues: $49.00 each (clothbound, $57.00).

Periodicals postage paid at Thousand Oaks, California, and additional offices.

Single issues of THE ANNALS may be obtained by individuals who are not members of The Academy for $19.00 each (clothbound, $29.00). Add $2.00 for shipping and handling on all pre-paid orders. Single issues of THE ANNALS have proven to be excellent supplementary texts for classroom use. Direct inquiries regarding adoptions to THE ANNALS c/o Sage Publications (address below).

All correspondence concerning membership in The Academy, dues renewals, inquiries about membership status, and/or purchase of single issues of THE ANNALS should be sent to THE ANNALS c/o Sage Publications, Inc., 2455 Teller Road, Thousand Oaks, CA 91320. Telephone: (805) 499-0721; FAX/Order line: (805) 499-0871. *Please note that orders under $30 must be prepaid.* Sage affiliates in London and India will assist institutional subscribers abroad with regard to orders, claims, and inquiries for both subscriptions and single issues.

Printed on recycled, acid-free paper

THE ANNALS

© 1999 *by* The American Academy *of* Political *and* Social Science

Editorial Office: 3937 Chestnut Street, Philadelphia, PA 19104.

For information about membership* (individuals only) and subscriptions (institutions), address:

SAGE PUBLICATIONS, INC.
2455 Teller Road
Thousand Oaks, CA 91320

From India and South Asia,	*From the UK, Europe, the Middle*
write to:	*East and Africa, write to:*
SAGE PUBLICATIONS INDIA Pvt. Ltd	SAGE PUBLICATIONS LTD
P.O. Box 4215	6 Bonhill Street
New Delhi 110 048	London EC2A 4PU
INDIA	UNITED KINGDOM

SAGE Production Staff: ERIC LAW, LISA CUEVAS, DORIS HUS, and ROSE TYLAK
*Please note that members of The Academy receive THE ANNALS with their membership.
International Standard Serial Number ISSN 0002-7162
International Standard Book Number ISBN 0-7619-2030-7 (Vol. 564, 1999 paper)
International Standard Book Number ISBN 0-7619-2031-5 (Vol. 564, 1999 cloth)
Manufactured in the United States of America. First printing, July 1999.

The articles appearing in THE ANNALS are indexed in *Academic Index, Book Review Index, Combined Retrospective Index Sets, Current Contents, General Periodicals Index, Public Affairs Information Service Bulletin, Pro-Views,* and *Social Sciences Index.* They are also abstracted and indexed in *ABC Pol Sci, America: History and Life, Automatic Subject Citation Alert, Book Review Digest, Family Resources Database, Higher Education Abstracts, Historical Abstracts, Human Resources Abstracts, International Political Science Abstracts, Journal of Economic Literature, Managing Abstracts, Periodica Islamica, Sage Urban Studies Abstracts, Social Planning / Policy & Development Abstracts, Social Sciences Citation Index, Social Work Research & Abstracts, Sociological Abstracts, United States Political Science Documents,* and/or *Work Related Abstracts, Westlaw,* and are available on microfilm from University Microfilms, Ann Arbor, Michigan.

Information about membership rates, institutional subscriptions, and back issue prices may be found on the facing page.

Advertising. Current rates and specifications may be obtained by writing to THE ANNALS Advertising and Promotion Manager at the Thousand Oaks office (address above).

Claims. Claims for undelivered copies must be made no later than twelve months following month of publication. The publisher will supply missing copies when losses have been sustained in transit and when the reserve stock will permit.

Change of Address. Six weeks' advance notice must be given when notifying of change of address to ensure proper identification. Please specify name of journal. **POSTMASTER:** Send address changes to: THE ANNALS of the American Academy of Political and Social Science, c/o Sage Publications, Inc., 2455 Teller Road, Thousand Oaks, CA 91320.

THE ANNALS

of The American Academy *of* Political *and* Social Science

ALAN W. HESTON, *Editor*
NEIL A. WEINER, *Assistant Editor*

———————— FORTHCOMING ————————

CIVIL SOCIETY AND DEMOCRATIZATION
Special Editors: Isidro Morales,
Guillermo De Los Reyes, and Paul Rich
Volume 565   September 1999

NETWORKS OF NOVELTY: THE SOCIAL
DIFFUSION OF IDEAS AND THINGS
Special Editors: Mary Durfee and Paul Lopes
Volume 566   November 1999

SCHOOL VIOLENCE
Special Editors: William G. Hinkle and Stuart Henry
Volume 567   January 2000

See page 2 for information on Academy membership and
purchase of single volumes of **The Annals.**

CONTENTS

BOOK DEPARTMENT CONTENTS

INTERNATIONAL RELATIONS AND POLITICS

AFRICA, ASIA, AND LATIN AMERICA

EUROPE

UNITED STATES

SOCIOLOGY

ECONOMICS

PREFACE

The juvenile court marks its hundredth anniversary this year. At the time of its creation, the juvenile court was heralded as one of the greatest advancements in the cause for children. While few will argue with the fact that the juvenile court has been a constructive force in promoting the welfare of children, the court has also been the subject of ongoing and increasingly severe criticism. The problems and abuses that plagued the juvenile court eventually reached the United States Supreme Court, whose decisions transformed the juvenile court from a social welfare institution into a court of law for young people. Now the juvenile court is faced with legislative policy changes resulting in a loss of jurisdiction over serious, chronic, and, in particular, violent delinquent acts. Also, the juvenile court's centennial arrives at a time when the voices calling for its abolition are growing louder and gaining support.

The articles in this volume had their roots in a symposium on the future of the juvenile court that was held at the University of Pennsylvania on 29-30 May 1997. The meeting was cosponsored by the university's School of Social Work and Law School. The participants were carefully selected and consisted of some of the country's leading juvenile justice policymakers, practitioners, researchers, and child advocates. The articles were written in the hopes of providing thoughtful and rational policy guidance to the heated and too often irrational debates taking place about the future of the juvenile court and related justice system for children.

The overall chairman of the symposium was the late Dr. Marvin Wolfgang, one of the world's leading criminologists and the person to whom this volume is dedicated.

Much has already been written about the future of the juvenile court. However, what has been written is largely limited to the role of the juvenile court in delinquency matters. The articles in this volume address this subject, but they go far beyond this one, albeit important, issue. The articles about the juvenile court's role in delinquency were written from theoretical and applied perspectives, with some authors offering different or opposing points of view. Two of the articles explore the role of the juvenile court in dependency, neglect, and related child maltreatment areas. One article includes a discussion about the role of the juvenile court in children's mental health. One of the authors examines the future of youth corrections, a critically important area interconnected with the juvenile court but often left out when considering the future of the court. Another article addresses the issues and concerns of young women who come into contact with the juvenile justice system, another area often overlooked in these debates.

Another important feature of this volume is that the authors are both highly respected academics and prominent practitioners. This blend of

8

perspectives and experience will, it is hoped, make the contents appealing to a broad audience.

This volume is dedicated to the memory of Marvin E. Wolfgang, preeminent criminologist, president of the American Academy of Political and Social Science, and dear colleague and friend. Throughout his long career, Dr. Wolfgang underscored in one or another way that the boy is the father to the man. It was this fundamental and driving principle that led Dr. Wolfgang to focus his formidable intellect on personal, social, and collateral developmental trajectories and transitions during the juvenile years and their relationship to delinquency and crime over the entire life course. This volume of *The Annals* advances Dr. Wolfgang's deep concerns in this regard one step further. It focuses attention on the many, complex, and often perplexing ways that the towering institution of the juvenile court can intervene, constructively or otherwise, in the developmental pathways of the youths who stand before or, as some might think, are enmeshed in it. Dr. Wolfgang fervently believed that the juvenile court had been placed, at its inception, on the right track in treating, supervising, and rehabilitating its young charges. While he rarely professed when it came to the public policy implications of his work, those of us who knew him understood that he embraced the reformative rather than punitive mission charged to the juvenile court. Youths could develop and change. They could reform. Those now working to reshape this historical mission, toward giving the juvenile court a coarser if not harsher adult bent, would almost certainly be challenged by Dr. Wolfgang to solidly justify this redirection. His challenge is ours. Much as Dr. Wolfgang focused on the trajectories and transitions in lives during their earliest and most vulnerable years, we focus on the past and potential future trajectories and transitions of the juvenile court and its relationship to those youngsters who come to know it.

IRA M. SCHWARTZ

ANNALS, *AAPSS*, **564**, July 1999

The Honest Politician's Guide to Juvenile Justice in the Twenty-First Century

By BARRY C. FELD

ABSTRACT: Within the past three decades, judicial decisions and legal changes have transformed the juvenile court from a nominally rehabilitative social welfare agency into a scaled-down, second-class criminal court that provides young offenders with neither therapy nor justice. The migration of African Americans from the rural South to the urban North that began three-quarters of a century ago, the macrostructural transformation of American cities and the economy over the past quarter of a century, and the current linkages in the popular and political culture between race and serious youth crime provide the impetus for get-tough policies to crack down on juveniles. The procedural and substantive convergence between juvenile and criminal courts has occurred because juvenile courts attempt to combine social welfare and criminal social control in one agency. If states uncouple social welfare from social control, then they can try all offenders in one integrated criminal justice system. But states must formally recognize youthfulness as a mitigating factor at sentencing. A youth discount—shorter sentences for reduced culpability— provides a practical administrative mechanism to recognize youthfulness as a mitigating factor.

Barry C. Feld is Centennial Professor of Law at the University of Minnesota Law School. He has written six books, most recently Bad Kids: Race and the Transformation of the Juvenile Court *(1999), and more than three dozen law review and criminology articles on various aspects of juvenile justice administration.*

THE public and politicians perceive a significant and frightening increase in youth crime and violence. Concerns about the inability of juvenile courts to rehabilitate chronic and violent young offenders while simultaneously protecting public safety accompany the growing fear of youth crime. Sensational media depictions of young criminals as a different breed of super-predators further heighten public anxiety. A desire to get tough, fueled in part by frustration with the intractability of crime, provides political impetus to crack down and transfer some young offenders to criminal courts for prosecution as adults and to strengthen the sanctioning powers of juvenile courts for the remaining delinquents.

Within the past three decades, judicial decisions, legislative amendments, and administrative changes have transformed the juvenile court from a nominally rehabilitative social welfare agency into a scaled-down, second-class criminal court for young offenders that provides them with neither therapy nor justice (Feld 1993a, 1997). This transformation occurred because of the migration of African Americans from the rural South to the urban North that began three-quarters of a century ago, the macrostructural transformation of American cities and the economy over the past quarter of a century, and the current linkages in the popular and political culture between race and serious youth crime (Feld 1998). Two competing cultural and legal conceptions of young people have facilitated the transformation. On the one hand,

legal culture views young people as innocent, vulnerable, fragile, and dependent children whom their parents and the state should protect and nurture. On the other hand, the legal culture perceives young people as vigorous, autonomous, and responsible almost adultlike people from whose criminal behavior the public needs protection.

The ambivalent and conflicted jurisprudence of youth enables policymakers selectively to manipulate the competing social constructs of innocence and responsibility to maximize the social control of young people. Over the past three decades, juvenile justice legal reforms have engaged in a process of criminological triage. At the soft end of juvenile courts' jurisdiction, reforms have shifted noncriminal status offenders out of the juvenile justice system into a hidden system of social control in the private sector mental health and chemical dependency industries. At the hard end of juvenile courts' jurisdiction, states transfer increasing numbers of youths into the criminal justice system for prosecution as adults. Juvenile court sentencing policies and practices escalate the punishments imposed on those delinquents who remain in an increasingly criminalized juvenile justice system.

In this article, I briefly describe the transformation of the juvenile court from a social welfare agency into a deficient criminal court. Second, I argue that juvenile courts' underlying idea is fundamentally flawed because in it the courts attempt to combine social welfare and penal social control in one agency. Because welfare and control functions embody inherent and irreconcilable contradictions, juvenile courts inevitably do both badly. If a state separates social welfare goals from criminal social control functions, then no need remains for a separate juvenile court. Rather, a state could try all offenders in one integrated criminal justice system. But children do not possess the same degree of criminal responsibility as adults. Adolescent developmental psychology, criminal law jurisprudence, and sentencing policy provide a rationale to formally recognize youthfulness as a mitigating factor when judges sentence younger offenders. A "youth discount" provides a sliding scale of criminal responsibility for younger offenders who have not quite learned to be responsible or developed fully their capacity for self-control. Combining enhanced procedural safeguards with formal mitigation of sentences provides youths with greater protections and justice than they currently receive in either the juvenile or criminal justice systems.

THE JUVENILE COURT

The juvenile court is the by-product of changes in two cultural ideas that accompanied modernization and industrialization a century ago: childhood and social control. Social structural changes associated with the shift from an agricultural to an urban industrial society, and the separation of work from the home, produced a new social construction of children as innocent, dependent, and vulnerable (Ainsworth 1991). Progressive child savers used the new imagery of childhood to advance a number of reform agendas: compulsory school attendance, child labor, and child welfare laws. A more modern, scientific conception of social control embraced positivist criminology and medical analogies to treat offenders rather than to punish them for their offenses. Positivism attempted to identify the antecedent variables that caused crime and deviance and challenged the classic formulation of crime as the product of blameworthy, free-will choices (Allen 1964, 1981). By attributing criminal behavior to external and deterministic forces, Progressive reformers reduced an actor's moral responsibility for crime and focused on efforts to reform rather than to punish the offender. The juvenile court combined the new conception of children with new strategies of social control to produce a judicial-welfare alternative to criminal justice, to remove children from the adult process, to enforce the newer conception of children's dependency, and to substitute the state as *parens patriae*. The juvenile court's rehabilitative ideal rested on several sets of assumptions about positive criminology, children's malleability, and the availability of effective intervention strategies to act in the child's best interests.

Procedure and substance intertwined in the juvenile court. Procedurally, juvenile courts used informal processes, conducted confidential hearings, and employed a euphemistic vocabulary to obscure and disguise the reality of coercive social control. Substantively, juvenile courts used indeterminate, nonpro-

·portional dispositions, emphasized treatment and supervision rather than punishment, and purportedly focused on offenders' future welfare rather than past offenses. Despite their benevolent rhetoric, however, the Progressive child savers who created the juvenile court deliberately designed it to discriminate, to Americanize immigrants and the poor, and to provide a coercive mechanism to distinguish between "our children" and "other people's children."

In their pursuit of the rehabilitative ideal, the Progressives situated the juvenile court on a number of cultural, legal, and criminological fault lines. They created several binary conceptions for the juvenile and criminal justice systems: either child or adult; either determinism or free will; either dependent or responsible; either treatment or punishment; either welfare or deserts; either procedural informality or formality; either discretion or the rule of law. The past three decades have witnessed a tectonic shift from the former to the latter of each of these pairs in response to the structural and racial transformation of cities, the rise in serious youth crime, and the erosion of the rehabilitative assumptions of the juvenile court.

THE TRANSFORMATION OF THE JUVENILE COURT

During the 1960s, the Warren Court's civil rights decisions, criminal due process rulings, and "constitutional domestication" of the juvenile court responded to broader structural and demographic changes taking place in America, particularly those associated with race and youth crime (Feld 1999). In the decades prior to and after World War II, black migration from the rural South to the urban North increased minority concentrations in urban ghettos, made race a national rather than a regional issue, and provided the impetus for the civil rights movement (Lemann 1992). The 1960s also witnessed the baby boom increases in youth crime that continued until the late 1970s. During the 1960s, the rise in youth crime and urban racial disorders provoked cries for "law and order" and provided the initial political impetus to get tough. Republicans seized crime control and welfare as wedge issues with which to distinguish themselves from Democrats, and crime policies for the first time became a central issue in partisan politics (Beckett 1997). As a result of sound-bite politics, symbols and rhetoric have come to shape penal policies more than knowledge or substance has. Since the 1960s, politicians' fear of being labeled soft on crime has led to a constant ratcheting-up of punitiveness.

The Supreme Court's due process decision responded to the macrostructural and demographic changes and attempted to guarantee civil rights, to protect minority citizens, and to limit the authority of the state. *In re Gault* (387 U.S. 1 [1967]) began to transform the juvenile court into a very different institution from that which the Progressives contemplated. *In re Gault* demonstrated the linkage between procedure and substance in the juvenile court and engrafted some formal procedures at trial onto the individualized treatment schema (Feld 1984). Although the Court did not intend its decisions to alter juvenile courts' therapeutic mission, in the aftermath of *In re Gault*, judicial, legislative, and administrative changes have fostered a procedural and substantive convergence with criminal courts (Feld 1993a, 1997). *In re Gault* shifted the focus of delinquency hearings from real needs to proof of legal guilt and formalized the connection between criminal conduct and coercive intervention. Providing a modicum of procedural justice also legitimated greater punitiveness in juvenile courts. Thus *In re Gault*'s procedural reforms provided the impetus for the substantive convergence between juvenile and criminal courts, so that today juvenile courts constitute a wholly owned subsidiary of the criminal justice system. It is a historical irony that race provided the initial impetus for the Supreme Court to expand procedural rights to protect minority youths' liberty interests, and now juvenile courts impose increasingly punitive sentences disproportionately on minority offenders. In *McKeiver* v. *Pennsylvania* (403 U.S. 528 [1971]), however, the Court denied to juveniles the constitutional right to jury trials in delinquency proceedings. *McKeiver* relied on the purported differences between juvenile courts' treatment and criminal courts' punishment to justify the procedural distinctions between the two systems.

Juvenile courts' procedural deficiencies

Unfortunately, *In re Gault* constituted an incomplete procedural revolution, and a substantial gulf still remains between the law on the books and the law in action. States continue to manipulate the fluid concepts of children and adults, or treatment and punishment in order to maximize the social control of young people. On the one hand, states treat juveniles just like adults when formal equality results in practical inequality. For example, states use the adult standard of "knowing, intelligent, and voluntary under the totality of the circumstances" to gauge juveniles' waivers of rights (*Fare* v. *Michael C.*, 442 U.S. 707 [1979]; Feld 1984), even though juveniles lack the legal competence of adults. Research on juveniles' waivers of *Miranda* rights (Grisso 1980) and waivers of their right to counsel provide compelling evidence of the procedural deficiencies of the juvenile court (Feld 1989, 1993b). On the other hand, even as juvenile courts have become more punitive, most states continue to deny juveniles access to jury trials or other rights guaranteed to adults (Feld 1988, 1995). Juvenile courts provide a procedural regime in which few adults charged with crimes and facing the prospect of confinement would consent to be tried.

Criminological triage

Simultaneously, juvenile courts' increased procedural formality have provided the impetus to adopt substantive criminological triage policies. This process entails diverting status offenders out of the juvenile system at the soft end, waiving serious offenders for adult criminal prosecution at the hard end, and punishing more severely the residual, middle range of ordinary delinquent offenders.

At the soft end, judicial and legislative disillusionment with juvenile courts' responses to noncriminal youths have led to diversion, deinstitutionalization, and decriminalization reforms (Feld 1993a, 1998). Deinstitutionalization reduced access to secure facilities for noncriminal offenders and provided the impetus to transfer many white, female, and middle-class youths whom juvenile courts formerly handled as status offenders into the private sector system of mental health and chemical dependency treatment and confinement (Schwartz 1989).

At the hard end, states transfer more juveniles to criminal courts. As a result of recent get-tough laws, judges, prosecutors, and legislators waive increasing numbers of younger offenders to criminal courts for prosecution as adults. The rate of judicial waiver increased 68 percent between 1988 and 1992 (Snyder and Sickmund 1995). Prosecutors in Florida alone transfer more juveniles to criminal court than do all of the juvenile court judges in the country together (Bishop and Frazier 1991). In an effort to crack down on youth crime, legislators exclude various combinations of age and offenses from juvenile courts' jurisdiction and then further expand the lists of excluded offenses and reduce the age of criminal responsibility.

The get-tough juvenile justice policies of the early 1990s reflect macrostructural, economic, and racial demographic changes in cities during the 1970s and 1980s; the emergence of the black underclass;

and the rise in gun violence and youth homicides (Massey and Denton 1993; Blumstein 1995). Between World War II and the early 1970s, semiskilled high school graduates could get well-paying jobs in the automobile, steel, and construction industries. Beginning in the 1970s, the transition from an industrial to an information and service economy reduced employment opportunities in the manufacturing sectors and produced a bifurcation of economic opportunities based on skills and education. During the post–World War II period, government highway, housing, and mortgage policies encouraged suburban expansion (Massey and Denton 1993). The migration of whites to the suburbs, the growth of information and service jobs in the suburbs, the bifurcation of the economy, and the deindustrialization of the urban core increased racial segregation and the concentration of poverty among blacks in the major cities (Wilson 1987, 1996). In the mid-1980s, the emergence of a structural underclass, the introduction of crack cocaine into the inner cities, and the proliferation of guns among youths produced a sharp escalation in black youth homicide rates (Blumstein 1995). The age-offense-race-specific increase in youth homicide provided further political impetus to get tough and to crack down on youth crime. In this context, because of differences in rates of offending by race, getting tough on violence meant targeting young black men. As a result of the connection in the public and political minds between race and youth crime, juveniles have become the symbolic

Willie Horton of the 1990s (Beckett 1997).

These get-tough waiver policies reflect juvenile courts' broader jurisprudential changes from rehabilitation to retribution. The overarching themes of these legislative amendments include a shift from individualized justice to just deserts, from offender to offense, from "amenability to treatment" to public safety, and from immature delinquent to responsible criminal. State legislatures use offense criteria in waiver laws as dispositional guidelines either to structure and limit judicial discretion, to guide prosecutorial charging decisions, or automatically to exclude certain youths from juvenile court jurisdiction (Feld 1987, 1995; Torbet et al. 1996).

These trends in waiver policy also reflect a fundamental cultural and legal reconceptualization of youth from innocent and dependent to responsible and autonomous. Politicians' sound bites, like "adult crime/adult time," reflect typical criminal policies that provide no formal recognition of youthfulness as a mitigating factor in sentencing. Once youths make the transition to the adult system, criminal court judges sentence them as if they are adults, impose the same sentences, send them to the same prisons, and even inflict capital punishment on them for the crimes they committed as children (Feld 1998; *Stanford* v. *Kentucky*, 492 U.S. 361 [1989]).

State legislators adopt social control policies within a binary framework: either child or adult, either treatment or punishment, either juvenile court or criminal court.

Unfortunately, jurisdictional bifurcation frustrates effective and rational social control and often results in a punishment gap when youths make the transition between the two systems. While violent young offenders receive dramatically more severe sentences as adults than they would have received as juveniles, chronic property offenders who constitute the bulk of youths judicially transferred actually get shorter sentences as adults than they would have obtained as delinquents had they remained within the juvenile system (Podkopacz and Feld 1995, 1996). Many of the recent changes in waiver laws represent an effort to improve the fit between waiver criteria and criminal court sentencing practices, to use juvenile prior records more extensively to enhance the sentences of young adult offenders, and to respond to career offenders and career criminality that begins in early adolescence but continues into adulthood (Feld 1998). Efforts to integrate juvenile and criminal court sentencing practices and records represent an effort to rationalize social control of serious and chronic offenders on both sides of the juvenile and criminal court line. The recent emergence of blended jurisdiction laws, intermediate sentencing options like extended jurisdiction prosecutions, and blended juvenile-criminal sentences provide examples of states' groping toward graduated, escalating sanctions for young offenders across the adolescent and criminal career developmental continuum (Feld 1995, 1998; Torbet et al. 1996).

Finally, the criminological triage process has resulted in increased punishment of those ordinary delinquents who remain within the jurisdiction of the juvenile justice system (Feld 1988; Sheffer 1995). Legislative preambles and court opinions explicitly endorse punishment as an appropriate component of juvenile sanctions. States' juvenile sentencing laws increasingly emphasize responsibility and accountability and provide for determinate and/or mandatory minimum sentences keyed to the seriousness of the offense (Sheffer 1995; Feld 1998; Torbet et al. 1996). These statutory provisions use principles of proportionality and determinacy to rationalize sentencing decisions, to increase the penal bite of juvenile sanctions, and to allow legislators symbolically to demonstrate their toughness.

Two general conclusions emerge clearly from empirical research evaluating juvenile court judges' sentencing practices. First, the "principle of offense"—present offense and prior record—accounts for most of the variance in juvenile court sentences that can be explained. Every methodologically rigorous study of juvenile court sentencing practices reports that judges focus primarily on the seriousness of the present offense and prior record when they sentence delinquents (Feld 1998). Second, after controlling for legal and offense variables, the individualized justice of juvenile courts produces racial disparities in the sentencing of minority offenders (Bishop and Frazier 1996). According to the juvenile court's treatment ideology, judges' discretionary decisions should disproportionally affect minority youths, because the Progressives intended judges to focus on youths' social circumstances rather than simply their offenses and designed them to discriminate between "our children" and "other people's children."

Evaluating juvenile correctional facilities for their effectiveness provides another indicator of the increased punitiveness of juvenile justice. Evaluations of juvenile correctional facilities in the decades following *In re Gault* reveal a continuing gap between the rhetoric of rehabilitation and the punitive reality (Feld 1977, 1981). Criminological research, judicial opinions, and investigative studies report staff beatings of inmates, the use of drugs for social control purposes, extensive reliance on solitary confinement, and a virtual absence of meaningful rehabilitative programs (Feld 1998; Parent et al. 1994). Despite rehabilitative rhetoric and a euphemistic vocabulary, the simple truth is that juvenile court judges increasingly consign disproportionately minority offenders to overcrowded custodial warehouses that constitute little more than youth prisons.

Evaluations of juvenile treatment programs provide little evidence that training schools, the most common form of institutional treatment for the largest numbers of serious and chronic delinquents, effectively treat youths or reduce their recidivism rates (Feld 1998). Despite these generally negative results, proponents of the traditional juvenile court continue their quest for the elusive rehabilitative grail and offer literature reviews, meta-analyses, or program descriptions that report that some interventions produce positive effects on selected clients under certain conditions. A recent comprehensive meta-analysis of 200 studies of interventions with serious juvenile offenders reported, "The average intervention effect for these studies was positive, statistically significant, and equivalent to a recidivism reduction of about 6 percentage points, for example, from 50% to 44%" (Lipsey and Wilson 1998, 330). Typically, positive treatment effects appear in small, experimental programs that provide an intensive and integrated response to the multitude of problems that delinquent youths present. Favorable results occur primarily under optimal conditions, for example, when mental health or other nonjuvenile correctional personnel provide services with high treatment integrity in well-established programs.

Even though some programs apparently are successful for some offenders under some circumstances and produce marginal improvements in the life chances of some juveniles, most states do not elect to provide these programs or services to delinquents generally. Rather, they confine most delinquents in euphemistically sanitized youth prisons with fewer procedural safeguards than adults enjoy. Thus, even if model programs can reduce recidivism rates, public officials appear unwilling to provide such treatment services when they face fiscal constraints, budget deficits, and competition from other, more politically potent interest groups. Organizational imperatives to achieve economies of scale mandate confining ever larger numbers of youths and thereby preclude the possibility of matching offenders with appropriate treatment programs.

THE INHERENT CONTRADICTIONS OF THE JUVENILE COURT

Juvenile courts punish rather than treat young offenders and use a procedural regime under which no adult would consent to be tried. The fundamental shortcoming of the juvenile court's welfare idea reflects a failure of conception and not simply a century-long failure of implementation. The juvenile court's creators envisioned a social service agency in a judicial setting and attempted to fuse its welfare mission with the power of state coercion. Combining social welfare and penal social control functions in one agency ensures that juvenile courts do both badly. Providing for child welfare represents a societal responsibility rather than a judicial one. Juvenile courts lack control over the resources necessary to meet child welfare needs exactly because of the social class and racial characteristics of their clients and because of the public's fear of "other people's children." In practice, juvenile courts almost inevitably subordinate welfare concerns to crime control considerations.

If we formulated child welfare programs ab initio, would we choose a juvenile court as the most appropriate agency through which to deliver social services, and would we make criminality a condition precedent to the receipt of services? If we would not initially choose a court to deliver social services, then does the fact of a youth's criminality confer upon the court any special competency as a welfare agency? Many young people who do not commit crimes desperately need social services, and many youths who commit crimes do not require or will not respond to social services. In short, criminality represents an inaccurate and haphazard criterion upon which to allocate social services. Because our society denies adequate help and assistance to meet the social welfare needs of all young people, juvenile courts' treatment ideology serves primarily to legitimate judicial coercion of some youths because of their criminality.

The attempt to combine social welfare and criminal social control in one agency constitutes the fundamental flaw of the juvenile court. The juvenile court subordinates social welfare concerns to criminal social control functions because of its inherently penal focus. Legislatures do not define juvenile courts' jurisdiction on the basis of characteristics of children for which the children are not responsible and for which effective intervention could improve their lives. For example, juvenile court law does not define eligibility for welfare services or create an enforceable right or entitlement based upon young people's lack of access to quality education, lack of adequate housing or nutrition, unmet health needs, or impoverished families—none of which are their fault. In all of these instances, children bear the burdens

of their parents' circumstances literally as innocent bystanders. Instead, states' juvenile codes define juvenile court jurisdiction based upon a youth's committing a crime, a prerequisite that detracts from a compassionate response. Unlike disadvantaged social conditions that are not their fault, criminal behavior represents the one characteristic for which adolescent offenders do bear at least partial responsibility. In short, juvenile courts define eligibility for services on the basis of the feature least likely to elicit sympathy and compassion, and they ignore the social structural conditions or personal circumstances more likely to evoke a greater desire to help. Juvenile courts' defining characteristic strengthens public antipathy to "other people's children" by emphasizing primarily that they are law violators. The recent criminological triage policies that stress punishment, accountability, and personal responsibility further reinforce juvenile courts' penal foundations and reduce the legitimacy of youths' claims to humanitarian assistance.

THE KID IS A CRIMINAL, AND THE CRIMINAL IS A KID

States should uncouple social welfare from social control, try all offenders in one integrated criminal justice system, and make appropriate substantive and procedural modifications to accommodate the youthfulness of some defendants. Substantive justice requires a rationale to sentence younger offenders differently from and more leniently than older defendants, a formal recognition of youthfulness as a mitigating factor. Procedural justice requires providing youths with full procedural parity with adult defendants and additional safeguards to account for the disadvantage of youth in the justice system. These substantive and procedural modifications can avoid the worst of both worlds, provide youths with protections functionally equivalent to those accorded adults, and do justice in sentencing.

My proposal to abolish juvenile courts constitutes neither an unqualified endorsement of punishment nor a primitive throwback to earlier centuries' vision of children as miniature adults. Rather, it honestly acknowledges that juvenile courts currently engage in criminal social control, asserts that younger offenders in a criminal justice system deserve less severe penalties for their misdeeds than do more mature offenders simply because they are young, and addresses many problems created by trying to maintain dichotomous and contradictory criminal justice systems based on an arbitrary age classification of a youth as a child or as an adult (Feld 1997).

Formulating a sentencing policy when the kid is a criminal and the criminal is a kid entails two tasks. First, I will provide a rationale for sentencing younger offenders differently from and more leniently than adult offenders. Explicitly punishing younger offenders rests on the premise that adolescents possess sufficient moral reasoning, cognitive capacity, and volitional control to hold them partially responsible for their behavior, albeit not to the same degree as adults. Developmental psychological research, jurisprudence, and criminal sentencing policy provide the rationale for why young offenders deserve less severe consequences for their misdeeds than do older offenders and justify formal recognition of youthfulness as a mitigating factor. Second, I will propose a youth discount—shorter sentences for reduced responsibility—as a practical administrative mechanism to implement youthfulness as a mitigating factor in sentencing.

The idea of deserved punishment entails censure and condemnation for making blameworthy choices and imposes sanctions proportional to the seriousness of a crime (von Hirsch 1976, 1993). Two elements—harm and culpability—define the seriousness of a crime. A perpetrator's age has relatively little bearing on assessments of harm—the nature of the injury inflicted, risk created, or value taken. But evaluations of seriousness also entail the quality of the actor's choice to engage in the criminal conduct that produced the harm. Youthfulness is a very important factor with respect to the culpability of a criminal actor because it directly affects the quality of choices. Responsibility for choices hinges on cognitive and volitional competence. Youths differ socially, physically, and psychologically from adults: they have not yet fully internalized moral norms, developed sufficient empathic identification with others, acquired adequate moral comprehension, or had sufficient opportunity to develop the ability to restrain their actions. They possess neither the rationality (cognitive capacity) nor the self-control (volitional capacity) for their criminal responsibility to be equated fully with that of adults. In short, their immaturity affects the quality of their judgments in ways that are relevant to criminal sentencing policy. Ultimately, a youth sentencing policy should enable young offenders to survive the mistakes of adolescence with their life chances intact.

Adolescence as a form
of reduced culpability

Certain characteristic developmental differences distinguish the quality of decisions that young people make from the quality of decisions by adults, and justify a somewhat more protective stance when states sentence younger offenders. Psychosocial maturity, judgment, and temperance provide conceptual prisms through which to view adolescents' decision-making competencies and to assess the quality of their choices (Cauffman and Steinberg 1995; Steinberg and Cauffman 1996; Scott 1992; Scott and Grisso 1997). Adolescents and adults differ in the quality of judgment and self-control they exercise because of relative differences in breadth of experience, short-term versus long-term temporal perspectives, attitudes toward risk, impulsivity, and the importance they attach to peer influences. These developmentally unique attributes affect youths' degree of criminal responsibility. Young people are more impulsive, exercise less self-control, fail adequately to calculate long-term consequences, and engage in more risky behavior than do adults. Adolescents may estimate the magnitude or probability of risks, may use a shorter time frame, or may focus on opportunities for gains rather than possibilities of losses differently from adults (Furby and Beyth-Marom 1992). Young people may discount the negative value of future consequences because they have more difficulty than adults in integrating a future consequence into their more limited experiential baseline (Gardner and Herman 1990). Adolescents' judgments may differ from those of adults because of their disposition toward sensation seeking, impulsivity related to hormonal or physiological changes, and mood volatility (Steinberg and Cauffman 1996; Cauffman and Steinberg 1995). Adolescents respond to peer group influences more readily than do adults because of the crucial role that peer relationships play in identity formation (Scott 1992; Zimring 1981). Most adolescent crime occurs in a group context, and having delinquent friends precedes an adolescent's own criminal involvement (Elliott and Menard 1996). Group offending places normally law-abiding youths at greater risk of involvement and reduces their ability publicly to withdraw. Because of the social context of adolescent crime, young people require time, experience, and opportunities to develop the capacity for autonomous judgments and to resist peer influence.

Developmental processes affect adolescents' quality of judgment and self-control, directly influence their degree of criminal responsibility and deserved punishment, and justify a different criminal sentencing policy. While young offenders possess sufficient understanding and culpability to hold them accountable for their acts, their crimes are less blameworthy than adults' because of reduced culpability and limited appreciation of consequences and also because their life circumstances understandably limit their capacity to learn to make fully responsible choices.

When youths offend, the families, schools, and communities that socialize them bear some responsibility for the failures of those socializing institutions. Human beings depend upon others to nurture them and to enable them to develop and exercise the moral capacity for constructive behavior. The capacity for self-control and self-direction is not simply a matter of moral luck or good fortune but a socially constructed developmental process that provides young people with the opportunity to develop a moral character. Community structures affect social conditions and the contexts within which adolescents grow and interact with peers. Unlike presumptively mobile adults, juveniles, because of their dependency, lack the means or ability to escape from their criminogenic environments.

Zimring (1982) describes the "semi-autonomy" of adolescence as a "learner's permit" that gives youths the opportunity to make choices and to learn to be responsible but without suffering fully the long-term consequences of their mistakes. The ability to make responsible choices is learned, and the dependent status of youth systematically deprives adolescents of chances to learn to be responsible. Young people's socially constructed life situation understandably limits their capacity to develop self-control, restricts their opportunities to learn and exercise responsibility, and supports a partial reduction of criminal responsibility. A youth sentencing policy would entail both shorter sentences and a higher offense-seriousness threshold before a state incarcerates youths than for older offenders.

Youth discount

The binary distinctions between children and adults that provide the basis for states' legal age of majority and the jurisprudential foundation of the juvenile court ignore the reality that adolescents develop along a continuum, and create an unfortunate either-or forced choice in sentencing. By contrast, shorter sentences for reduced responsibility represent a more modest and readily attainable reason to treat young offenders differently from adults than the rehabilitative justifications advanced by Progressive child savers. Protecting young people from the full penal consequences of their poor decisions reflects a policy to preserve their life chances for the future, when they presumably will make more mature and responsible choices. Such a policy both holds young offenders accountable for their acts because they possess sufficient culpability and mitigates the severity of consequences because their choices entail less blame than those of adults.

Sentencing policy that integrates youthfulness, reduced culpability, and restricted opportunities to learn self-control with penal principles of proportionality would provide younger offenders with categorical fractional reductions of adult sentences. If adolescents as a class characteristically make poorer choices than adults, then sentencing policies should protect young people from the full penal consequences of their bad decisions. Because youthfulness constitutes a universal form of reduced culpability or diminished responsibility, states should treat it categorically as a mitigating factor, without regard to nuances of individual developmental differences. Youth development is a highly variable process, and chronological age is a crude, imprecise measure of criminal maturity and the opportunity to develop the capacity for self-control. Despite the variability of adolescence, however, a categorical youth discount that uses age as a conclusive proxy for reduced culpability and shorter sentences remains preferable to any individualized inquiry into the criminal responsibility of each young offender. Developmental psychology does not possess reliable clinical indicators of moral development that equate readily with criminal responsibility and accountability. For young criminal actors who are responsible, to some degree, clinical testimony to precisely tailor sanctions to culpability is not worth the burden or diversion of resources that the effort would entail. Because youthful mitigated criminal responsibility is a legal concept, there simply is no psychiatric analogue to which clinical testimony would correspond. Rather, a youth discount categorically recognizes that

criminal choices by young people are to some degree qualitatively different from those of adults and constitute a form of partial responsibility without any additional clinical indicators.

This categorical approach would take the form of an explicit youth discount at sentencing, a sliding scale of criminal responsibility. A 14-year-old offender might receive, for example, 25-33 percent of the adult penalty; a 16-year-old defendant, 50-66 percent; and an 18-year-old adult, the full penalty, as currently occurs (Feld 1997). The deeper discounts for younger offenders correspond to the developmental continuum and their more limited opportunities to learn to be responsible and to exercise self-control. Because reduced culpability provides the rationale for youthful mitigation, younger adolescents bear less responsibility and deserve proportionally shorter sentences than older youths. With the passage of time, increased age, and more numerous opportunities to develop the capacity for self-control, social tolerance of criminal deviance and claims for youthful mitigation decline. Discounted sentences that preserve younger offenders' life chances require that the maximum sentences they receive remain very substantially lower than those imposed on adults. Capital sentences and draconian mandatory minimum sentences—for example, life without parole—have no place in sentencing presumptively less blameworthy adolescents. Because of the rapidity of adolescent development and the life-course-disruptive consequences of incarceration, the rationale for a youth discount also supports requiring a higher in/out threshold of offense seriousness and culpability as a prerequisite for imprisonment.

Only states whose criminal sentencing laws provide realistic, humane, and determinate sentences that enable a judge actually to determine real-time sentences can readily implement a proposal for explicit fractional reductions of youths' sentences. One can know the value of a youth discount only in a sentencing system in which courts know in advance the standard, or going rate, for adults. In many jurisdictions, implementing a youth discount would require significant modification of the current sentencing laws, including adoption of presumptive sentencing guidelines with strong upper limits on punishment severity, elimination of all mandatory minimum sentences, and introduction of some structured judicial discretion to mitigate penalties based on individual circumstances. Attempts to apply youth discounts idiosyncratically within the flawed indeterminate or mandatory-minimum sentencing regimes that currently prevail in many jurisdictions runs the risk of simply reproducing all of their existing inequalities and injustices.

VIRTUES OF AN INTEGRATED CRIMINAL JUSTICE SYSTEM

A graduated age-culpability sentencing scheme in an integrated criminal justice system avoids the inconsistencies associated with the binary either-juvenile-or-adult drama currently played out in judicial waiver proceedings and in prosecutorial charging decisions, and it introduces proportionality to the sentences imposed on the many youths currently tried as adults. It also avoids the punishment gap when youths make the transition from one justice system to the other, and it ensures similar consequences for similarly situated offenders. Adolescence and criminal careers develop along a continuum; the current bifurcation between the two justice systems confounds efforts to respond consistently to young career offenders. A sliding scale of criminal sentences based on an offender's age as a proxy for culpability accomplishes simply and directly what the various blended-jurisdiction statutes attempt to achieve indirectly (Feld 1995). A formal policy of youthfulness as a mitigating factor avoids the undesirable forced choice between inflicting undeservedly harsh penalties on less culpable actors and doing nothing about the manifestly guilty.

An integrated justice system also allows for integrated record keeping and enables officials to identify and respond to career offenders more readily than the current jurisdictional bifurcation permits. Even adolescent career offenders deserve enhanced sentences based on an extensive record of prior offending. But an integrated justice system does not require integrated prisons. The question of how long differs from questions of where and what. States should maintain age-segregated youth correctional facilities both to protect younger offenders from adults and to protect geriatric prisoners from younger inmates. Virtually all young offenders will return to society, and the state should provide them with resources for self-improvement because of its basic responsibility to its citizens and its own self-interest. A sentencing and correctional policy must offer youths room to reform and provide opportunities and resources to facilitate young offenders' constructive use of their time.

Finally, affirming partial responsibility for youth constitutes a virtue. The idea of personal responsibility and accountability for behavior provides an important cultural counterweight to a popular culture that endorses the idea that everyone is a victim, that all behavior is determined, and that no one is responsible. The juvenile court elevated determinism over free will, characterized delinquents as victims rather than perpetrators, and subjected them to an indeterminate quasi-civil commitment process. The juvenile court's treatment ideology denied youths' personal responsibility, reduced offenders' duty to exercise self-control, and eroded their obligations to change. If there is any silver lining in the current cloud of get-tough policies, it is the affirmation of responsibility. A culture that values autonomous individuals must emphasize both freedom and responsibility. A criminal law that bases sentences on blameworthiness and responsibility must recognize the physical, psychological, and socially constructed differences between youths and adults. Affirming responsibility forces politicians to be honest when the kid is a criminal and the criminal is a kid. The real reason states bring young offenders to juvenile courts is not to deliver social services but because the offenders committed a crime. Once politicians recognize that simple truth, then justice can follow.

References

Ainsworth, Janet E. 1991. Re-imagining Childhood and Re-constructing the Legal Order: The Case for Abolishing the Juvenile Court. *North Carolina Law Review* 69:1083-133.

Allen, Francis A. 1964. Legal Values and the Rehabilitative Ideal. In *The Borderland of the Criminal Law: Essays in Law and Criminology*. Chicago: University of Chicago Press.

———. 1981. *Decline of the Rehabilitative Ideal*. New Haven, CT: Yale University Press.

Beckett, Katherine. 1997. *Making Crime Pay: Law and Order in Contemporary American Politics*. New York: Oxford University Press.

Bishop, Donna and Charles Frazier. 1991. Transfer of Juvenile to Criminal Court: A Case Study and Analysis of Prosecutorial Waiver. *Notre Dame Journal of Law, Ethics & Public Policy* 5:281-302.

———. 1996. Race Effects in Juvenile Justice Decision-Making: Findings of a Statewide Analysis. *Journal of Criminal Law & Criminology* 86:392-413.

Blumstein, Alfred. 1995. Youth Violence, Guns, and the Illicit-Drug Industry. *Journal of Criminal Law & Criminology* 86:10-36.

Cauffman, Elizabeth and Laurence Steinberg. 1995. The Cognitive and Affective Influences on Adolescent Decision-Making. *Temple Law Review* 68:1763-89.

Elliott, Delbert and Scott Menard. 1996. Delinquent Friends and Delinquent Behavior: Temporal and Developmental Patterns. In *Delinquency and*

Crime: Current Theories, ed. J. David Hawkins. New York: Cambridge University Press.

Feld, Barry C. 1977. *Neutralizing Inmate Violence: Juvenile Offenders in Institutions*. Cambridge, MA: Ballinger.

———. 1981. A Comparative Analysis of Organizational Structure and Inmate Subcultures in Institutions for Juvenile Offenders. *Crime & Delinquency* 27:336-63.

———. 1984. Criminalizing Juvenile Justice: Rules of Procedure for Juvenile Court. *Minnesota Law Review* 69:141-276.

———. 1987. Juvenile Court Meets the Principle of Offense: Legislative Changes in Juvenile Waiver Statutes. *Journal of Criminal Law & Criminology* 78:471-533.

———. 1988. Juvenile Court Meets the Principle of Offense: Punishment, Treatment, and the Difference It Makes. *Boston University Law Review* 68:821-915.

———. 1989. The Right to Counsel in Juvenile Court: An Empirical Study of When Lawyers Appear and the Difference They Make. *Journal of Criminal Law & Criminology* 79:1185-346.

———. 1993a. Criminalizing the American Juvenile Court. In *Crime and Justice: A Review of Research*, ed. Michael Tonry. Vol. 17. Chicago: University of Chicago Press.

———. 1993b. *Justice for Children: The Right to Counsel and the Juvenile Court*. Boston: Northeastern University Press.

———. 1995. Violent Youth and Public Policy: A Case Study of Juvenile Justice Law Reform. *Minnesota Law Review* 79:965-1128.

———. 1997. Abolish the Juvenile Court: Youthfulness, Criminal Responsibility, and Sentencing Policy. *Journal of Criminal Law & Criminology* 88:68-136.

———. 1998. Juvenile and Criminal Justice Systems' Responses to Youth Violence. *Crime and Justice: A Review of Research* 24:189-261.

———. 1999. *Bad Kids: Race and the Transformation of the Juvenile Court*. New York: Oxford University Press.

Furby, Lita and Ruth Beyth-Marom. 1992. Risk Taking in Adolescence: A Decision-Making Perspective. *Developmental Review* 12:1-44.

Gardner, William and Janna Herman. 1990. Adolescents' AIDS Risk Taking: A Rational Choice Perspective. In *Adolescents and the AIDS Epidemic*, ed. William Gardner, Susan G. Millstein, and Bruce Leroy Cox. San Francisco: Jossey-Bass.

Grisso, Thomas. 1980. Juveniles' Capacities to Waive *Miranda* Rights: An Empirical Analysis. *California Law Review* 68:1134-66.

Lemann, Nicholas. 1992. *The Promised Land: The Great Black Migration and How It Changed America*. New York: Vintage Books.

Lipsey, Mark W. and David B. Wilson. 1998. Effective Intervention for Serious Juvenile Offenders. In *Serious and Violent Juvenile Offenders: Risk Factors and Successful Interventions*, ed. Rolf Loeber and David P. Farrington. Thousand Oaks, CA: Sage.

Massey, Douglas and Nancy Denton. 1993. *American Apartheid: Segregation and the Making of the Underclass*. Cambridge, MA: Harvard University Press.

Parent, Dale G., Valerie Lieter, Stephen Kennedy, Lisa Livens, Daniel Wentworth, and Sarah Wilcox. 1994. *Conditions of Confinement: Juvenile Detention and Corrections Facilities*. Washington, DC: Department of Justice, Office of Juvenile Justice and Delinquency Prevention.

Podkopacz, Marcy Rasmussen and Barry C. Feld. 1995. Judicial Waiver Policy and Practice: Persistence, Seriousness and Race. *Law & Inequality: A Journal of Theory and Practice* 14:73-178.

———. 1996. The End of the Line: An Empirical Study of Judicial Waiver. *Journal of Criminal Law & Criminology* 86:449-92.

Schwartz, Ira M. 1989. *(In)justice for Juveniles: Rethinking the Best Interests of the Child*. Lexington, MA: Lexington Books.

Scott, Elizabeth S. 1992. Judgment and Reasoning in Adolescent Decision Making. *Villanova Law Review* 37:1607-69.

Scott, Elizabeth S. and Thomas Grisso. 1997. The Evolution of Adolescence: A Developmental Perspective on Juvenile Justice Reform. *Journal of Criminal Law & Criminology* 88:137-89.

Sheffer, Julianne P. 1995. Serious and Habitual Juvenile Offender Statutes: Reconciling Punishment and Rehabilitation Within the Juvenile Justice System. *Vanderbilt Law Review* 48:479-512.

Snyder, Howard and Melissa Sickmund. 1995. *Juvenile Offenders and Victims: A National Report*. Washington, DC: Department of Justice, Office of Juvenile Justice and Delinquency Prevention, National Center for Juvenile Justice.

Steinberg, Laurence and Elizabeth Cauffman. 1996. Maturity of Judgment in Adolescence: Psychosocial Factors in Adolescent Decision Making. *Law and Human Behavior* 20:249-72.

Torbet, Patricia, Richard Gable, Hunter Hurst IV, Imogene Montgomery, Linda Szymanski, and Douglas Thomas. 1996. *State Responses to Serious and Violent Juvenile Crime: Research Report*. Washington, DC: Department of Justice, Office of Juvenile Justice and Delinquency Prevention, National Center for Juvenile Justice.

von Hirsch, Andrew. 1976. *Doing Justice*. New York: Hill & Wang.

———. 1993. *Censure and Blame*. New York: Oxford University Press.

Wilson, William Julius. 1987. *The Truly Disadvantaged*. Chicago: University of Chicago Press.

———. 1996. *When Work Disappears: The World of the New Urban Poor*. New York: Knopf.

Zimring, Franklin. 1981. Kids, Groups and Crime: Some Implications of a Well-Known Secret. *Journal of Criminal Law & Criminology* 72:867-902.

———. 1982. *The Changing Legal World of Adolescence*. New York: Free Press.

ANNALS, *AAPSS*, **564**, July 1999

Is There a Jurisprudential Future for the Juvenile Court?

By KATHERINE HUNT FEDERLE

ABSTRACT: This article considers the arguments for abolition of the juvenile court and suggests that its proponents may not go far enough in their proposals to dismantle the juvenile court's delinquency jurisdiction. While eliminating the juvenile court's delinquency jurisdiction may be justifiable given the court's emphasis on punishment and control, any such proposal also must account for the institutional effects on the court. Particularly, proponents of abolishing the court's delinquency jurisdiction on grounds that it is a flawed criminal court must consider whether that criticism also provides justification for abolition of the juvenile court's status offense jurisdiction since status offenders also are subject to state control for their behaviors. Moreover, even if a separate juvenile court is retained, proponents of abolishing the court's delinquency jurisdiction must take into account the institutional consequences of changing the court's caseload. In light of the juvenile court's social control functions, the use of state power and authority over petty and noncriminal juvenile offenders, and the implications for a coherent account of rights, this article suggests that abolition requires a more significant restructuring than has been previously suggested.

Katherine Hunt Federle is associate professor of law and director of the Justice for Children Project at the Ohio State University College of Law. She was a Prettyman Fellow at Georgetown University Law Center from 1984 to 1986. She was the chair of the American Bar Association Family Law Section's Committee on Juvenile Law and Dependency and participated in drafting the ABA's Standards for Representing Children in Abuse and Neglect Cases. She has written numerous articles on the rights of children.

A juvenile court system grounded in notions of rehabilitation and reform seems to have little relevance in a society where children commit increasingly violent—and spectacularly public—criminal acts. While such incidents may undermine public support for and confidence in the juvenile court, they also diminish the political viability of a separate juvenile justice system.

This changed political reality is reflected in recent congressional proposals to try more minors as adults and to enhance penalties for those who remain in the juvenile justice system. Recent changes in state laws also have enabled the transfer of more minors to adult criminal courts for trial. By lowering the age at which a minor may be tried as an adult, expanding the list of crimes for which a minor may be tried in criminal court, and changing the transfer process, many states have limited the jurisdictional reach of the juvenile court (Parent et al. 1997).

Nevertheless, the justification for measures designed to protect the public from juvenile crime seems unfounded. Juvenile crime generally and, relevantly, violent juvenile crime have been declining. Between 1994 and 1996, the violent crime arrest rate for juveniles declined 12 percent (Snyder 1997). Murder arrest rates also have shown a significant decline, dropping 14 percent alone between 1995 and 1996 (Snyder 1997). The juvenile arrest rate for property crimes also reached its lowest point in a decade when, in 1996, there were approximately 2400 arrests for every 100,000 youths in the United States (Snyder 1997).

Less than one-half of 1 percent of all youths between the ages of 10 and 17 were arrested for violent crimes (Snyder 1997).

While it appears specious to ground arguments for abolition of the juvenile court in public safety concerns, there are other, legitimate reasons for advancing abolitionist claims. In this issue of *The Annals*, Professor Barry Feld makes several compelling arguments in support of these claims that the juvenile court should be abolished. Nevertheless, there are certain aspects of his proposal that require further amplification.

For example, Feld focuses solely on the juvenile court's delinquency jurisdiction without considering the structural consequences of removing these cases from the juvenile court. Additionally, his proposal for a sentencing structure that accounts for the youthfulness of the offender may simply perpetuate, rather than alleviate, systemic inequality. Additionally, Feld's argument for abolishing the juvenile court fails to account for the concomitant value of rights and the change, if any, to the child's status as a rights holder that would result from abolition.

This article, then, begins by reviewing Feld's proposal to try all juvenile offenders in an integrated criminal justice system. It then focuses on the arguments favoring abolition of the court's delinquency jurisdiction and questions the narrowness of the proposal in terms of the court's bureaucratic and institutional frameworks. The article then discusses the feasibility of a youth discount and suggests that such a discount may actually perpetuate the illegitimate uses of state power. Finally, this article considers abolition of the juvenile court in terms of the rights of children and argues that the real value in trying children in one integrated criminal justice system lies in the recognition of children as rights holders.

THE STRUCTURAL CONSEQUENCES OF ABOLISHING DELINQUENCY

In his article, Feld argues for abolition of the court's delinquency jurisdiction because the juvenile court has become, he claims, a "deficient criminal court." As evidence of the juvenile court's criminalization, Feld points to the removal of status offenders from the juvenile court through diversion, deinstitutionalization, and decriminalization, curtailing judicial discretion by implementing more determinate sentencing schemes grounded in principles of accountability and punishment; to changes in waiver statutes to emphasize the seriousness of the offense and retribution; and to a general procedural restructuring that primarily advantages the state by maximizing social control of juveniles.

As a consequence, diversion and waiver policies and practices leave behind "ordinary" juvenile offenders who commit less serious crimes. Nevertheless, those minors who have been neither diverted nor waived are treated more punitively than adults accused of the same crimes because of the increased emphasis on punishment and accountability in the juvenile justice system.

Feld, however, does not believe that we should revive the juvenile court's traditionally rehabilitative underpinnings. According to Feld, the juvenile court is an unsuitable child welfare agency because the criterion on which services are allocated—criminality—is not a rational one. Furthermore, the juvenile court's social welfare objectives are inevitably subordinated to its criminal social control goals because of the emphasis on accountability and punishment. Thus the very way in which children obtain services—by committing a criminal act—is also most likely to elicit a punitive response. Feld, therefore, argues that the punitive aspects of the juvenile court system usurp its rehabilitative foundations.

Consequently, Feld argues that there is no compelling reason to maintain a separate juvenile court. He thus proposes the abolition of the juvenile court's delinquency jurisdiction and argues for an integrated criminal court to handle all criminal matters involving youths. For Feld, the creation of a single criminal court is a more "honest" response to juvenile crime because it is an explicit acknowledgment of social control. It is advantageous to the state as well as the child for it ensures that like offenders will be punished similarly but nevertheless provides procedural protections often lacking in the juvenile court. Finally, a single criminal court system also promotes individual responsibility by holding youths accountable for their actions.

However, any argument for abolition of the court's delinquency jurisdiction would seem to support the elimination of the juvenile court's status offense jurisdiction as well. Although diversion and deinstitutionalization policies have removed many status offenders from the jurisdiction of the juvenile court, the court continues to handle a surprising number of status offense cases. In fact, the extent to which status offenders have actually been diverted and deinstitutionalized may be overstated while the number of status offenders actually processed within the juvenile justice system may be understated. In 1995, juvenile courts petitioned and formally disposed of an estimated 146,400 status offense cases, an increase of 77 percent over the number of cases handled in 1986 (Sickmund et al. 1998). The case rate also increased by 63 percent between 1986 and 1995 (Sickmund et al. 1998).

Additionally, in 9900 of the cases petitioned as status offenses in 1995, the juvenile court ordered the minor detained (Sickmund et al. 1998). Although this signifies a decline of 22 percent in the use of detention since 1986, it represents a 37 percent increase since 1991 (Sickmund et al. 1998). Although only half of all status offense cases resulted in an adjudication, and most of those resulted in a disposition of probation, 16 percent still resulted in a placement outside the home in a residential facility (Sickmund et al. 1998). Interestingly, most of the minors placed outside the home had been adjudicated for ungovernability or for running away (Sickmund et al. 1998).

Although the number of status offense cases is dwarfed by the number of delinquency cases handled by juvenile court (of which there were an estimated 1 million in 1995) (Sickmund et al. 1998), status offense cases still constitute a significant part of the court's caseload. It also is apparent, despite diversion and deinstitutionalization mandates, that status offenders continue to be detained or institutionalized or both. Moreover, these practices disproportionately affect African American youths, who experience higher case and detention rates, and girls, who are more likely to be charged with running away from home than are boys (Sickmund et al. 1998). Finally, because of urban-rural dichotomies that often result in regional variations in crime rates, status offenses may be viewed more seriously by a particular juvenile court. Consequently, one would expect differences in the way some juvenile courts respond to status offenders.

Some commentators, including the Institute of Judicial Administration and the American Bar Association, have argued forcefully for elimination of status offenses. These arguments generally have turned on notions of gender equity and a recognition that such intervention is ineffective (Institute of Judicial Administration and American Bar Association 1980). But status offenses also most directly implicate the juvenile court's social welfare functions. The behavior is not criminal, and the articulated justifications for intervention have explicitly focused on improving the child. Abolition of the court's status offense jurisdiction, then, seems particularly appropriate if one accepts the premise that the juvenile court is an unsuitable child welfare agency; thus any proposal to abolish the court on these grounds seems inevitably to require a reexamination of the court's status offense jurisdiction.

Retention of the court's status offense jurisdiction and elimination of its delinquency jurisdiction also have institutional ramifications. Bureaucratic institutions are as a general matter self-protective and self-perpetuating. Therefore, it is unlikely that the juvenile court system will downsize simply because approximately 1.5 million delinquency cases have been removed to the criminal justice system. Rather, the system is more likely to respond by filling the void created by the removal of delinquency cases with other types of proceedings, like status offenses. Thus, while it is possible to talk about eliminating only the court's delinquency jurisdiction, inevitably we must consider what role a reconstructed juvenile court will continue to play and whether it has a continuing social welfare function.

YOUTH DISCOUNTS AND SYSTEMATIC INEQUALITY

The idea that the juvenile court has had a social welfare function at all leads to a second point in Feld's argument for abolition, namely, to treat youthfulness as a mitigating factor at the sentencing phase of a criminal proceeding. The argument for a youth discount is that adolescents, while they have sufficient moral reasoning and cognitive capacity to merit punishment, nevertheless lack the degree of culpability warranting imposition of full responsibility for their criminal activity. In other words, minors deserve leniency because of their youth, so the sentences imposed must be considerably less than those for adult offenders. Under such circumstances, life sentences and capital punishment would be inappropriate.

According to Feld, to ensure that youths receive these discounted sentences, and to avoid the problems of discretion and subjectivity, the states should categorically treat youth as a mitigating factor by creating age-based discounts. Of course, such discounts could be valid only in those jurisdictions that already impose "realistic, humane, and determinate sentences" on adults.

Setting aside questions about the political feasibility of a youth discount, the primary objection to this proposal is the real possibility that a youth discount would ultimately prove disadvantageous. To understand why this may be so, it is useful to articulate some assumptions about state power, the law's violence, and the courts. Returning, for a moment, to Feld's argument for abolition, he notes that the states manipulate the concepts of childhood and adulthood to "maximize the social control of young people." This is an important point, for the institutional structure we call the juvenile court may be used to deflect a deeper examination of structural inequality. Furthermore, the existence of a separate court not only provides an excuse for avoiding state responsibility; it also masks the illegitimate exercise of the state's coercive power.

For example, whether the juvenile court ever really had a social welfare function is debatable. This is not to say that some individuals in the juvenile justice system were not sincerely concerned about the welfare of children with whom they came into contact; in fact, many of the reformers were and are sincerely concerned with the welfare of the children they serve. But from its inception, the focus of the juvenile court has been on children of the poor. This focus was supported by an underlying belief that these children and their parents could be subject to a different level of state coercion simply because of their poverty (Garrison 1983). Consequently, these children and their families were subjected to a level of state coercion that was not and has not been replicated among middle- and upper-middle-class families (Garrison 1983). In this sense, then, the juvenile court's social welfare function has always been one of social control.

If the goal is social control, then one can clearly see that the court's institutional function is to obscure the use of state coercion. Abolition of the juvenile court thus removes a structural impediment, enabling us to see more clearly the state's use of its coercive power while permitting us to question and challenge the state's exercise of that power.

Moreover, by returning minors to the criminal justice system, we may then confront the consequences of state coercion and violence in that system. There is little doubt that, in the criminal justice system, the state uses its power to coerce compliance and sanction deviance. Sometimes that power is even used to authorize an act of state violence in the form of an execution. But the use of the state's power to control and/or punish crime obscures a separate social control function that has classist and, inevitably, racist implications.

The problem is that the use of that power is often masked by bureaucratization and routinization. That is, the power of the state congeals in bureaucratic institutions, like its courts, and is inherently a part of the bureaucratic structure. Consequently, the exercise of that power becomes so routine that it is invisible to those within the institution. This is particularly problematic when the use of that power has discriminatory and marginalizing effects. Because the exercise of that power has become virtually invisible through its routinization, it has become hard to see its illegitimacy.

By abolishing the juvenile court and returning certain young offenders to the criminal justice system, we unmask the social control function not only of the juvenile court but also of the criminal court. Returning minors to criminal court thus enables us to reexamine the functions of the criminal court and to critically appraise the state's use of coercion and violence in the criminal justice system. In turn, this should force us to ask some hard questions about the appropriate use of state power and the legitimacy of state coercion and violence.

Although significant numbers of children are transferred to the criminal court system (perhaps as many as 176,000 each year [Sickmund 1994]), we have not directly questioned the state's use of its power over these children because of the talismanic effects of waiver. Waiver, whether by judicial determination, the exercise of prosecutorial discretion, or statutory exclusion, sends an unmistakable message that these children are somehow different, that they rightly belong in the adult system. Moreover, waiver itself is an institutional exercise of power that becomes so routine it is invisible. But by returning all juvenile offenders to the criminal justice system, we should begin to see that not all criminal behavior warrants the state's use of its coercive power.

The problem with a youth discount, then, is that it can continue to mask the racist and classist implications of the state's power. That is, discounting a sentence for the offender's youth suggests that the maximum sentence itself is valid and may legitimately be imposed. In this sense, youth discounts may validate existing models of state coercion and violence. Perhaps this is why Feld included in his proposal the caveat that youth discounts may be used only in those criminal justice systems that are humane. But it is not clear why we would need a youth discount in an enlightened justice system in the first instance. Therefore, we need to be able to define and create a criminal justice system that is just and humane.

To do so, we must decide when, if at all, the state may use coercion and violence and we must consider whether the state's use of its power in this way actually masks racism and classism. The question, then, is not whether some offenders deserve leniency because of their youth but whether the state must assume responsibility for institutional and structural inequities. Bringing all minors into the adult system enables us to ask these difficult questions. But the notion of a youth discount will ultimately prove disadvantageous because it masks the state's use of its power to engage in social control. Therefore, it is important that we do not make the same mistakes with the criminal court that we made with the juvenile court. Only by examining the relationship between structural inequality and the state's use of coercion for social control may we begin to move toward a more just and rational criminal justice system.

THE VALUE OF RIGHTS
IN THE ABOLITION DEBATE

Finally, abolishing the juvenile court may enable us to see that children should have status as rights holders. The juvenile court's emphasis on rehabilitation and reform not only masks the coercive effects of state intervention but also permits the state to do things to children on the grounds that it is in the children's best interests. Of course, coercive state interventions rarely benefit those at whom such interventions are aimed and often do more harm than good (Federle 1994). Moreover, claiming to act on behalf of a child allows the claimant to do certain things without regard to the rights of that individual. Consequently, children often experience coercive and even punitive sanctions under the guise of best interests (Federle 1994).

Because the state claims to act on behalf of children, the rights that children may have are often overlooked. If children nevertheless benefited from a more paternalistic approach, it would be difficult to argue that they needed such rights. But children have not been advantaged by the state's claims to be acting on their behalf (Federle 1995). In fact, many paternalistic interventions have not only failed to improve the lives of children but may actually have disadvantaged them (Federle 1995). Consequently, grounding claims in child protection simply underscores the need for a coherent account of the rights of children.

Moreover, rights have an independent value. To have a right is to have power; to be a rights holder is to be a powerful individual who commands respect from others (Federle 1995). Rights enable the rights holder to demand attention and to seek legal redress from a society in which the rights holder may have been excluded or marginalized. Empowering children by recognizing that they have rights thus will have benefits that reach beyond the judicial system. If we recognize children as beings worthy of respect, we may actually reduce their victimization (Federle 1995).

Although criticisms of the juvenile court as an inferior criminal court are valuable, ultimately they do not help us see the problems of a judicial system that does not purport to protect and vindicate the rights of children. Furthermore, proposals focusing only on abolition of the court's delinquency jurisdiction fail to account for institutional and bureaucratic realities. From a rights perspective, however, the abolition of the juvenile court may prove advantageous. By freeing us from a disabling conception of children as vulnerable and dependent, we may begin to see how rights can empower. Any discussion of abolition, then, should take into account the importance and value of rights.

References

Federle, Katherine Hunt. 1994. Looking for Rights in All the Wrong Places: Resolving Custody Disputes in Divorce Proceedings. *Cardozo Law Review* 15:1523-66.

———. 1995. Looking Ahead: An Empowerment Perspective on the Rights of Children. *Temple Law Review* 68:1585-605.

Garrison, Marsha. 1983. Why Terminate Parental Rights? *Stanford Law Review* 35:423-96.

Institute of Judicial Administration and American Bar Association. 1980. *Standards for Juvenile Court, Noncriminal Misbehavior, Standard 1.1.* Chicago: American Bar Association.

Parent, Dale, Terence Dunworth, Douglas McDonald, and William Rhodes. 1997. *Key Legislative Issues in Criminal Justice: Transferring Serious Juvenile Offenders to Adult Courts.*

Washington, DC: Department of Justice, National Institute of Justice.

Sickmund, Melissa. 1994. *How Juveniles Get to Criminal Court*. Washington, DC: U.S. Department of Justice, Office of Juvenile Justice and Delinquency Prevention.

Sickmund, Melissa, Anne L. Stahl, Terrence A. Finnegan, Howard N.

Snyder, Rowen S. Poole, and Jeffrey A. Butts. 1998. *Juvenile Court Statistics 1995*. Washington, DC: Department of Justice, Office of Juvenile Justice and Delinquency Prevention.

Snyder, Howard. 1997. *Juvenile Arrests 1996*. Washington, DC: Department of Justice, Office of Juvenile Justice and Delinquency Prevention.

ANNALS, *AAPSS*, **564**, July 1999

Shackled in the Land of Liberty: No Rights for Children

By WANDA MOHR, RICHARD J. GELLES,
and IRA M. SCHWARTZ

ABSTRACT: This article addresses the rights of children in areas of juvenile justice, child welfare, and mental health. Although a large proportion of the juvenile court's business includes child welfare and mental health cases, these important areas are rarely considered by authors concerned with the future of the juvenile court. In mental health, children have few, if any, rights. Yet, they are often subjected to abuse and constraints that would constitute major civil rights violations if they were adults. In child welfare, children have some basic rights, but they are often dependent upon the virtually unbridled discretion of child welfare and other administrative officials. More often than not, the juvenile court plays a perfunctory role in the process and merely rubber-stamps recommendations made by child welfare personnel. The article discusses the implications of these issues and how they should be addressed in the future.

Wanda Mohr is an assistant professor at the University of Pennsylvania School of Nursing and is best known for her research into the private psychiatric hospital scandal of the 1980s and 1990s.

Richard J. Gelles holds the Joanne and Raymond Welsh Chair of Child Welfare and Family Violence in the School of Social Work at the University of Pennsylvania.

Ira M. Schwartz serves on the board of Pennsylvania Partnerships for Children and is a member of the National Association of Deans and Directors of Schools of Social Work and the Council on Social Work Education.

T HE United Nations Convention on the Rights of the Child represented an international resolution concerned with safeguarding the physical, social, cultural, and religious rights of children, and it established a new legal regime for the protection of such rights. The convention was held in 1989 and was passed by the U.N. General Assembly, and then it passed out of the collective consciousness of the U.S. government. Despite the support of the National Association of Social Workers and warnings emanating from the National Commission on Children about the status of children's rights in the United States, supporting legislation has not been ratified by the Senate or advanced by either the Bush or Clinton administrations.

The children of the richest country in the world continue to occupy a position in a no-man's-land between chattel and constitutionally protected citizen. This ambiguous situation ensures that children are denied some of the most basic rights available to adults and other citizens of free societies.

One of those basic rights is the right of free expression. Yet, because of antiquated notions rooted in property rights law, children are often denied the rights to adequate representation and, in some instances, to express their views in judicial and administrative proceedings, either directly or through a representative or appropriate body. In this article, we discuss some of the ways that the denial of this basic freedom plays out in the juvenile justice, child welfare, and mental health systems. We illustrate how the neglect of children's rights, their invisibility, and their lack of representation in present systems lead to the inevitable abuses of the same children who should receive protection within those systems under the Fourteenth Amendment to the Constitution. We also discuss the changes that must be enacted in the policy arena to ensure that children's mistreatment ceases and that they can lead lives free of fear and chaos.

THE JUVENILE JUSTICE SYSTEM

The juvenile court "was part of a general movement directed toward removing adolescents from the criminal law process and creating special programs for delinquent, dependent, and neglected children" (Platt 1977, 10). At the time of its creation, it was heralded as one of the greatest advances in the cause for troubled children (10). It was premised on the *parens patriae* philosophy assuming the state's authority to protect those who cannot protect themselves. In contrast to the adult criminal justice system, which operates under a primarily punitive and just-deserts rubric, the fundamental canon of the juvenile justice system in the United States has traditionally put an emphasis on individualized treatment and rehabilitation.

Reform efforts by social crusaders during the Progressive Era led to the establishment of the nation's first formal juvenile court in Chicago in 1899. The concept spread rapidly, and "by 1917 juvenile court legislation had been passed in all but three states and by 1932 there were over 600 independent juvenile courts throughout the United States" (Platt 1977, 10).

The Chicago juvenile court and the others that were modeled after it were envisioned to be less like courts and more like social welfare agencies. Their primary concern was for the general welfare of troubled and wayward children. As a result, the juvenile courts were given broad authority over virtually all forms of child and adolescent behavior and cases, including delinquency, status offenses, and child neglect and dependency. The legislation that created juvenile courts presumed a system in which justice and the promise of the emerging social and behavioral sciences would work together to rehabilitate all manner of delinquent, dependent, or neglected children (Levine and Levine 1970).

The juvenile courts operated free from the due process and adversarial legal proceedings that characterized the adult criminal courts. These, it was felt, were an impediment to making decisions that were in "the best interests" of the child. Instead, the juvenile court focused on determining the causes of a child's misbehavior or problems and, with the help of professionals skilled in child guidance, providing proper diagnosis and treatment. As a result, juvenile court judges and other professionals (for example, social workers, probation officers, psychologists, and psychiatrists) were given broad discretion in making decisions about the disposition and treatment of cases involving children.

Predictably, the unbridled discretion given to judges and other "helping professionals" coupled with the informality and secrecy of the juvenile court proceedings resulted in serious due process failures and abuse. For example, children were found guilty of offenses based upon hearsay. They did not have the benefit of counsel and could not cross-examine witnesses. Typically, no record was kept of the proceedings, proceedings that took place behind closed doors. Then, despite the avowed emphasis on treatment and rehabilitation, children were routinely deprived of their liberty and provided with little or no meaningful services. Many were sent off to institutions characterized by hard labor, highly regimented schedules, and an absence of meaningful education and treatment programs. Oftentimes, they were institutions where children were mistreated and exploited by ill-trained and uncaring staff.

The problems confronting the juvenile justice system were widespread, with scandals surfacing in states throughout the country. Eventually, the federal government, the U.S. Supreme Court, and others took action. For example, a series of Supreme Court decisions in the late 1960s and 1970s provided young people with many of the same due process and procedural safeguards accorded adults (Schwartz 1989). At about the same time, the Senate Subcommittee to Investigate Juvenile Delinquency launched an in-depth inquiry into the juvenile justice system, culminating in the enactment of the federal Juvenile Justice and

Delinquency Prevention Act of 1974. Also, such groups as the National Advisory Committee on Juvenile Justice, the Institute for Judicial Administration/American Bar Association, and the Commission on Accreditation of the American Correctional Association issued standards for juvenile justice.

These developments changed the face of juvenile justice in the United States. The legal processing and handling of juveniles in delinquency matters began to mirror that in the adult criminal courts. Juveniles were given access to legal representation and the right to cross-examine witnesses, and they could be found guilty of crimes only based upon the same legal standard (beyond a reasonable doubt) used in the adult criminal courts (Feld 1997). Also, records were kept of the proceedings. The federal government, through the Office of Juvenile Justice and Delinquency Prevention, made funds available to the states as an incentive to change juvenile justice policies and practices. This change included such things as removing status offenders from secure detention and youth correction facilities, removing juveniles from adult jails, and encouraging the development of community-based alternatives to juvenile prisons (Schwartz 1989; Binder and Polan 1991; Ohlin 1998).

Child advocates and critics of the juvenile justice system applauded these developments. Unfortunately, history has shown that their hopes and dreams for reforms were never fully realized. The so-called due process revolution did transform the juvenile court from being a social welfare institution into a court of law. Young people were given many of the same protections and due process guarantees accorded adults. However, researchers have found that large numbers of children who appeared in the juvenile courts in some states did not have lawyers (Feld 1997). Many of these children, it was discovered, were encouraged to waive their right to counsel even though research has shown that they often did not understand the meaning and implications of that decision (Feld 1997). Although status offenders were removed from secure facilities, their numbers were offset by the incarceration of more young people for minor and petty delinquent acts. Moreover, there is evidence that many status offenders, as well as other troubled children, were propelled into private inpatient psychiatric and substance abuse facilities where they were essentially confined against their will with virtually no legal protections (Schwartz, Jackson-Beeck, and Anderson 1984).

One hundred years of the juvenile court

The year 1999 marks the hundredth anniversary of the juvenile court. Child advocates, juvenile court judges, and other juvenile justice professionals had been anticipating and planning for this event for years. However, as 1999 drew closer, the prospects for a celebration of the juvenile court and its prospects for the future dimmed. Enthusiasm dampened because the voices calling for the juvenile court's abolition were gaining support. Also, and more important, it was becoming clear that this once sacred institution had lost much of the support it had enjoyed from the public and from elected public officials.

The juvenile court always had its critics, particularly in the academic community. Barry Feld, for example, has studied and written extensively about the juvenile court and its failings. He is a strong proponent of the abolitionist argument, and his work, perhaps more than that of any other scholar, has influenced the thinking and debates about the juvenile court and its failings. Feld finds little justification for the juvenile court given the procedural convergence between the juvenile and adult criminal courts and given the fact that most states have altered the purpose of their juvenile courts to take on a punishment role (Feld 1997).

Although Feld and a few other prominent academics have played an influential role in the current debates, public fear about juvenile crime, and violent crime in particular, has had just as much or more of an impact on the most recent assault on the juvenile justice system and on the erosion in the juvenile court's jurisdiction. For example, throughout the 1990s there have been daily media accounts of drive-by shootings, horrific crimes committed by young children, and senseless shootings and killings by teenagers on school grounds. Juvenile homicides jumped to 3790 in 1993, more than double the number committed less than 10 years earlier (Strom, Smith, and Snyder 1998). This prompted

lawmakers in virtually every state to overhaul their juvenile justice statutes. The statutory changes were designed to crack down on juvenile law violators by treating more of them like adults. The slogan "Adult crime deserves adult time" became popularized and seemed to be the guiding principle for policymaking. At the same time, penalties were stiffened for young people who were kept in the juvenile justice system.

Forty-one states now allow or require transfer of children 14 years old or younger to criminal court under certain conditions. In Indiana, children as young as 10 years old can be waived to criminal court if they are charged with manslaughter or murder. Twelve states do not set any minimum age for criminal prosecution. Oklahoma expressly allows children tried as adults to be incarcerated with adults upon conviction, regardless of the child's age (Klein 1998). These legislative changes have resulted in a significant increase in the number of young people tried in the adult criminal courts and who have received adultlike sentences.

On 1 January 1999, the Juvenile Justice Reform Act of 1998 took effect in Illinois, ironically, the state that gave birth to the rehabilitative philosophy. This act expands certain kinds of record keeping in schools, mandating that certain information, such as serious disciplinary infractions involving weapons and drug use, are kept and disclosed to law enforcement on request. The act also requires state police to develop a statewide database to identify and track juvenile offenders. All children aged 10 and older who are arrested for felony offenses will be fingerprinted, while those arrested for Class A and B misdemeanors may be fingerprinted and included in the database. It also increases the maximum amount of time that police can detain a youth before he or she is charged, from 6 hours to 12 hours for all crimes and 24 hours for a crime of violence. It changes the maximum time for which a juvenile offender can be held in custody before being tried from 15 to 30 days, and, paralleling practices in the adult criminal justice system, it provides for judges to place conditions upon a juvenile offender as part of his or her release prior to trial. Clearly, these changes, coupled with legislation previously enacted, reshape the state's juvenile justice system in ways never envisioned by its creators.

Juvenile justice reforms: Back to the future

The due process reforms injected into the legal handling of children in the juvenile courts were necessary and represented significant advances in the cause for children. However, the child advocates and reformers who championed these issues never envisioned that the procedural convergence between the juvenile and adult criminal courts would ultimately raise the question about whether a separate court for children would be needed for delinquency matters. They also failed to recognize the limitations of the social sciences and, when it occurred, grossly underestimated the impact of the implosion of the so-called rehabilitative ideal. Just as important, they did not anticipate or have adequate responses to the rise in juvenile violence and the public outrage it engendered. The child savers who invented the juvenile justice system a century ago are probably spinning in their graves knowing that children are once again being incarcerated in adult jails and prisons. Aside from the fact that preliminary research indicates that this practice is counterproductive and does little, if anything, to enhance public safety (Bishop and Frazier 1996), it signals a return to policies and practices that existed before the turn of the century.

The debate about the current and future role, if any, of the juvenile court in delinquency matters is vitally important. Despite its importance, however, this debate is incomplete because it fails to take into account the current and future role of the juvenile court in child abuse and neglect matters. Proposals for reform, if they are going to receive serious consideration and have any chance to be implemented, must take these matters into account. It is simply not adequate to recommend, as some do, that delinquency matters be handled in the adult criminal courts and that child abuse and neglect issues be handled as civil matters.

There are many lessons to be learned from the attempts to reform juvenile justice. Reformers who want to address the legal and service delivery issues confronting children in the child welfare and mental health systems would be well advised to carefully examine these lessons and the implications they may have.

SHACKLED IN THE LAND OF LIBERTY

CHILD WELFARE

U.S. law and tradition grant parents broad discretion in how they rear their children. In *Smith* v. *Organization of Foster Families for Equality and Reform* (431 U.S. 816 [1977]), the U.S. Supreme Court held that the Fourteenth Amendment gave parents a "constitutionally recognized liberty interest" in maintaining the custody of their children "that derives from blood relationship, state law sanction, and basic human right." This interest is not absolute, however, because the state has power and authority to exercise *parens patriae* duties to protect citizens who cannot fend for themselves.

The state may attempt to limit or end parent-child contact and make children eligible for temporary or permanent placement or adoption when the parents (1) abuse, neglect, or abandon their children; (2) become incapacitated in their ability to be a parent; (3) refuse or are unable to remedy serious, identified problems in caring for their children; or (4) experience an extraordinarily severe breakdown in their relationship with their children (for example, owing to a long prison sentence). Cognizant that severing the parent-child relationship is an extremely drastic measure, the U.S. Supreme Court held in *Santosky* v. *Kramer* (455 U.S. 745 [1982]) that a court may terminate parental rights only if the state can demonstrate with clear and convincing evidence that a parent has failed in one of these four ways. Most state statutes also contain provisions for parents to voluntarily relinquish their rights. The state also has the authority to return a child to his or her parents. This occurs once a determination is made that it would be safe to return the child home and that the child's parents would be able to provide appropriate care.

Although the juvenile court is involved in each step in this process, child welfare agencies are responsible for investigating and managing cases of child maltreatment. Nonetheless, the juvenile court is responsible for making the final decisions about whether children are removed from their parents, whether they are returned to their parents, where children are placed (for example, with relatives, in foster care, or in residential treatment), and terminating parental rights and adoptions.

The ideal role of the juvenile, family, or dependency court in child welfare matters is to balance parents' constitutional rights to be free from undue and unwarranted interference in raising their children with the dependent child's rights to protection from harm. Child protection is bolstered by the state's ability to seek ex parte orders or stipulations to allow a child to be removed from what is deemed an unsafe caretaking environment. State laws also allow hospitals to place holds of various lengths on children in order to protect the children and allow for an investigation of the children's care situations.

Ex parte orders and holds are short-term efforts designed to protect children. If a medical evaluation or a child protective evaluation concludes that a child is at risk and should be removed from the caregiving environment, the matter is placed before a juvenile or family court judge or master for a hearing. The hearing proceeds in a typical adversarial style.

Before we examine a child's rights and representation in a child welfare legal action, it is important to look at the institutional and cultural context of the child welfare system. For at least the last 100 years, the abuse and neglect of children has been responded to by private and public social welfare institutions and agencies and not by the criminal justice system. The case that has been most widely written on is the case of Mary Ellen Wilson, a neglected child discovered in New York City in 1874. Mary Ellen had been beaten with a leather thong and allowed to go ill clothed in cold weather (for a complete discussion, see Gelles 1996, 1997). Mary Ellen's case was initially investigated by Etta Wheeler, a "friendly visitor" who worked for St. Luke's Methodist Mission. The New York police declined to become involved, as there was no evidence that a crime had been committed. Legend has it that Mary Ellen's case was argued in court by the Society for the Prevention of Cruelty to Animals (SPCA) because Mary Ellen was a member of the "animal kingdom." In fact, the court accepted the case because the child needed protection. The SPCA did not represent Mary Ellen, but private societies for the prevention of cruelty to children were established after the case received broad coverage in the New York City newspapers.

In the years after the Mary Ellen case, child abuse and neglect came to be defined as a social problem in need of a social welfare response. Unless a homicide took place, and even when a child was killed, the institution responsible for investigating cases, responding, and protecting was a social welfare institution. In spite of the fact that some acts of child abuse are clearly acts of felony assault and violate criminal codes, the criminal justice system, from the police, to prosecutors, to criminal courts, are rarely directly involved in such a case.

As a consequence of social welfare institutions' taking priority over child welfare cases, the legal cases do not result in an adversarial proceeding pitting the state against the offenders, as would, for example, a case of domestic violence. Rather, the legal proceedings involve a state, county, or local department of child welfare versus the parents or caretakers of the alleged victim.

The cultural context that led to the creation of this system and continued support of the system revolves around the constitutional stipulation that parents should be free from undue interference in raising their children. In addition, deep cultural convictions, values, and ideologies support child maltreatment as a child welfare issue, not a criminal justice issue. The core ideological value is that children do best when raised by their biological parents. One version of this ideology is the notion that even the best foster or adoptive family is not better for a child than a marginal biological family. Thus, for more than 100 years, the main focus of child welfare has been to rehabilitate or help families so they can raise their children. At the turn of the last century, family preservation was the province of the settlement house movement. The most recent attempts to keep maltreated children with their biological caregivers are support for intensive family preservation and family support programs.

As noted, there is at least a theoretical tension between parents' rights and child protection. However, the underlying ideology of the child welfare system is that the best placement for children is with their parents. Permanency, while theoretically allowing for a number of alternative placements (such as legal guardianship, adoption, or congregate care), is typically conceptualized as keeping a child with his or her parents or achieving reunification. Similarly, although child welfare institutions promote the ideology of making decisions that are in "the best interests of the child," almost always the best interests are assumed to be achieved if the child is raised by his or her biological caregivers.

An example of this ideological commitment can be seen in the institutional interpretation of the reasonable efforts clause of the Adoption Assistance and Child Welfare Act of 1980. This law required that states make "reasonable efforts" prior to the placement of a child in foster care or to make it possible for a child to return to his or her home. The law never actually defined the terms "reasonable" and "efforts." Nonetheless, child welfare workers, supervisors, administrators, attorneys, and judges often interpreted this law to mean that the state had an obligation to make every possible effort to keep a child in the home or return a child there. Some state child welfare statutes do in fact require every possible effort. As noted earlier, the Supreme Court ruled in *Santosky* v. *Kramer* that states could terminate parents' rights only if there was clear and convincing evidence that parents had abused, neglected, or abandoned their children; were incapacitated; refused or were unable to remedy problems in caring for their children; or experienced a severe breakdown in their relationship with their children. Thus parents who make a "reasonable effort" to care for their children would not have their parental rights terminated.

The mandate for child welfare agencies and family, juvenile, or dependency courts is to find a balance between parents' constitutional rights and children's rights. In executing this mandate, the agencies and courts appear to have achieved a level playing field. However, appearances are not only deceiving; they are false. The playing field is hardly level and is clearly tilted in favor of parents' rights.

By ideology and practice, the child welfare system and the courts lean toward preserving the family and keeping children with, or returning children to, their biological parents. The standard in most court proceedings is whether the state can prove by clear and convincing evidence that parents or caretakers are unfit. Of course, the same state agency has as its goal the preservation of that family. The agencies and the courts operate from the assumptions that children do best when cared for by biological parents, that parents want to be caring and adequate parents, and that existing programs to assist parents are effective, and, when not effective, that the shortfall is due to insufficient resources for the programs or the caseworker's implementing the program inappropriately. All things being equal, it is felt that a child's best interests are served if the child can remain with or be returned to his or her biological caretakers.

The legal representation that children's best interests receive is another example of how uneven the family court playing field is. With the exception of emergency ex parte proceedings, the parents will have legal representation. If there are two caretakers, each may have a representative. Attorneys employed by the state or county child welfare agency represent the state. At stake are the parents' constitutional rights and the child's best interest. Yet the child often has no trained legal counsel. At present, in only half of the states does state law require the child to have an attorney represent the child at dispositional or termination proceedings. In the other half of the states, the representation is either by a court-appointed special advocate or a guardian *ad litem*. In only 30-40 percent of the states does a child welfare statute define the role of the child's lawyer; in the majority of the states, the role is not defined. Thus, in at least half of the states, children in child welfare cases are not represented by an attorney. While there are well-trained court-appointed

special advocates and guardians *ad litem*, it is often the case that the representative of the child is untrained and unaware of federal and state law as well as existing precedents. It is not altogether uncommon to find that attorneys who represent children are equally unfamiliar with controlling legislation and precedent (Peters 1997).

Taking a wider look at child welfare legal proceedings, we also see the minimal legal protections and safeguards that are offered children. It was not until 1974 that the federal government even recommended (as part of a requirement for federal child abuse and neglect funding) that children have a guardian *ad litem* represent their legal interests. Two Supreme Court decisions also demonstrate the minimal protections offered children. In *Suter* v. *Artist* (503 U.S. 347 [1992]), the Supreme Court ruled that the federal Adoption Assistance and Child Welfare Act of 1980, which articulates standards for states to receive Title IVE funding, does not create rights for children enforceable in an action nor does the law create an implied private cause for action. In *DeShaney et al.* v. *Winnebago County Department of Social Services et al.* (489 U.S. 189 [1989]), the Court affirmed that if a state child welfare agency fails to protect an individual (in this case, a minor child) against a caretaker's violence (in this case, a father), the state agency is not responsible for the harm done to the child. Failure of a state agency to protect an individual against private violence does not constitute a violation of due process.

The implication of this decision is that state agencies cannot be held liable for failing to protect a child from harm, even if they are aware the child may be at risk.

In the absence of Supreme Court precedent that federal law provides legal guarantees for children and that children involved with the child welfare system have a right to be protected, the legal rights of children have been advanced by a series of class action suits against state and local child welfare agencies. At present, at least 27 states and many more localities are under court order to improve child welfare services. However, there is little consistency in the suits or court stipulations. In Alabama, for example, the state is obliged to provide more family preservation services; in Connecticut, the state has been ordered to give more weight to child safety. Thus, even class action suits fail to provide clear support for children's rights and best interests (or at least bring to the issue differing conceptions of children's "best interests").

For at least 100 years, the main thrust of the child welfare system has been to provide social and psychological resources so that children can be raised without interference by the government. While the child welfare system is criticized from all directions, one consistent concern is that children are often removed from families without cause or that families that can be helped are not afforded that opportunity (Wexler 1991; Guggenheim 1999). Those who demonstrate concern for children harmed even after they have been identified by the child welfare system are labeled "child savers," a term designed to be pejorative in this case.

The child welfare system has been in crisis for nearly three decades. The response to the crisis is a "round up the usual suspects" call for more resources, more workers, and reorganization of child welfare bureaucracies. New federal legislation, the Adoption and Safe Families Act of 1997, attempted to create more balance in the system by identifying instances where reunification efforts did not have to be made for families, by requiring states to seek termination of parental rights when children had been in out-of-home care for 15 of the previous 22 months, and by mandating that states do concurrent planning, rather than planning only for reunification and then seeking alternatives when such plans failed or were deemed inappropriate. In Florida, Arkansas, and Michigan, plans are in place or are being developed to transfer child protection investigations from child welfare agencies to the sheriffs or police. There seems to be a subtle change to move child maltreatment from a social welfare issue to a criminal issue.

What impact the Adoption and Safe Families Act and current changes regarding investigations will have is to be determined. What is clear, however, is that children and their "best interests" are given minimal consideration in child welfare proceedings. The child welfare system remains a system where the client is the parent, where the parent's legal rights are primary, and where a child's developmental best interests are rarely represented or given careful and appropriate weight.

THE MENTAL HEALTH SYSTEM

Meeting the needs of children with mental health problems has always been a challenge. It is a long-standing national issue that has received much attention but little action (Ross 1995). In 1970, the National Institute of Mental Health (U.S. Department of Health, Education, and Welfare 1970) pointed out that less than 1 percent of the disturbed children in our society were receiving any kind of treatment, and less than half of these were getting adequate help. In that same year, the Joint Commission on the Mental Health of Children (1970) referred to this country's lack of commitment to children and youths as a "national tragedy." Eight years later, the President's Commission on Mental Health (1978) was still calling attention to the fact that children and adolescents were not receiving mental health services commensurate with their needs. A decade later, the Office of Technology Assessment estimated that only 20-30 percent of children identified to be in need of services actually receive any care. Much of that care is considered to be overly restrictive when rendered in institutional settings and disorganized and fragmented when executed in community settings (Mental Health Association 1989; Macro International 1992).

There is also evidence documenting the growing number of youths with serious emotional disorders who come into contact with the juvenile justice system (Friedman and Kutash 1992). But given the existing state of mental health knowledge, expertise, and resources, it is highly doubtful if the mental health system has the capability to meet the needs of these young people.

Complicating the issue of service provision to mentally ill children is the vagueness of the diagnostic criteria involved in determining whether a child does or does not have a mental illness or whether the child is engaging in delinquent behavior for some other underlying reason. For this determination to be made, professionals rely on the American Psychiatric Association's *Diagnostic and Statistical Manual of Mental Disorders* (*DSM*). Since its development, the *DSM* has been a source of controversy and critique. Major difficulties include the *DSM*'s (1) lack of theoretical foundation, (2) lack of precision, (3) failure to consider context, and (4) lack of consequential validity. With respect to lack of theory, scholars in child development (Jensen and Hoagwood 1997; Richters and Cicchetti 1993) posit that the *DSM* is of questionable use in diagnosing children in that the manual's categories represent a collection of symptoms that are downward extensions of adult psychosocial functioning.

Also complicating the picture in mental health service provision is the movement to managed care for the mentally ill within both the private and public sectors. In addition to the management of care system contracts, behavioral health care is increasingly being outsourced, or contracted out, to private providers.

The ultimate impact of these developments is unclear. Preliminary reports in Massachusetts indicate that outsourcing resulted in lower mental health expenditures for children at the same time that the use of acute residential inpatient treatment for children and adolescents escalated. Between October 1992 and May 1995, total expenditures for this purpose rose 774 percent, expenditures per recipient increased 67 percent, and the number of children and adolescents placed in these settings climbed by 423 percent (Jaspen 1998). This suggests that the cost savings some health care policy experts and others had hoped for in this area may not be realized. Just as troubling is that the Massachusetts experience suggests there may be cost shifting, with more children being propelled into the most costly, most restrictive, and most questionable types of treatment where they have little protection under the law.

*Children's rights in
    the mental health system*

The complex relationship of children to the mental health system is rooted in three underlying and competing interests (Hopcroft 1985). The first of these is the interest in the sacredness of the family; in preserving the autonomy of parents in determining and providing for the best interests of their children; and in preserving the particular personal and cultural values of the family. The second is the state's interest in protecting the child, in preventing or controlling unwanted behavior, and in providing a system of mental health care. The third interest is the child's interest in being cared for, loved, and helped to become an autonomous individual with the rights and privileges of an adult (Hopcroft 1985).

Laws and rules governing the psychiatric hospitalization of minors vary considerably from state to state. However, the overall policy that governs this area was set by the U.S. Supreme Court's decision in *Parham v. J.R.* (442 U.S. 584) in 1979. In handing down this decision, the Supreme Court essentially declared that children do not have the same constitutional rights as adults. According to *Parham v. J.R.*, the U.S. Constitution allows involuntary hospitalization of a minor without judicial review if the child's legal custodian consents, the treating clinicians concur, and the clinicians periodically review the need for continued inpatient treatment.[1] Individual states are free to grant their own citizens additional rights, so this disenfranchisement of children plays itself out differently in different states. In Massachusetts, for example, children have the right to court-assigned counsel in certain civil and quasi-criminal cases, but the role of that counsel is very narrow. According to sections 39F and 29 of chapter 119 of the Massachusetts Annals of Law (Law Co-operative, 1994), the attorney does not advocate the child's position to the court; rather, the attorney must "advocate to the court the disposition of the case the lawyer believes will serve the best interest of the child, even when that position is contrary to the client's expressed wishes." At the same time, however, according to section 38 of chapter 210 of the Massachusetts annals, the attorney must also "inform the court of the client's contrary views and the lawyer's reasons for believing that they will not serve the client's best interest." Thus representation by counsel at a commitment hearing is not commensurate with the same idea of due process for children as it is for adults. By attenuating the role of counsel, the Commonwealth of Massachusetts risks erroneous commitment of children to a most restrictive setting without the benefit of the same protection afforded other citizens.

In Florida, the Fourth District Court of Appeal in West Palm Beach recently became the first to apply the state's laws on involuntary commitment under the Baker Act to Minors (Smith 1998). Under this decision, children under the age of 18 are entitled to the same precommitment hearing as adults to determine whether they are dangerous and whether there are less severe alternatives to commitment. In most states, however, the avenues for relief are not as formal as those available to adults, and, without adequate provisions for judicial review, children can languish in facilities for unspecified lengths of time and suffer the most basic deprivation of their rights as human beings.

Nowhere was this more dramatically illustrated as during the years of the for-profit psychiatric hospital scandal (Mohr 1997, 1998). Public hearings in Texas revealed patterns of widespread and consistent abuse against patients, the majority of whom were children and adolescents.

The abuse included unwarranted and excessively lengthy institutionalization; withholding access to mail and telephone; censoring mail, telephone conversations, and visits; restricting access to parents and clergy; forced medications and unwarranted mechanical restraints; restrictions on personal items of clothing; and a panoply of abusive and punitive procedures and actions that were dispensed at staff members' whims and for which there was no therapeutic justification. Despite charges of criminal and civil rights violations and clear causes for action including battery, false imprisonment, and assault, among others, the U.S. Department of Justice did not pursue legal actions on behalf of the former patients, leaving any further litigation to private attorneys (Borreson 1997).

Mental health care for adults

The U.S. Supreme Court continues to recognize involuntary commitment as an option based on two legal theories. First, under its police power, the state has the authority to protect the community from the dangerous acts of the mentally ill; and second, under its *parens patriae* powers, the state can provide care for citizens who cannot care for themselves, such as some mentally ill people. Almost all states have commitment laws for adults that vary from state to state, but most laws permit commitment of the mentally ill on the following grounds: dangerousness to self or others; mental illness and need for treatment; and inability to provide for basic needs. The states recognize the patient's right to legal counsel, and court commitment is made before a judge or jury in a formal hearing. Once hospitalized, adult psychiatric patients have the following rights, among others: (1) the right to communicate with people outside of the hospital through correspondence, telephone, and personal visits; (2) the right to keep clothing and personal effects with them in the hospital; (3) the right to religious freedom; (4) the right to education; (5) habeas corpus; (6) the right to independent psychiatric examination; (7) the right not to be subjected to unnecessary mechanical restraints; (8) the right to periodic review of status; (9) the right to legal representation; (10) the right to privacy; (11) the right to informed consent; (12) the right to treatment; (13) the right to refuse treatment; and (14) the right to treatment in the least restrictive setting. Unlike their child counterparts, under the Baker Act, and upheld by the Supreme Court, adults are entitled to an impressive array of judicial protections and procedural rights.

In addition, voluntary admission status at a public or private facility is completely voluntary in most states, and this status may be terminated at any time, with or without notice by the patient or the superintendent of the facility. However, voluntary admission status is generally not an option for children under the age of 16 because they are not considered to be competent, although they are competent to make a decision involving such serious matters as having an abortion. Moreover, unlike the strict confidentiality that applies to adult records, in a number of states children's legal custodians can access their medical records at any time without their permission.

*Children's mental
   health care in practice*

Children who are mentally ill are dually disadvantaged: they are children and therefore powerless, and they are mentally ill and therefore both powerless and noncredible. Leaf (1996) asserts that committing teenagers to private mental hospitals has become increasingly popular and is frequently used to manage troublesome adolescent behavior (1688). Some parents appear willing to take the step of committing their children to psychiatric institutions due to behavior that clearly does not require such treatment, and these children are often powerless to prevent it.

For years before the egregious events of the for-profit psychiatric hospital scandals, former patients were reporting abuses at the hands of staff as well as violations of their basic rights. Despite civil lawsuits and repeated investigations by states into reported abuses, the abuses continue. The most unacceptable outcome of these abuses is the deaths that have occurred as a result of the inappropriate restraint of children. During 1998, deaths were reported in North Carolina (T.S., male, aged 15), Arizona (E.C., female, aged 15), Massachusetts (M.S., male, aged 16), and Connecticut (A.M., male, aged 11). In a special series by the *Hartford Courant*, results from a 50-state survey on the use of restraints confirmed 142 deaths occurring during or shortly after restraint or seclusion in the past decade. Twenty-six percent of these deaths involved children. Because these cases go unreported for the most part, the actual number is estimated to be much higher, as high as 50-150 each year, according to the Harvard Center for Risk Analysis (Weiss 1998).

CONCLUSION

As we noted at the outset of this article, the rights of children in the United States fall somewhere between protected citizen and property. At no time in a child's involvement in the juvenile justice system, child welfare system, or mental health system is the child afforded the same rights and constitutional protections that an adult would receive. Nonetheless, there is considerable variation between these three institutions in terms of how clearly children's rights are codified and articulated.

Children's rights in the juvenile justice system are relatively well defined. The Supreme Court decision in In re Gault (387 U.S. 1 [1967]) established precedent for due process and representation for children who are involved with the juvenile court.

Children's rights in the child welfare and mental health systems are much less defined and clear. Contrary to prevailing thought and assumptions, children's rights in child welfare proceedings are not well articulated. Children's best interests, while theoretically the central focus of child welfare proceedings and actions, often take a backseat to parents' rights. While children are represented in child welfare action, this representation does not come up to creating a level playing field that balances parents' constitutional rights and children's rights to protection. The system designed to protect children from violence often subjects them to violence via lack of safety and permanence.

A change is in the offing in the child welfare system, as a number of states have begun to transfer the responsibility for child maltreatment investigations from child welfare agencies to the police or sheriff's departments. This transfer may well result in more cases of child maltreatment being prosecuted in criminal courts rather than family or juvenile courts. How this will affect children's rights and safety is unknown and will remain unknown unless such policy changes are evaluated.

The transfer of child maltreatment cases from child welfare agencies to the criminal justice system may provoke strong objection. The objection will arise because no less than one-half of child maltreatment reports are due to neglect, and poverty is a leading cause of neglect as well as a major cause of physical abuse. Many child and family advocates will argue that families should be helped and not prosecuted because the real underlying problem is poverty. However, poverty is also a major correlate of juvenile delinquency, and juveniles are not relieved of their responsibility for criminal behavior because they have been raised in families and communities suffering from poverty and oppression.

Children have rights to protection and permanence. At the moment, the child welfare system does not adequately assure children these rights. The fact that as many as 27 states are involved in child welfare litigation demonstrates how widespread the problem of children's lack of protection and permanence is in the United States.

It is also worth noting that approximately 20 percent of children in the child welfare system are in institutional settings. These children are often placed in institutional settings against their will and are defined as being in need of treatment. While in these settings, they are often subject to virtually the same restrictions on their liberty and treatment protocols as are juvenile delinquents committed to public and private youth correction facilities. In fact, it is not uncommon for youths in the child welfare system to be placed in the same facilities where they may or may not be separated from the delinquents. Also, child welfare cases in institutional settings are often placed for an indeterminate period of time. Indeterminate placements or sentences are generally not allowed for adults or delinquent youths but are a normal part of the child welfare system.

Finally, children in the mental health system have the least rights of all children. The *Parham* decision reasserts parents' rights to have their children committed to a mental health facility if a "competent" mental health professional provides an appropriate diagnosis. Clearly, some parents are acting in their children's best interests when they seek placement of their children in a mental health facility. However, some parents opt for such placements as part of an attempt to control their children and win a parent-child conflict. The mental health professional's diagnosis that results in such a placement may not conform to science or best practice. There needs to be some kind of assurance that children are placed in mental health facilities for medical reasons and that children's rights are not violated by such placements.

Once children are placed, there are additional abuses and restrictions that violate children's basic rights and needs.

One thing is clear: when the state acts on the basis of *parens patriae*, it is not certain that children's rights, needs, and basic protections are considered or assured. We continue to assume that parents and the state are single-minded in their goal of protecting children and providing for their best interests. The actual operation of the juvenile justice, child welfare, and mental health systems provides ample evidence that there are many exceptions to this rule and the end result is much violence and harm inflicted on the children we claim we are trying to protect.

Note

1. The Court held that a formal judicial hearing is not required for involuntary hospitalization of juveniles and that parental consent and independent medical judgment

agreeing with the need for psychiatric hospitalization are constitutionally sufficient.

References

Adoption and Safe Families Act. 1997. 111 Stat. 2115.

Adoption Assistance and Child Welfare Act. 1980. 42 U.S.C. §§ 670 et seq.

Binder, Arnold and Stephen Polan. 1991. The Kennedy-Johnson Years, Social Theory, and Federal Policy in the Control of Juvenile Delinquency. *Crime & Delinquency* 37:242-61.

Bishop, Donna M. and Charles E. Frazier. 1996. The Transfer to Criminal Court: Does It Make a Difference? *Crime & Delinquency* 42:171-83.

Borreson, Stephen. 1997. Fraud Suits Still Haunt Hospital Giant. *Texas Lawyer* 12(46):24-28.

Feld, Barry C. 1997. Abolish the Juvenile Court: Youthfulness, Criminal Responsibility and Sentencing Policy. *Journal of Criminal Law & Criminology* 88:68-136.

Friedman, Robert and Krista Kutash. 1992. Challenges for Child and Adolescent Mental Health. *Health Affairs* 11(3):125-36.

Gelles, Richard J. 1996. *The Book of David: How Preserving Families Can Cost Children's Lives.* New York: Basic Books.

———. 1997. *Intimate Violence in Families.* Thousand Oaks, CA: Sage.

Guggenheim, Morton. 1999. Comments on Children, Children's Rights and the Child Welfare System. Paper presented at the second symposium of the Journal of Constitutional Law, University of Pennsylvania, Philadelphia.

Hopcroft, Thomas E. 1985. Civil Commitment of Minors to Mental Institutions in the Commonwealth of Massachusetts. *New England Journal on Criminal and Civil Confinement* Summer: 542-92.

Jaspen, B. 1998. Psychiatric Systems Post More Growth Despite Consolidation. *Modern Healthcare* 28(21):54.

Jensen, Peter S. and Kimberly Hoagwood. 1997. The Book of Names: DSM-IV in Context. *Development and Psychopathology* 9(2):231-49.

Joint Commission on the Mental Health of Children. 1970. *Crisis in Child Mental Health: Challenges for the 1970s.* New York: Harper & Row.

Klein, Eric K. 1998. Dennis the Menace or Billy the Kid: An Analysis of the Role of Transfer to Criminal Court in Juvenile Justice. *American Criminal Law Review* 35:371-410.

Leaf, Samuel. 1996. How Voluntary Is the Commitment of Minors? Disparities in the Treatment of Children and Adults Under New York Civil Commitment Law. *Brooklyn Law Review* 62:1687-722.

Levine, Murray and Adeline Levine. 1970. *A Social History of Helping Services: Clinic, Court, School, and Community.* New York: Appleton-Century-Croft.

Macro International, Inc. 1992. *Final Report: Community-Based Mental Health Services for Children in the Child Welfare System.* Report no. HHS-001-91-0016-01. Washington, DC: Department of Health and Human Services.

Mental Health Association. 1989. *Final Report and Recommendations of the Invisible Children Project.* Alexandria, VA: Mental Health Association.

Mohr, Wanda K. 1997. The Outcomes of Corporate Greed. *Image: Journal of Nursing Scholarship* 29(1):39-47.

———. 1998. Experiences of Patients Involved in the Texas Hospital Scandal. *Perspectives in Psychiatric Care* 34(4):5-17.

Ohlin, Lloyd E. 1998. The Future of Juvenile Justice Policy and Research. *Crime & Delinquency* 44(1):143-53.

Peters, Jean Koh. 1997. *Representing Children in Child Protective Proceedings: Ethical and Practical Dimensions.* Charlottesville, VA: LEXIS Law.

Platt, Anthony M. 1977. *The Child Savers: The Invention of Delinquency.* Chicago: University of Chicago Press.

President's Commission on Mental Health. 1978. *Report to the President.* Washington, DC: Government Printing Office.

Richters, John E. and Dante Cicchetti. 1993. Mark Twain Meets DSM-III(R): Conduct Disorder, Development, and the Concept of Harmful Dysfunction. *Development and Psychopathology* 5(1-2):5-31.

Ross, Catherine J. 1995. Disposition in a Discretionary Regime: Punishment and Rehabilitation in the Juvenile Justice System. *Boston College Law Review* 36:1037-101.

Schwartz, Ira M. 1989. *(In)justice for Juveniles: Rethinking the Best Interest of the Child.* Lexington, MA: Lexington Books.

Schwartz, Ira M., M. Jackson-Beeck and R. Anderson. 1984. The "Hidden" System of Juvenile Control. *Crime & Delinquency* 30:371-85.

Smith, Stephanie. 1998. Appeals Panel Breaks Ground by Extending Procedural Rights to Minors. *Palm Beach Daily Business Review,* 4 Nov.

Strom, Kevin J., Steven K. Smith, and Howard N. Snyder. 1998. *State Court Processing Statistics, 1990-94: Juvenile Felony Defendants in Criminal Courts.* Washington, DC: Department of Justice.

U.S Department of Health, Education, and Welfare. National Institute of Mental Health. 1970. *Report on the State of Mental Health, 1970.* Mental Health Publication no. 5027. Washington, DC: Government Printing Office.

Weiss, Eric M. 1998. Deadly Restraint: A Nationwide Pattern of Death. *Hartford Courant,* 11-15 Oct.

Wexler, Richard. 1991. *Wounded Innocents: The Real Victims of the War Against Children.* Buffalo, NY: Prometheus.

Delinquency and Desert

By STEPHEN J. MORSE

ABSTRACT: This article addresses the moral and legal responsibility that may fairly be attributed to mid and late adolescents who commit criminal offenses and how adolescents' responsibility should affect the law's response. It offers a robust theory of responsibility that is rooted in our current moral theories and practices of blame and punishment. Next the article reviews the psychosocial and developmental literature to determine whether or to what degree mid to late adolescents are morally responsible for their conduct and whether they are less responsible than adults. Finally, the article considers the dispositional consequences implied by the theory of responsibility in general and by what we know about adolescents in particular. It concludes that neither data nor common sense can resolve the normative issue of juvenile responsibility.

Stephen J. Morse is Ferdinand Wakeman Hubbell Professor of Law and professor of psychology and law in psychiatry at the University of Pennsylvania. His scholarly interests are criminal law and mental health law.

NOTE: This article was presented as a paper at the symposium The Future of the Juvenile Court, sponsored by the John D. and Catherine T. MacArthur Foundation and the University of Pennsylvania and held at the University of Pennsylvania Law School in May 1997. For their excellent comments, the author would like to thank the symposium organizer, Dean Ira Schwartz; the commentators on the paper, Professor Alfred Blumstein, Professor James B. Jacobs, and Ms. Jane Tewksbury; and the many participants who offered suggestions. The paper was also presented at the Legal Studies Workshop at the University of Pennsylvania Law School. The author thanks his commentator, Leo Katz, and his other colleagues for their help. Finally, he thanks Kevin Reitz and Paul Robinson for their characteristically thoughtful comments. The present article is an abbreviated version of Immaturity and Irresponsibility, *Journal of Criminal Law & Criminology*, 88:15-67 (1997), which is reprinted here with permission.

O UR image of teenage offenders vacillates. We see them as wayward youths, as kids gone wrong, who nonetheless are not bad. This image is of the teen as a victim. They are misguided, immature, insufficiently socialized, but not evil. What they need is a therapeutic response that will permit natural maturation and socialization to set them on the right path. In contrast, we also see teen offenders as hostile predators, the products of unfortunate environments and perhaps heredity, who have little or no human sympathy or regard. This image is of the teen as a full-fledged criminal. Because they are evil and fully responsible, teens must be punished to satisfy just deserts and to protect the public. At the extreme, they deserve to be executed. In the anecdotal reports that fill the media and that often drive public policy, it is not hard to find either image.

The image of the teen offender as a criminal seems currently to predominate. Mid to late adolescence is a high-risk age for offending, especially violent offending (Elliott 1994), and the increased availability and common use of weapons (10-11) make teen violence particularly frightening. Although violent crime rates, including rates of violent juvenile crime (Sickmund, Snyder, and Poe-Yamagata 1997, 16-19), are down in most major cities of the United States, the public still fears teen violence. Pictures of schoolyard shootings and gang slaughter fill our minds. We are warned that a cohort of "superpredators" will soon emerge as the inevitable result of demographic variables (Bennett, DiIulio, and Waters 1996, 26-29).

The legislative and judicial reaction to public concern about serious and violent teen offenders has been substantial. Since 1992, 47 states and the District of Columbia have made changes in their laws governing the response to serious and violent juvenile offenders (Torbet et al. 1996; Singer 1996). The rate at which they are being removed from the juvenile justice system and prosecuted in the criminal justice system has skyrocketed. The traditional confidentiality of juvenile court proceedings and records is yielding to greater openness.

Critics of these changes believe that they are unfair to juveniles because juveniles are not fully responsible for their offenses and that the changes will not protect public safety because a criminal justice response will simply harden the antisocial tendencies already exhibited. They wish the juvenile justice system would adopt more flexible dispositional options that would give kids a genuine chance to grow up straight, while simultaneously exerting enough control over them to protect the public.

The common law treated people 14 years old as fully responsible. Many think the common law was wise; many disagree. This article addresses the claim that adolescent offenders are not fully responsible moral and legal agents. I make the assumption, which is almost universally shared in Anglo-American criminal jurisprudence, that desert based on moral fault is at least a necessary precondition for the punishment of youthful offenders. The focus on desert is not intended to gainsay the importance of other juvenile justice goals, such as prevention or reform. Depending on one's theory of punishment, such goals may be of great importance. But these other goals will be addressed only as they relate to the article's central question: the moral and ultimately legal responsibility of adolescent offenders.

We cannot think sensibly about this issue unless we first have in place a robust theory of responsibility generally. Only then will we be able to consider the relation of what we know about juveniles developmentally and psychosocially to ascriptions of responsibility to juveniles. Part 1 therefore offers a theory of responsibility, rooted in our current moral theories and actual practices of blaming and punishing. Part 2 explores whether juveniles meet the test of responsibility provided in part 1. In particular, to determine which juveniles deserve mitigation, it reviews psychosocial and developmental variables that differentiate juveniles from adults. Part 3 addresses the dispositional consequences that parts 1 and 2 imply. I conclude that neither common sense nor behavioral science data resolve the issue of juvenile responsibility. How we should respond to juvenile offenders is ultimately a moral judgment that must be derived from our best normative account of responsibility.

1. THINKING ABOUT RESPONSIBILITY

This part begins by explaining the law's concept of the person and how the legal conceptions of responsibility and excusing flow from the account of personhood. It then offers an account of what we are doing when we hold people responsible. Finally, it offers a broader view of the criteria of responsibility.

The law's concept of the person and responsibility

Intentional human conduct, that is, action, unlike other phenomena, can be explained both by physical causes and by reasons for action. Although physical causes explain the movements of galaxies and planets, molecules, infrahuman species, and all the other moving parts of the physical universe, only human action can also be explained by reasons. It makes no sense to ask a bull that gores a matador, "Why did you do that?" but this question makes sense and is vitally important when it is addressed to a person who sticks a knife into the chest of another human being. It makes a great difference to us if the knife wielder is a surgeon who is cutting with the patient's consent or a person who is enraged at the victim and intends to kill him.

When one asks about human action, "Why did she do that?" two distinct types of answers may therefore be given. The reason-giving explanation accounts for human behavior as a product of intentions that arise from the desires and beliefs of the agent. The second, mechanistic type of explanation treats human behavior as simply one more phenomenon of the universe, subject to the same natural, physical laws that explain all phenomena.

The social sciences, including psychology and psychiatry, are uncomfortably wedged between the reason-giving and the mechanistic accounts of human behavior. Sometimes they treat behavior objectively, treating it as primarily mechanistic or physical; other times, the social sciences treat behavior subjectively, as a text to be interpreted. Yet other times, they engage in an uneasy amalgam of the two. What is always clear, however, is that the domain of the social sciences is human action and not simply the movements of bodies in space.

Law, unlike mechanistic explanation or the conflicted stance of the social sciences, views human action as almost entirely reason governed. The law's concept of a person is that of a practical reasoning, rule-following being, most of whose legally relevant movements must be understood in terms of beliefs, desires, and intentions. As a system of rules to guide and govern human interaction—the legislatures and courts do not decide what rules infrahuman species must follow—the law presupposes that people use legal rules as premises in the practical syllogisms that guide much human action. The legal view of the person is not that all people always reason and behave consistently rationally according to some preordained, normative notion of rationality. It is simply that people are creatures who act for and consistently with their reasons for action and who are generally capable of minimal rationality according to mostly conventional, socially constructed standards.

The law's concept of responsibility follows logically from its conception of the person and the nature of law itself. As a system of rules that guides and governs human interaction, law tells citizens what they may and may not do, what they must or must not do, and what they are entitled to. Unless human beings were creatures who could understand and follow the rules of their society, the law would be powerless to affect human action. Rule followers must be creatures who are generally capable of properly using the rules as premises in practical reasoning. It follows that a legally responsible agent is a person who is so generally capable, according to some contingent, normative notion both of rationality itself and of how much capability is required. These are matters of moral, political, and, ultimately, legal judgment, about which reasonable people can and do differ. Whatever might be the conclusion within a polity, the debate is about human action—intentional behavior guided by reasons.

Criminal law criteria exemplify the foregoing analysis. Most substantive criminal laws prohibit harmful conduct. Effective criminal law requires that citizens must understand what conduct is prohibited, the nature of their conduct, and the consequences for doing what the law prohibits. Homicide laws, for example, require that citizens understand that unjustifiably killing other human beings is prohibited, what counts as killing conduct, and that the state will inflict pain if the rule is violated. A person incapable of understanding the rule or the nature of her own conduct, including the context in which it is embedded, could not properly use the rule to guide her conduct. For example, a person who delusionally believed that she was about to be killed by another person and kills the other in the mistaken belief that she must do so to save her own life does not rationally understand what she is doing. She, of course, knows that she is killing a human being and does so intentionally. In addition, in the abstract, she probably knows and endorses the moral and legal prohibition against unjustified killing. In this case, however, the rule against unjustifiable homicide will be ineffective because she delusionally believes that her action is justifiable.

The general incapacity properly to follow the rule is what distinguishes the delusional agent from people who are simply mistaken but who have the general ability to follow the rule. We believe that the delusional person's failure to understand is not her fault because she lacked the general capacity to understand in this context. In contrast, the person capable of properly following the rule is at fault if she does not do so.

Holding responsible

My explanation and justification of holding people responsible and blaming them is an internal account, an interpretation of our practices as I find them. My task is to determine if our practices are internally coherent and consistent with moral theories that we accept. Although I acknowledge that responsibility and blame are social constructs, my account is not purely pragmatic. I am concerned with when it is fair to hold people responsible, to blame them, and to express our blame through sanctioning responses. When it is fair individually and socially to respond in these ways will depend on facts about the agent and the situation and on moral theory.

The internalist account I am defending asserts that to hold someone morally responsible and to blame that person is to be susceptible to a range of appropriate emotions, such as resentment, indignation, or gratitude, just in case that agent breaches or complies with a moral obligation we accept, and to express those emotions through appropriate negative or positive practices, such as blame or praise.[1] Moral responsibility criteria and practices are not simply behavioral dispositions to express positive and negative reinforcers. They reflect moral propositional attitudes toward the agent's conduct. For example, an appropriate responsive expression of blaming language is rarely intended simply as a negative reinforcer, emitted solely to decrease the probability of a future breach of moral expectations. It also essentially conveys the judge's attitude that the agent has done wrong. Because holding an agent morally responsible expresses a morally propositional attitude, it is not a species of noncognitive and purely emotional response. Moral responsibility practices are not solely propositional, however; they are not just descriptions of wrongdoing, of the breach of expectations. Again, holding people morally responsible involves the susceptibility to a set of reactive emotions that are inherently linked to the practices that express those emotions. It is one thing to say that behavior breached a moral expectation. This is an example of objective description. It is another to hold the agent morally responsible for that behavior, which involves a complex of emotions and their expression that have the force of a judgment.

The reactive account theorizes that we hold people morally responsible if they breach a moral expectation that we accept. A moral expectation that we accept is one that can be normatively defended by reason. Assuming that some reasonable measure of agreement can be reached about the content of the criminal law's prohibitions, the question is, When is it just or fair to feel and express a reactive emotion in response to a breach of the expectation that a prohibition reflects? The expressions of the negative reactive emotions, which can in theory range from the mildest expressions of disapproval to the most punitive sanctions, all are likely to impose pain on the recipient, and, if morality has any requirements, it at a minimum necessitates having good reason to harm another human being. Morality and our law are firmly committed to a theory of desert that holds that it is unfair to hold responsible and sanction a person who is not at fault. We are committed to this principle at the deepest level. Accordingly, it would be unjust to express a negative moral reactive attitude either to an agent who did not breach an obligation we accept or to an agent who lacked the capacity when she breached to understand and be guided by good, normative reason. To be at fault, an agent must actually breach an expectation and must have general normative competence and the general ability at the time to be guided by it. Moral and legal responsibility and blaming practices track this account.

For example, children lack normative competence because they are generally unable to grasp the good reasons not to breach an expectation. The agent acting under duress and some people with mental disorders may have general normative competence, but they may be unable to be guided by it in specific circumstances because, respectively, the choice they face is too hard or because they are unable fully to comprehend what they are doing. It would be unfair to hold responsible and blame such people, because they do not deserve it.

The criteria for responsibility and excuse

The law and morality alike exculpate either because an agent has not violated a moral prohibition or obligation we accept or because the agent has violated the norm but is generally or situationally normatively incompetent. In criminal law terms, the former case includes all doctrines that deny prima facie liability, such as the absence of a voluntary act or the absence of appropriate mens rea resulting from ignorance or mistake; the latter includes the excusing affirmative defenses, such as legal insanity, duress, and infancy. In this subsection, I focus on the latter. I argue that the law and morality include two generic excusing conditions: nonculpable irrationality (or normative incompetence) and nonculpable hard choice. An agent who is nonculpably irrational or faces a sufficiently hard choice when she breaches a moral obligation is not at fault and does not deserve to be blamed and punished.

Rationality or normative competence is the most general, important prerequisite to being morally responsible.[2] More specifically, it means that the agent has the general capacity to understand and to be guided by the reasons that support a moral prohibition that we accept. The agent can be incapable of rationality in two different respects: the agent either is unable rationally to comprehend the facts that bear on the morality of his action or is unable rationally to comprehend the applicable moral or legal code. For example, the delusional self-defender is unable rationally to comprehend the most morally relevant fact bearing on her culpability—whether her life is genuinely threatened. An agent unable rationally to understand morally what she is doing cannot grasp and be guided by the good reason not to breach a moral and legal expectation we accept.

What is the content of rationality that responsibility requires? As part of the normative, socially constructed practice of blaming, there cannot be a self-defining answer. A normative, moral, and political judgment concerning the content and degree of rationality is necessary. Nonetheless, some guide is possible. I do not have an exalted or complicated notion of rationality, but most generally it includes the ability, in Susan Wolf's words, "to be sensitive and responsive to relevant changes in one's situation and environment—that is, to be flexible" (Wolf 1990, 69). It is the ability to perceive accurately, to get the facts right, and to reason instrumentally, including weighing the facts appropriately and according to a minimally coherent preference ordering. Put yet another way, it is the ability to act for good reasons and it is always a good reason not to act (or to act) if doing so (or not doing so) will be wrong. Notice that it is not necessary that the defendant acted for a good, generalizable reason at the time of the crime. Most offenders presumably do not, or they would not have offended. The general normative capacity to be able to grasp and be guided by reason is sufficient.

After much thought, I have come to the conclusion that normative competence should require the ability to empathize and to feel guilt or some other reflexive reactive emotion. Most of the time when the desire to do harm arises, a police officer is not at one's elbow. The cost of future official detection, conviction, and punishment for most crime is relatively slight compared to the immediate rewards of satisfying one's desires, especially if one is a dispositionally steep time discounter. Unless one is able to put oneself affectively in another's shoes, to have a sense of what a potential victim will feel as a result of one's conduct, and is able at least to feel the anticipation of unpleasant guilt for breach, one will lack the capacity to grasp and be guided by the primary rational reasons for complying with moral expectations (Deigh 1995). Once again, it is not required that the defendant actually empathized and felt guilt at the time of the crime. Most wrongdoers presumably do not experience such states at the time of the crime. A general capacity to feel these emotions is sufficient to render the agent normatively rational.[3]

A highly controversial question is whether desires or preferences in themselves can be irrational.[4] It is, of course, true that having desires that most people consider irrational is likely to get someone into trouble, especially if the desires and situations that tempt an agent are strong. Nonetheless, I conclude that even if desires can be construed as irrational, irrational desires do not deprive the agent of normative competence unless they somehow disable the rational capacities just addressed or they produce an internal hard-choice situation distinguishable from the choices experienced by people with equally strong, rational desires. In other words, if the agent with irrational desires can comprehend the morally relevant features of her conduct, she can be held responsible if her irrational desires are the reasons she breaches an expectation we accept.

Hard choice as an excusing condition requires that the defendant was threatened with harm unless she did something even more harmful than the harm threatened. If a person of reasonable firmness would have yielded under the circumstances, we conclude that the choice was too hard to have expected the defendant to resist. Although the agent may have breached an expectation we accept, we think it is unfair to blame and

punish her, because the choice to do the right thing was too hard to make under the circumstances. The law requires that the threat be made by a human being, but why should it matter if the threat is made by another person or arises as a result of naturally occurring, impersonal circumstances? Moreover, why should a threat of death or grievous bodily harm be necessary, as the law now requires? People of reasonable firmness are more likely to find such threats too hard to bear, compared to threats of lesser physical and psychological harm, but why exclude the latter a priori?

Agents who appear to be incapable of reasonable firmness present an apparently problematic case for the hard-choice excuse. An easy choice for most people may be subjectively very difficult for them. How should such cases be analyzed? Remember, to begin, that the "person of reasonable firmness" standard does not mean that everyone who is not dispositionally of reasonable firmness will be excused. The standard is normative. Those who are fortunate enough to be especially brave and those who are of average braveness will be able to meet it quite readily. Those who are of less than average dispositional firmness will have more trouble resisting when they should. Still, if we judge that the person had the general capacity to comply with the reasonable-firmness standard, even if it is harder for her than for most, then she will be held responsible if she yields when a person of reasonable firmness would have resisted. This is true of most objective standards in the law: people with less than average ability to meet them are still held to that standard if they are generally capable of meeting them. The legal result comports with common sense and ordinary morality. When important moral expectations are involved—for example, be careful; don't harm others under weakly threatening conditions—we believe it is fair to expect fellow citizens capable of meeting reasonable standards to comply (Hart 1968).

What should be done, however, with the person we do not think capable of complying, such as the extreme coward who is placed in the threatening situation through no fault of her own? Justice demands an excuse in such cases, but on what theory? One possibility is that the person's general capacity for rationality is disabled. For example, the fear of bodily injury may be so morbid that any threat creates anxiety sufficient to block the person's capacity to grasp and be guided by good reason. Another way of analyzing the case is as an example of internal hard choice. The real threat here that creates the hard choice is not of the lesser physical harm itself; instead, it is the threat of such supremely dysphoric inner states that renders the choice so hard for this agent.[5] A model of hard choice created by the threat of internal dysphoria may be the best explanation of why we might want to excuse in an array of cases that are often thought to require a volitional or control excuse, such as the pedophile, pyromaniac, compulsive gambler, drug addict, and similar cases. In all, the predisposition causes intense desires, the frustration of which threatens the agent with great dysphoria. Perhaps a person of reasonable firmness faced with sufficient dysphoria would yield.

I prefer to analyze these cases in terms of irrationality.[6] The hard-choice model is plausible, but, at the most practical level, it will often be too difficult to assess the degree of threatened dysphoria that creates the hard choice. Assessing the capacity for rationality is not an easy task, but it is a more commonsense and commonly made assessment. Second, it is not clear that the fear of dysphoria would ever be sufficient to excuse the breach of important expectations, except in precisely those extreme cases in which we would assume that the agent's rational capacity was essentially disabled. In sum, if an excuse is to obtain in the case of the coward or the other cases mentioned, once again, the generic incapacity for rationality or hard choice will explain why we might want to excuse.

I have argued that irrationality, defined to include the capacity for empathy and guilt, and hard choice are the essential excusing conditions. A rational agent not faced with a hard choice may fairly be blamed and punished if she breaches an expectation that we accept. It is not hard to understand why lack of the general capacity for rationality and hard choice are excusing conditions. Either condition will make it too hard for the agent properly to follow the rule, to comply with the expectation, because she will be unable either to grasp or to be guided by the good reasons not to offend.

Perhaps there should be other conditions required for responsibility in

addition to the capacity for rationality and the absence of a hard choice.
Many variables may make it easier
or harder for the agent to meet moral
obligations.[7] It is harder to conform
to the requirements of morality and
the criminal law if an agent has characteristics that predispose to objec-
tionable behavior and lacks characteristics that are self-protective.
Impulsivity and hot temper are
examples of the former; successful
self-control strategies and good judgment are examples of the latter. An
agent with many of the worrisome
characteristics and few of the self-
protective variables will surely be at
greater risk for breaching expectations, especially if circumstances are
provoking or tempting. If an agent
lacks protective predispositions and
is exposed to a criminogenic environment, it will, all else being equal, be
considerably harder for the agent to
avoid offending than for a person
who is more fortunately endowed
and exposed to a more benign environment. If anger-provoking or evil-
tempting situational variables never
arise, one is both lucky and less likely
to engage in harm-doing. These
observations are almost tautologi-
cally true, however, and tell us little
about excusing in general.

But not all variables that make it
harder to behave rightly are prereq-
uisites for responsibility. Even a
combination of unfortunate dispositions and situational variables will
not necessarily excuse. A hot-blooded
person who is sorely, but legally
inadequately provoked will not have
an excuse if she kills the provoker,
even if she both lacks self-control and
appears out of control. Morality and

the law alike set a minimum standard for what is required for responsible action, and not everything that
would help an agent to behave well is
or should be included in the standard. As long as an agent possesses
the minimum requirements for normative competence, she is capable of
meeting moral obligations, and it is
not unfair to hold her responsible,
even if it is harder for her than for
others. Moreover, the justice of holding people to high standards of
regard for the rights and interests of
others is especially warranted in
cases involving serious harm-doing,
because such situations give agents
the strongest possible reasons to
avoid breaching moral expectations.

Proponents who wish to expand
the criteria for responsibility must
also provide a fuller theory of excusing and an account of why particular
variables ought to be included as
excusing conditions. Although the
bad luck of lacking self-protective
variables and being exposed to
highly criminogenic situations
should generate sympathy and caution before blaming and punishing,
variability of good fortune is an inevitable aspect of the human condition,
and bad luck is not an excuse unless
it produces an excusing condition,
such as lack of normative competence. Anger at harm-doers and sympathy for victims should not lead us
to overestimate the normative competence of harm-doers, but sympathy
for harm-doers should also not lead
us to underestimate their normative
competence.

The view of responsibility I have
presented is not necessarily an all-
or-none, bright-line concept. There

can be almost infinite degrees of normative competence or hardness of choice, and, correspondingly, in principle, responsibility could be arrayed along an almost infinitely subdivided continuum. But human beings are epistemologically incapable of evaluating these normative criteria with such subtle precision. Thus the law does adopt a bright-line test. But rough mitigating doctrines are possible and may be the appropriate vehicles for addressing the moral relevance of those variables that make flying straight harder. I have argued that, for just this reason, the law should adopt a generic, mitigating partial excuse (Morse 1998). If mitigation is justified in an individual case, however, it must be because the genuine criteria for excuse—irrationality and hard choice—are sufficiently, albeit not fully, present. Thus criminogenic predispositions will be relevant only if they compromise the general capacity for normative competence. If they do, a strong case for mitigation obtains.

I have argued that the incapacity for rationality and hard choice are the excusing and mitigating conditions that best account for the moral and legal world that we have and that they provide a coherent and justifiable account of our practices. Many alternative explanations have been given, however. Among these are the belief that determinism or causation undermines responsibility, that excused people lack free will or do not intend to do what they do, that excused people have no capacity for choice, and that excused people are out of control or lack the capacity to control their behavior. Most of

these, in my opinion, are either incorrect, confusing, question begging, or conclusory, and none in fact coherently accounts for the excusing and mitigating conditions that law and morality employ. For example, it would be preposterous to believe that the behavior of children is caused or determined but that the behavior of adults is not and that that is why children are excused. None of these adequately justifies why juveniles should be held less responsible. To explain in detail why each of the alternatives is unsuccessful would exceed the limits of this article, but I have provided the full explanation elsewhere (Morse 1997).

2. THE MORAL AND LEGAL RESPONSIBILITY OF JUVENILES

This part first considers a common strategy for addressing the responsibility of juveniles: identifying an alleged difference between juveniles and adults and assuming that the empirical difference makes a moral difference. Then, based on the analysis of part 1, this part suggests why juveniles may be in general less morally responsible than adults and how the legal system and researchers can take practical account of such differences.

Begging the question

The question of juvenile responsibility is not simply whether juveniles are generally different from adults. Surely they are in many ways. The real issue is whether they are morally different, and that depends on whether a moral theory that we accept dictates that the variables that behaviorally distinguish juveniles should also diminish their responsibility. Difference is not necessarily diminution, after all, and to assume otherwise is to beg the question.

A standard strategy reviews the research on the developmental and psychosocial variables that apparently distinguish juveniles from adults and identifies the approximate age at which the distinction no longer seems to obtain. The explicit or implicit conclusion is that many of these variables diminish responsibility, but the conclusion is simply assumed, and that is the difficulty. Many of the variables may seem to be attractive candidates for diminishing responsibility, but until the argument is proved, we can have little sense of the force of the assumption.

One possibility is that a proposed variable is reducible to normative incompetence. The task in this case is to show why the variable diminishes normative competence. The second possibility is that the concept of normative competence should be expanded so that the behavioral difference should make a moral difference. The task here is to show why, according to some moral theory, normative competence should be so expanded. In both cases, a further task is to explain why adults who are indistinguishable from juveniles should not be treated the same as juveniles according to the moral theory that treats juveniles as a class differently.

For example, if juveniles are not rational, it is a simple matter to explain why they are not responsible, as we already excuse adults who are

sufficiently irrational. But, to take a common example, suppose juveniles as a class are more subject to peer pressure than adults. This does not appear to raise a problem with an agent's general capacity for normative competence, but should it excuse for some other reason? If so, is there good reason not to excuse the smaller proportion of adults who may be as subject to peer pressure as the average juvenile?

A related question that is often begged is the moral and legal relevance of the observation that juveniles are allegedly more changeable than adults, either through normal developmental processes or through interventional strategies. Adolescence is a stage of dynamic psychological change, and for this and other reasons adolescents may be especially amenable to treatment. Many self-protective variables may be precisely those that undergo developmental change and that can be strengthened. It is assumed without question that the differential plasticity of juveniles should affect our moral and legal response. But the proper response to juvenile harmdoers depends entirely on our theories justifying intervention in their lives. If we believe that pure retributivism should guide our response, everything will depend on moral responsibility; if we are pure consequentialists, moral responsibility is of no consequence; if we are mixed theorists, desert is a necessary condition for punishment and sets limits, but it is not sufficient for punitive intervention. The relevance of plasticity must therefore be assessed according to the applicable theory of intervention in general and a theory of punishment in particular.

If responsibility is treated as a matter of retrospective moral evaluation, as I suggested it essentially is and should be, then the plasticity or amenability to treatment of a variable is irrelevant to whether it diminishes moral responsibility. Responsibility should be mitigated or excused if a variable that diminishes responsibility was operative at the time of harm-doing, whether or not this characteristic is alterable, and vice versa. It is hard to imagine what moral theory would suggest that plasticity per se should reduce responsibility. To the extent that fault is a necessary or sufficient condition for full responsibility, plasticity is irrelevant. Thus a pure retributivist can justify full negative sanctions for a fully responsible juvenile, even if the juvenile will grow out of the characteristic that predisposed her to wrongdoing. Similarly, the pure retributivist can justify lesser sanctions for a partially responsible juvenile, even if she will not grow out of the characteristic that predisposes her to criminal conduct.

Plasticity might be highly relevant, however, to a mixed or purely consequential theory of punishment or social intervention. For example, according to a mixed theory, specific prevention may justify a less punitive response for a fully responsible juvenile wrongdoer—say, a shorter incarceration—because she will mature or it is easier speedily to alter her antisocial tendencies, but the lenience will not be based on diminished desert. Alternatively, if one is a purely consequential theorist, on

general and specific prevention grounds, one could justify lengthier incarceration for a partially responsible but highly dangerous juvenile who is unlikely to change for the better.

With these considerations in mind, we are ready to turn to the question of the moral responsibility of juveniles.

The criteria for juvenile responsibility

This section considers the moral responsibility of adolescents from an explicitly retrospective, morally evaluative stance. In other words, it explores the degree to which adolescents can fairly be blamed and punished for their wrongdoing on the ground of moral desert. A consistent strategy of this section is to examine the law's response to adult offenders who possess juvenile characteristics and to consider whether kids who are morally like adults should be treated as kids and whether adults who are morally like kids should be treated as adults. The section does not address the good consequences that might flow from treating adolescents as responsible as, or less responsible than, adults who commit the same deeds. Some of the consequential implications are considered in the next part.

Let us begin by narrowing the question. Young children rarely commit crimes in response to hard choices, and they lack many of the necessary attributes of rationality, including a developed capacity for empathy. Moreover, young children infrequently commit serious crimes. Consequently, the issue of full or substantial responsibility is not seriously in contention for young children. Mid adolescents do commit serious crimes, however, and in many respects they may appear to meet the criteria for rationality. The moral and legal responsibility of mid and late adolescents is thus the critical moral and practical issue.

Many able scholars have reviewed the literature concerning potential legally relevant differences between adolescents and adults (Feld 1999, 287-330; Grisso 1996; Scott, Reppucci, and Woolard 1995; Steinberg and Cauffman 1996; see also Woolard, Reppucci, and Redding 1996). I shall make the simplifying assumption that the near consensus of their findings represents the most accurate current assessment of those differences. In brief, the literature indicates that the formal reasoning ability and the level of cognitive moral development of mid adolescents differs little from adults. Further, on narrowly conceived cognitive tasks performed under laboratory conditions that concern decisions about medical treatment, there is little difference in outcome between mid adolescents and adults. As a class, however, adolescents (1) have a stronger preference for risk and novelty; (2) subjectively assess the potentially negative consequences of risky conduct less unfavorably; (3) tend to be impulsive and more concerned with short-term than long-term consequences; (4) subjectively experience and assess the passage of time and time periods as longer; and (5) are more susceptible to peer pressure. All five differences diminish with maturation throughout adolescence, with most disappearing by mid to late adolescence, but they do appear robust for adolescents as a class. It is crucial to remember, however, that a finding of a statistically significant difference between groups does not mean that there is no overlap between them. In fact, the adolescent and adult distributions on these variables overlap considerably: large numbers of adolescents and adults are indistinguishable on measures of these variables.

Mid-adolescent and adult formal reasoning, including instrumental reasoning, are indistinguishable, but these other differences allegedly affect adolescent judgment and self-control. Adolescents make serious mistakes as a result of developmental immaturity that they would not make under similar circumstances after they mature. Consequently, many argue, adolescents should be protected from the full consequences of their immature mistakes, lest their lives be ruined by developmental factors they would outgrow in the normal course of life (Zimring 1982). It is well to remember, however, that all these characteristics are matters of degree, and, by mid adolescence, most juveniles are probably able to control them to a substantial degree, although it may be harder for them than for adults.

Before continuing, we must consider the relevance of the research concerning adolescence to juvenile criminal responsibility. Most of the research summarized earlier investigated adolescent decision making and behavior in general and risk taking in particular; it did not examine adolescent criminal behavior.[8] Adolescent criminal conduct for the most part involves the intentional infliction of harm: the offender intentionally killed, inflicted grievous bodily harm, raped, stole, destroyed, or burned. That is, it is the adolescent's conscious object to cause in the immediate future precisely the harm the law prohibits. Unless serious adolescent offenders are specially unlucky or unskillful, they are practically certain to produce the harm that is their conscious objective and they know it. The intentional harmdoer knows that the conduct invades the interests of others; those interests may be given little value or otherwise ignored or rationalized away, but they must be present to the adolescent agent's mind. Adolescents can surely commit crimes of risk creation, such as reckless homicide, but primarily serious crimes of intention raise the issues that concern us. For crimes of serious risk creation, the risk is immediate and, once again, the risked result will be present to the adolescent's mind.

Risky conduct in general is different in important ways from conduct intended to cause immediate harm: risky conduct often is not criminal or seriously so; it often affects primarily the risk taker; often the probability of the harm risked may not be high; and, finally, often the risked result is a long-term, rather than an immediate, consequence. For example, adolescents intentionally drive too fast and engage in other forms of bravado, but much conduct of this sort is not criminal, much of the risk is to themselves, and the probability of a serious harm, such as death, is not high; they intentionally experiment with drugs, but they face only the longer-term and low-probability risks of endangering their ultimate social success and health; they intentionally engage in unprotected sex, but such behavior is not criminal and creates again the longer-term, low-probability risk of disease and pregnancy; and so on. The harms risked are serious, but the risky conduct does not demonstrate substantial antisocial potential, and in none of these cases is the result practically certain. When an adolescent (or anyone else) decides whether to engage in risky conduct, the potential harm does not weigh as heavily as the adolescent's gratification. The latter is certain; the former is not. Moreover, if one is driven by a desire for gratification, it is easier to fail sufficiently to weigh the interests of others whom one does not desire to harm and to underestimate the longer-term risk one's conduct produces.

If risky conduct is statistically normal for adolescents, treating adolescents as criminals or protocriminals may appear to be criminalizing normality, but this is not the case. Again the law does not criminalize or seriously criminalize much risk-creating conduct. More important, no matter how much adolescents may prefer risk, it can scarcely be claimed that serious crime is the statistically normal mode that adolescents use to express their preference for risk. To treat an adolescent murderer, rapist, arsonist, or the like as simply a kid in search of risk and to suggest that we should consider decriminalizing such conduct among kids is neither justified by the data nor morally warranted.

In sum, the relevance of the research on adolescent immaturity and poor judgment to intentional criminal behavior is unclear. The desire for immediate gratification is likely to exert more influence when the potential harm is uncertain (and not criminal) than when it is intended (and criminal). What is more, the moral reason not to engage in conduct is vastly stronger and more immediate when the harm is intended rather than risked (Wallace 1994), which explains why we consider intentional harm-doing more culpable than risky harm-doing. Although poor judgment may be characteristic of adolescent risk taking, there is no evidence that such judgment also infects intentional criminal behavior, and adolescents have stronger reason to avoid poor judgment when intentional criminal behavior is contemplated. If the primary variable that adolescent offenders underestimate is the risk of getting caught for their wrongdoing, this is hardly reason to think that they are less responsible. Moreover, recent research suggests that adolescents respond to the incentive structure of the juvenile and criminal law much as adults do (Levitt 1998).

On empirical and normative grounds, the poor judgment that characterizes adolescent decision making generally may not apply as fully to serious criminal conduct as it does to the behaviors that the research on difference studied. Indeed, because the vast majority of adolescents do not commit the most serious criminal offenses, even in criminogenic environments, it is difficult to assert that poor adolescent judgment is strongly predisposing to such offenses. For the present, however, I wish to make the assumption that, in comparison to the case of adults, poor judgment more substantially affects the criminal conduct of adolescents as a class.

The potential excusing or mitigating force of these factors that I have lumped together as poor judgment does not depend on determinism, lack of free will, lack of choice, lack of intention, a defect in the will, irresistible impulse, or the formal inability to control oneself. Nonetheless, they surely all increase the probability that an agent will engage in risky or harmful behavior; they all decrease the probability that an agent will exercise her full capacity for normative competence when she probably should. When tempted by the rewards of risky or harmful conduct, the agent will either ignore or underweight the reasons not to engage in this conduct, although she may have general normative competence. Thus these factors decrease the probability. The question is whether these developmental characteristics of adolescence are reducible to sufficient, nonculpable defects in the capacity for rationality or whether they should excuse for other reasons.

It appears, however, that the variables that distinguish adolescents from adults are not components of moral rationality. An impulsive agent or one especially subject to peer pressure, for example, may have the general capacity for normative competence. In this respect, these variables may be like other characteristics, such as hot temper or greed, that are also not components of the general capacity for normative competence but that may make it harder to exercise this capacity. If so, these variables would excuse only if they disabled the agent's capacity for rationality to a sufficient degree to warrant exculpation. Thus we need to know the effect of these variables on the capacity for rationality and we need some sense of how much disability is sufficient to excuse.

At the extreme, the case for excuse based on such variables seems plausible. A thoroughly impulsive person, for whom the desire becomes the deed, with no mediating thought whatsoever, who has tried without success to overcome this characteristic, may in fact lack the general capacity for normative competence.[9] A totally other-directed, dependent person lacking any sense of autonomous selfhood may be similarly situationally disabled when peer pressure is strongly brought to bear. These by definition are extreme cases, however, and no one seriously argues that mid to late adolescents as a class meet this description. It is a matter of degree. The strength of these variables is directly proportional to the degree of difficulty an agent will experience in exercising the general capability for rationality.

It will be instructive to consider why these variables have no formal excusing force whatsoever for adults, except in extreme cases that are typically assimilated to mental disorder, such as impulse control disorders or the like. A highly impulsive or peer-oriented adult will be held fully culpable for wrongdoing potentiated by impulsivity or peer pressure. Indeed, many people will tend to condemn wrongdoers for these characteristics. The reason, I believe, is that we think that, except at the extremes, agents with these characteristics are sufficiently able to grasp and to be guided by good reason when they are considering wrongdoing. It may be harder for them to be guided by good reason, but they are nonetheless capable. After all, potential violation of moral expectations gives an agent supremely good reason to exercise the rational capacity the agent possesses.

Our moral and legal response to such variables is a product of our commonsense understanding of human behavior, filtered through our moral theory of how much capacity for normative competence an agent must possess to be held responsible. Everyone has been in a situation that made it harder to be guided by the general capacity for rationality. Stress, fatigue, rage, and a host of other variables that can undermine rationality are ever present features of the human condition, as is the frequent desire to do wrong when in such states. Few people have been able to avoid wrestling with demons. Nonetheless, we know that virtually everyone, virtually always, is able to exercise the general capacity for rationality and does not do wrong. Our moral conclusion is that the adult wrongdoer may be held accountable unless the agent's capacity for rationality is extremely and nonculpably disabled.

A substantial minority of adults is similar to mid to late adolescents on the variables that distinguish the age cohorts as classes. A regrettable number of adults are immature and have dreadful judgment. We do not excuse that minority of adults. Why, therefore, should adolescents be treated differently? Adults obviously have more experience with the consequences of their behavior and life experience generally and some mature as a result, but many do not. Impulsive or peer-oriented adults probably have always learned less from experience than their more mature counterparts. Moreover, it does not take very much life experience and moral subtlety to understand how killing, raping, burning, stealing, and so on affect others.

A second reason for treating adolescents differently might be that immaturity is an inevitable normal developmental characteristic of the adolescent but is not a developmental characteristic of adulthood. This, too, is true, but its moral relevance is obscure. Whether a behavioral variable that makes it harder to grasp and be guided by the general capacity for good reason is a feature of normal development or a dismaying outcome of a failure to mature, the variable is present. Moreover, one can hardly morally fault an adult for having a characteristic that is itself a product of developmental failure. Do we really believe that when we ask a chronically immature adult to grow up, he or she has the potential to change her character very much? Do we really believe that telling a dependent adult to become more independent will somehow render the person less vulnerable to peer pressure? We can ask an immature or dependent adult to change his or her behavior, provide the proper incentives to maximize the chance that this will happen, and expect that some behavior might change when something important is at stake. But the same is true of adolescents. Moreover, it may be harder for an adult to change behavior by fighting against the grain because the dispositions are longer standing and more ingrained.

Should adolescents and similar adults be treated morally alike? If adults who possess the usually distinguishing adolescent characteristics can fairly be held accountable and no individualized mitigating or excusing claims are permitted, why should mid to late adolescents as a class be held less accountable on the basis of these characteristics? Conversely, if these variables do sufficiently undermine the capacity for normative competence to warrant mitigation or excuse for mid to late adolescents as a class, then should adult wrongdoers not be permitted to make individualized excusing claims based on these variables?

My analysis of the distinguishing variables implies that they do not undermine the general moral responsibility of an agent because they are not inconsistent with possessing the general capacity for normative competence concerning the gross, obviously wrong conduct constituting serious criminal offenses. At most, they make it harder for the agent to exercise the general capacity for normative competence. For example, consider again adolescent vulnerability to peer pressure. We know that adolescents are more likely than adults to commit crime in groups and that juvenile gangs are common. There can be no doubt that youths defining their fluid adolescent identities in terms of their peers will find it harder to consider the interests of those their peers wish to harm. Indeed, there will often be reasons and rituals to help the potential adolescent wrongdoer devalue and demonize victims or otherwise rationalize her conduct. But most such adolescents surely retain the general normative competence to understand and be guided by the reasons that killing, raping, burning, stealing, and so on are wrong, even when the pressure of peers motivates them to ignore or underweight these reasons.

Although I conclude that the distinguishing characteristics canvassed so far are not themselves part of normative competence and they probably do not undermine the general capacity for normative competence, the research has not addressed a potentially critical distinguishing variable: the capacity for empathy, which I have claimed is a component of normative competence. Although adolescents have adequate formal reasoning powers and understanding of the content of the moral rules, and sufficient life experience to understand the facts, including the consequences of the serious crimes that concern us, they may lack the general capacity for empathy that is a component of full moral agency. Put another way, although adolescents may be highly subject to peer pressure, they are also

developmentally self-centered, a quality that will usually diminish with normal maturation.[10] The research literature is not altogether clear on this question, but it seems to be a plausible assumption. If this is correct, then adolescents as a class may be less responsible moral agents in general and might deserve mitigation, if not full excuse.

Once again, however, the comparison to adults will be instructive. The law does not excuse full-fledged psychopaths,[11] who are apparently completely incapable of empathy and guilt as a result of genetic or developmental variables. On my theory of responsibility, such people should be excused, and I wish to proceed as if the law followed. After all, if it is really morally acceptable to hold genuine psychopaths fully accountable, the argument for holding adolescents less responsible on the basis that they are not fully empathetic is anemic at best. Assuming, then, that insufficient empathy undermines moral agency generally, it appears that morality and the law should treat adolescents and similarly situated adults alike. We cannot blame the adolescent for the lack, because it is a normal developmental characteristic. But we can hardly blame the adult either. The capacity for empathy is not the sort of characteristic one can easily work on and alter, like one's handwriting or manners. It is not even the type of characteristic, like impatience or hot temper, that one can learn techniques to control, if not remove. Finally, we must ask how much lack of capacity for empathy is required to justify mitigation or excuse. Do adolescents lack it this much? Should not adults who do so also be entitled to make a mitigating claim similar to that made for adolescents?

I have reached no conclusion about whether mid to late adolescents as a class should be treated as less responsible than adults. My analysis does lead me to conclude, however, that we must very carefully identify why adolescents might be treated differently, and if fairness requires differential treatment for the class, it also requires that adults with the same responsibility-diminishing characteristics be treated equally.

3. IMPLICATIONS AND RECOMMENDATIONS

This brief part considers the adjudicative and dispositional consequences that follow from concluding that mid- to late-adolescent serious offenders as a class should not be distinguished from their adult counterparts. I propose to explore these issues selectively and suggestively, rather than comprehensively.

If we conclude that mid- to late-adolescent offenders as a class are as morally responsible as adults, desert alone would furnish no basis for differential response, although other punitive and penological goals might. For example, dangerousness and amenability to treatment may distinguish adolescents, and a system that considered consequential concerns in addition to desert might well conclude that these factors should be examined to determine the appropriate disposition.

The more difficult question is how the law should respond if dynamic developmental factors produce diminished general capacity for normative competence in large numbers of mid- to late-adolescent serious offenders. Let us assume that adolescents as a class are less responsible because they exhibit responsibility-diminishing attributes, such as a lack of fully developed capacity for empathy, that are a normal feature of their developmental stage.

First, consider the adjudication of culpability. One response is entirely to individualize the desert determination for adolescent offenders in order to determine which offenders are not fully responsible. After all, not all adolescents are alike, even if they are distinguishable from adults as a class. The conclusion that adolescents are distinguishable from adults must depend on the ability reliably and validly to measure the distinguishing variables in the study samples. If there are no reliable and valid measures of these variables, we cannot conclude that the classes are distinct. If such measures are available, as they must be to warrant the underlying conclusion of difference, then any individual can be measured. A profile of potentially responsibility-diminishing attributes could thus be obtained for any adolescent offender, and the score could be compared to the distributions for adolescents and adults. Such individualization might be difficult, involving subtle judgments about an offender's cognitive and emotional status, but perhaps justice demands the attempt. No test score can dictate culpability, of course, but it would provide evidence that could be used to argue for greater or lesser guilt. Such evidence would be more objective, however, than the usual sources, such as the clinical evaluations of mental health professionals and others.

Second, if adolescents are less responsible as a class, the law might adopt a rebuttable presumption of partial responsibility for adolescent offenders. Fairness and efficiency should require the prosecution to prove beyond a reasonable doubt that a particular adolescent defendant was fully responsible. Although another level of burden of persuasion could be used, liberty and stigma are essentially at stake in determining if an adolescent is fully responsible or not. These are precisely the interests that *In re Winship* (379 U.S. 358 [1970]) identified as requiring the reasonable-doubt standard. It is plausible to assume that in cases of obvious immaturity or where the evidence of immaturity is strong, the prosecution would either accept that mitigation was warranted or would be unable to bear its persuasion burden. Where the evidence of maturity is strong, it suggests that this adolescent defendant has passed the stage of development that warrants mitigation. In this case, full responsibility would be both justifiable and provable. Marginal cases are probably the largest category, because the overlap between mid to late adolescents and adults is so large. In these cases, the prosecution will most often be unable to bear the persuasion burden, and the presumption of partial responsibility will prevail. This is as it should be in a system that prefers

incorrect attributions of innocence (or lesser culpability) to incorrect attributions of guilt (or greater culpability). Assuming that we can reasonably assess the attributes that distinguish adolescents, such a system would allow us to individualize, with a strong presumption in favor of partial responsibility.

The individualization described is analogous to the current juvenile court waiver or transfer authority. It differs, however, because it would be premised entirely on culpability, rather than on public safety or, alas, on concerns for vengeance. If blameworthiness is a necessary precondition of punishment, then less responsible adolescent defendants should not be fully punished, no matter how dangerous they are or how dreadful their deeds. In addition, under the regnant mixed theory of punishment, which holds that desert is necessary but not sufficient to justify punishment, a fully responsible adolescent offender need not be fully punished unless there is good consequential reason for doing so.

Finally, I concluded at the close of part 2 that if most or all adolescents are only partially morally responsible, then similarly situated adults should be treated similarly. I recognize that the law may adopt a bright line based on age to avoid the expense of individualization. Thus, if subjection to peer pressure does somehow excuse and juveniles are more subject as a class, there might be reason not to try to identify the small group of juveniles that is not especially subject to peer pressure. The search for efficiency in adjudicating juveniles then errs on the side of leniency. But this argument need not be symmetrical. Should adult adjudication err on the side of severity and unfairness in the search for efficiency? We generally hold that it is better to acquit the guilty than to convict the innocent. Should not efficiency yield to the need to individualize for the small class of adults with the same characteristics as juveniles who therefore might not be fully responsible? If new variables do not reduce to standard excusing conditions, questions like these must be addressed fully.

Now let us consider the dispositional consequences. Assume first that some form of individualization was performed and a minority of adolescent offenders were found fully responsible. They should be treated according to whatever theory of punishment was dominant. What seems clear in these cases, however, is that the considerations that presumptively apply to adolescents do not apply to them. Further developmental maturation is not required to achieve the full capability for responsibility. Thus the system should apply the same dispositional considerations that it applies to adult offenders. This is not to suggest that especially vulnerable but responsible adolescents should be incarcerated with more hardened adult (or adolescent) offenders (or, for that matter, that especially vulnerable adults should be incarcerated with more hardened offenders of any age). No prisoner should be subject to avoidable brutalization, but responsible adolescents would otherwise be treated like responsible adults.

Assume, now, that individualization results in mitigation or that all adolescents are conclusively presumed to warrant mitigation. In this case, developmental variables have resulted in partial responsibility, and a sensible dispositional response would take account of those variables. In other words, wrongdoing in these cases is in substantial measure a product of juvenile immaturity that will be outgrown under proper conditions. Once outgrown, the wrongdoer is far less likely to make such mistakes in the future. The question, of course, is, What possible dispositions will facilitate maturation and protect the public from dangerous juveniles? Reformatories and prisons, especially if they are brutal, are hardly the types of environments that provide the firm but caring discipline and the graded freedom and responsibilities that give adolescents the best chance to develop mature, good reason. On the other hand, less secure institutions may be insufficient for protection, and the adolescent offender's usual environment might be more criminogenic than prophylactic. Although there are quite solid empirical findings about the general characteristics of treatment programs that work (Lipsey 1997; Lipsey and Wilson 1998), valid classification of offenders is difficult,[12] and we are seldom sure about which of the various therapeutic interventions that might be tried works specifically for whom. The disposition of adolescents should facilitate maturation to the fullest extent possible, but this will not be a simple task.

What should we do about partially responsible adolescents until the doctor comes with a dispositional cure? Attempts to individualize terms of incarceration based on differential desert are likely to be well-meaning but misguided shams. Perhaps the best we can do is some legislatively mandated reduction in punishment for all partially responsible adolescents.[13] The balance of just deserts and public safety could be obtained by an inverse relation between the seriousness of the offense and the reduction mandated: more serious crimes would receive less reduction, and vice versa. In addition to maximizing public protection within a scheme of punishment reduction for partial responsibility, this proposal seems presumptively fair because serious crimes present the potential wrongdoer with the strongest possible reason to bring whatever rational capability could be brought to bear on the intention to harm another.

I wish to emphasize in conclusion that my primary focus on the implications of adolescent responsibility does not exhaust the range of considerations that a sensible justice system might consider when adjudicating and mandating dispositions for serious adolescent offenders. But to the extent that desert is a necessary precondition for and a limit on punishment, it cannot be ignored.

Notes

1. The following defense draws directly and liberally from Wallace's Strawsonian, reactive account in Wallace 1994, 51-83.

2. I state this criterion in alternative terms—rationality or normative competence—because the concept of rationality is associated with so much historical, conceptual, and philosophical disagreement that the term distracts many people. As I explain later in this article, I mean nothing exalted or essential by the term. It is simply a commonsense term used to cover a congeries of human capacities without which morality and human flourishing in general would be difficult. If the term seems too broad, I am perfectly comfortable with the term "normative competence."

3. Paul Robinson has pointed out in a personal communication that some people may systematically suppress their capacity to empathize and feel guilt. If so, they retain the general capacity and are responsible for inactivating it. Professor Robinson correctly points out that it may be difficult to distinguish those who suppress a capacity they retain from those who do not have the capacity. This difficulty may be overstated, however. An examination of an offender's range of relationships should make it easier to determine if the capacity generally exists. A terrorist may squelch any empathy or guilt for the victims of her terror, but she may demonstrate with her compatriots that she retains the general capacity.

4. Nozick (1993) notes, "At present, we have no adequate theory of the substantive rationality of goals and desires" (139-40).

5. I have explored such a model for inner coercion at length elsewhere. See Morse 1994.

6. Competing explanations based on volitional problems typically are conceptually confused or lack empirical support. Morse 1994, 1658-59.

7. See Morse 1994, 1605-10, for a discussion of variables that make it harder or easier for the agent to fly straight.

8. Grisso (1996, 238-42) suggests that more empirical research is needed before we can confidently conclude that differential legal treatment of mid to late adolescents is warranted. Scott, Reppucci, and Woolard (1995, 238) note only a single study comparing adult and adolescent decision making concerning criminal conduct.

9. Impulsivity is often considered a characteristic of adolescence and a predisposing cause of dangerous and criminal conduct. For example, dispositional impulsiveness may in part explain the higher accident rate among adolescents. Consequently, it is worth noting

that despite apparent consensus that the disposition to act with less forethought or with steeper time discounting is involved, impulsivity is difficult to define and to measure. Parker and Bagby 1997, 142-43. See McCown and De-Simone 1993, 5. Dickman (1993, 153) claims that many of the inconsistencies in the impulsivity literature can be resolved by inferring the specific cognitive processes in which subjects differ.

10. Hoffman (1991) discusses the development of the capacity for empathy and its relation to moral principles and judgment.

11. See *Model Penal Code* 1962, sec. 4.01(2).

12. For example, if lack of the capacity for empathy diminishes responsibility, incarceration term and treatment decisions would have to distinguish between normal developmental situations and psychopathy, which can be very difficult.

13. I suggested (and rejected) such an approach for mentally abnormal but legally sane adults long ago (Morse 1979). I have recently revived the idea, however (Morse 1998). The suggestion in the text follows the revival.

References

Bennett, William John, John J. DiIulio, Jr., and John P. Waters. 1996. *Body Count: Moral Poverty and How to Win America's War Against Crime and Drugs*. New York: Simon & Schuster.

Deigh, John. 1995. Empathy and Universalizability. *Ethics* 105:743-63.

Dickman, Scott. 1993. Impulsivity and Information Processing. In *The Impulsive Client: Theory, Research and Treatment*, ed. William G. McCown, Judith L. Johnson, and Myrna B. Shure. Washington, DC: American Psychological Association Press.

Elliott, Delbert S. 1994. *Youth Violence: An Overview*. Philadelphia: University of Pennsylvania, School of Social Work, Center for the Study of Youth Policy; Ft. Lauderdale, FL: Nova South Eastern University, Shepard Broad Law Center; Salt Lake City:
University of Utah, Graduate School of Social Work.

Feld, Barry. 1999. *Bad Kids: The Transformation of the Juvenile Court*. New York: Oxford University Press.

Grisso, Thomas. 1996. Society's Retributive Response to Juvenile Violence: A Developmental Perspective. *Law and Human Behavior* 20(June):229-47.

Hart, Herbert Lionel Adolphus. 1968. *Punishment and Responsibility: Essays in the Philosophy of Law*. New York: Oxford University Press.

Hoffman, Martin L. 1991. Empathy, Social Cognition, and Moral Action. In *Handbook of Moral Behavior and Development*, ed. William M. Kurtines and Jacob L. Gewirtz. Hillsdale, NJ: Lawrence Erlbaum.

Levitt, Steven D. 1998. Juvenile Crime and Punishment. *Journal of Political Economy* 106(6):1156-85.

Lipsey, Mark. 1997. Effective Intervention for Serious Juvenile Offenders: A Synthesis of Research. Vanderbilt University. Manuscript.

Lipsey, Mark W. and David B. Wilson. 1998. Effective Intervention for Serious Juvenile Offenders: A Synthesis of Research. In *Serious and Juvenile Offenders: Risk Factors and Successful Interventions*, ed. Rolf Loeber and David P. Farrington. Thousand Oaks, CA: Sage.

McCown, William G. and Philip A. DeSimone. 1993. Impulses, Impulsivity, and Impulsive Behaviors: A Historical Review of a Contemporary Issue. In *The Impulsive Client: Theory, Research and Treatment*, ed. William G. McCown, Judith L. Johnson, and Myrna B. Shure. Washington, DC: American Psychological Association Press.

Model Penal Code (Proposed Official Draft). 1962. Philadelphia: American Law Institute.

Morse, Stephen J. 1979. Diminished Capacity: A Moral and Legal Conundrum. *International Journal of Law and Psychiatry* 2:271-98.

———. 1994. Culpability and Control. *University of Pennsylvania Law Review* 1587-660.

———. 1997. Immaturity and Irresponsibility. *Criminal Law and Criminology* 88:15-67.

———. 1998. Excusing the New Excuse Defenses: A Legal and Conceptual Review. In *Crime and Justice*, ed. M. Tonry. Vol. 23. Chicago: University of Chicago Press.

Nozick, Robert. 1993. *The Nature of Rationality*. Princeton, NJ: Princeton University Press.

Parker, James D. and R. Michael Bagby. 1997. Impulsivity in Adults: A Critical Review of Measurement Approaches. In *Impuslivity: Theory, Assessment, and Treatment*, ed. Christopher D. Webster and Margaret A. Jackson. New York: Guilford Press.

Scott, Elizabeth S., N. Dickon Reppucci, and Jennifer L. Woolard. 1995. Evaluating Adolescent Decision Making in Legal Contexts. *Law and Human Behavior* 19(June):221-44.

Sickmund, Melissa, Howard N. Snyder, and Eileen Poe-Yamagata. 1997. *Juvenile Offenders and Victims: 1997 Update on Violence*. Washington, DC: Department of Justice, Office of Juvenile Justice and Delinquency Prevention.

Singer, Simon I. 1996. *Recriminalizing Delinquency: Violent Juvenile Crime and Juvenile Justice Reform*. New York: Cambridge University Press.

Steinberg, Lawrence and Elizabeth Cauffman. 1996. Maturity of Judgment in Adolescence: Psychosocial Factors in Adolescent Decision Making. *Law and Human Behavior* 20(June):249-72.

Torbet, Patricia McFall, Richard Gable, Hunter Hurst IV, Imogene Montgomery, Linda Szymanski, and Douglas Thomas. 1996. *State Responses to Serious and Violent Juvenile Crime*. Washington, DC: Department of Justice, Office of Juvenile Justice and Delinquency Prevention.

Wallace, R. Jay. 1994. *Responsibility and the Moral Sentiments*. Cambridge, MA: Harvard University Press.

Wolf, Susan R. 1990. *Freedom Within Reason*. New York: Oxford University Press.

Woolard, Jennifer L., N. Dickon Reppucci, and Richard G. Redding. 1996. Theoretical and Methodological Issues in Studying Children's Capacities in Legal Contexts. *Law and Human Behavior* 20(June):219-28.

Zimring, Franklin E. 1982. *The Changing World of Adolescence*. New York: Free Press.

ANNALS, *AAPSS*, **564**, July 1999

The Fork in the Road to Juvenile Court Reform

By GORDON BAZEMORE

ABSTRACT: Juvenile justice reform efforts seeking a more criminalized juvenile court and justice system, as well as those aimed at revitalizing the individual treatment mission, have been one-dimensional in their failure to address the multiple justice needs of communities associated with youth crime, and they have been insular in their singular focus on the needs and risks of offenders. In the late 1990s, a growing number of juvenile justice professionals began to embrace a third, more holistic vision for reform based on a normative concern with repairing the harm caused by crime to individuals and relationships and a commitment to victims, communities, and offenders as primary stakeholders in the justice process. This article considers the implications of emerging practice based on a restorative community justice model for systemic reform in the context, content, and structure of juvenile justice and the response to youth crime.

Gordon Bazemore is currently a professor of criminal justice at Florida Atlantic University. His recent publications appear in Justice Quarterly, Crime & Delinquency, *the* Justice System Journal, *and the* Journal of Sociology and Social Welfare. *He is the coeditor of* Restorative Juvenile Justice: Repairing the Harm of Youth Crime *and is currently the principal investigator of a national action research project funded by the Office of Juvenile Justice and Delinquency Prevention to pilot restorative justice reform in several jurisdictions.*

YOGI Berra once advised a group of baseball managers and sports writers, "When you come to the fork in the road, take the fork." Although no one knows exactly what Mr. Berra really meant, in the 1990s, a number of juvenile justice professionals seem to have concluded that they have indeed come to a fork in the road. One apparent path leads toward the vision of a criminalized juvenile court and juvenile justice system. For some, this path implies a merger of adult and juvenile courts into one court, with punishment as its primary mandate and a focus on ensuring due process in adjudication and proportionality in sanctions (Feld 1990).[1] The other path seems to continue, to some extent, with business as usual, attempting to shore up the traditional treatment mission of the court. Advocates of this path have responded to juvenile justice critics with an effort to revitalize and expand court services and increase funding and efficiency through a focus on what works best in the rehabilitation of specific populations of offenders (Krisberg 1988; Palmer 1992).

Facing this choice, some juvenile justice professionals seem to try to walk (or ask their employees to walk) on both paths, at least for a period of time. Others have appeared to have more literally "taken the fork," if by this we mean rejecting both the traditional treatment and the new punitive models as the primary paths for juvenile justice and seeking to build completely new roads, which would, it is hoped, lead to different destinations. One such destination is a partnership with communities based upon a new response to youth crime more reliant on citizens, community groups, and socializing institutions than on juvenile justice professionals in expert roles. Acknowledging the multiple expectations communities have of juvenile justice agencies, as well as the traditional concern with the needs and risks presented by offenders, proponents of this third way have argued that crime victims and communities should be viewed as stakeholders in response to youth crime.

The purpose of this article is to briefly outline this alternative framework for a future response to youth crime and describe the new role for the juvenile court and justice system intervention that it implies. Restorative community justice is a problem-oriented effort to engage victims and citizens in healing and in community building, reparative efforts that attempt to give responsibility for justice solutions as much as possible back to citizens and community groups.[2] In describing the restorative community justice path toward systemic reform in the response to youth crime, I suggest that the current crisis in juvenile justice offers an opportunity for a dramatic transformation in the juvenile court and justice system. The crisis also presents dangers that restorative justice programs may simply be added on to juvenile justice agencies aimed at continuing down the road toward an increasingly punitive response, the road of a revitalized yet incomplete treatment mission, or a winding road that pursues both and moves increasingly away from the very communities that justice systems were designed to serve.

THE LOSS OF COMMUNITY COMPETENCE AND THE RISE OF CRIME CONTROL EXPERTS

You can observe a whole lot just by watching.

—Yogi Berra

Why the new turn to community in response to youth crime, and why the questioning of the mission and role of juvenile justice? If Monsieur Berra's reflections about history and research are as cogent as his aforementioned travel advice, those who have watched the evolution of juvenile justice systems in the past three decades will have observed a profound change in the role and responsibility assumed by government in the response to crime, conflict, and trouble. Indeed, most baby boomers and older generations can recall a time when adults in their communities took responsibility for looking after and imposing informal controls on neighborhood children other than their own. Moreover, there were numerous informal means of resolving disputes and disturbances peacefully, as well as mechanisms for sanctioning behavior that exceeded tolerance limits without recourse to formal court processes. In effect, community members, with the encouragement and support of schools, neighborhood police, and other institutions, often took care of problems that now end up in juvenile and criminal justice systems.

Not all of these informal processes afforded the respect for diversity in culture and lifestyle we would now demand. It can be argued, however, that something important was lost as communities seemed to abandon their responsibility for many problems that now find their way onto juvenile court dockets. While community social control and problem-solving efforts can simply be written off as nostalgic memories of a different era, it is also possible to examine ways in which juvenile justice intervention may have contributed to a weakening of the capacity of citizens, socializing institutions such as families and schools, and community groups to respond to youth trouble and deviance. Moreover, it can be argued that expansion of the government role in these matters has contributed to a kind of learned helplessness and powerlessness in raising young people and resolving disputes (McKnight 1995).

Numerous case examples and research studies illustrate how efforts to centralize, professionalize, and expand juvenile justice and social services sent messages to communities to leave matters to the experts. James Q. Wilson's classic study of Eastern and Western City police departments (1967) was in this regard a harbinger for what soon became more intrusive, centralized juvenile justice systems with broader mandates. In this 1960s comparison, Wilson showed that the more professional, by-the-book responses to delinquent and troublesome young people in Western City, which involved formal processing at a centralized intake facility, resulted in a much higher rate of court referrals (and official arrest records) than was the case with the less professional, and less formal, neighborhood-based approach of Eastern City officers.

Three decades of juvenile justice experience in trying to minimize the harmful effects of formal court processing by developing diversion programs can also teach important lessons about the intrusiveness, expansiveness, and counterproductive impacts of some well-intended social service interventions (Polk 1984). Diversion is generally viewed by researchers and juvenile justice critics as a failure because of a process known as net widening, in which programs meant to serve as community alternatives to court actually expand the number of youths going to court (Schur 1972; Ezell 1992). However, another critique would point not to net widening per se as the problem. Rather, by widening government nets and ignoring the need to strengthen community nets (Braithwaite 1994; Moore and O'Connell 1994), juvenile justice policymakers uncritically expanded system intervention. In doing so, they also failed to distinguish between interventions that build or enhance bonding and strengthen youth-adult relationships and those interventions that further stigmatize and exclude young people and isolate youths from conventional adults. Though well intended, many diversion programs necessarily had the latter effect. More important, these programs sent messages to citizens and communities that government services were available that could solve many of the problems that families,

schools, and other community groups were experiencing with young people, thereby usurping the community's responsibility and undercutting its role.

Today, an increasing number of jurisdictions appear to be establishing, or reestablishing, centralized juvenile court intake facilities, now labeled assessment centers. As they do so, juvenile justice professionals are encouraging police officers to bring youths in for diagnosis, classification, screening, and (ultimately) possible detention and court referral, rather than adjusting cases informally at the neighborhood level. In addition, a number of judges and some policymakers are now advocating that the juvenile court take back its jurisdiction over status offenders (young people who are runaways, truants, and the like but have not committed criminal offenses), a jurisdiction relinquished in most of the country in the 1970s. As these developments occur, the implications of Wilson's study, and of the diversion experience, for an expanding government role and a diminished community role in the response to youth trouble are becoming even more apparent.[3]

Those watching juvenile justice systems in the past three decades will have also observed that administrators of these systems find themselves under growing pressure from policymakers and increasingly at odds with the communities they serve. The crisis has been brought on by decades of increased funding, expansion, and apparent improvements in technical efficiency that, ironically, appear to have left justice systems even less capable of addressing the basic expectations that communities have of them. Many juvenile justice agencies and administrators can rightfully claim that constantly increasing caseloads have limited their effectiveness, even as funding has increased. But if it is acknowledged that at least some juvenile justice agencies and programs remain underfunded, it must also be said that they are underconceptualized.

THE BOX OF PUNISHMENT
AND TREATMENT

Sometimes, I feel like my only option is to send the kid to jail or send him to the beach.
—A juvenile court judge

Currently, when a crime is committed, three primary questions are asked: who did it, what laws were broken, and what should be done to the offender (Zehr 1990)? The latter question is generally followed with another question about the most appropriate punishment or treatment approach to promote rehabilitation. The question of punishment or treatment has been a primary preoccupation of juvenile justice dialogue for the past four decades.[4] Moreover, the policy lenses of treatment and punishment limit the possibilities for juvenile court intervention and place unnecessary blinders on visions for juvenile justice reform. Although there is, of course, nothing wrong with treatment and punishment per se, as guiding philosophies for juvenile justice intervention, these responses are incomplete, and neither punishment nor treatment approaches alone or together seem capable of garnering public support for a viable juvenile court and justice system.

The popularity of the new retributive justice paradigm in juvenile courts is not due to the efficiency or effectiveness of punishment. Indeed, punishment is an expensive response to crime that is often overused or inappropriately used. Punishment typically causes offenders to focus on themselves rather than their victims, and increasing its severity may have little or no impact if we have miscalculated the extent to which sanctions such as incarceration are actually experienced by offenders as punitive (Wright 1991; Crouch 1993). While the punitive approach to crime may appease the public demand for retribution, it is not concerned with reintegrating offenders or with restoring peace and a sense of safety in communities. Moreover, as the experience with transferring juveniles to adult court indicates, neither the threat nor the reality of punishment seems to have a deterrent effect on recidivism.

In the minds of policymakers and the public, however, punitive sanctions appear to be at least somewhat related to the offense. In contrast, treatment modalities appear solely related to the needs of the offender. Treatment in juvenile justice programs, for example, typically asks little of offenders beyond participating in counseling, remedial services, or recreational programs. There is little in the message of the treatment response that attempts to communicate to an offender that he or she has harmed someone and should take action to repair damages wreaked upon the victim. Faced with the choice between approaches that seem to provide only benefits to offenders and punishments that appear on the surface to provide consequences for crime and affirm community standards, many average citizens, policymakers, and crime victims will choose the latter.

As closed-system paradigms, both the individual treatment and retributive justice models are conceptually and practically insular and one-dimensional. Treatment and punishment models are one-dimensional because they reduce justice intervention to a simplistic choice between helping or hurting offenders. They are insular because they are essentially offender focused. Neither punishment nor treatment addresses the specific needs of crime victims or the needs and risks of victimized communities, and both fail to engage victims and other citizens as stakeholders in the justice process. Whether treatment or punishment is emphasized, the offender is the passive and solitary recipient of intervention or service. Increasingly reliant on secure facilities, treatment programs, and professional experts, most juvenile justice systems effectively exclude community members from what could be meaningful roles in a more effective response to crime:

Treatment and punishment standing alone are not capable of meeting the intertwined needs of the community, victim, offender and family. For the vast majority of the citizenry, juvenile justice is an esoteric system wrapped in a riddle. Support comes from understanding, understanding from involvement and participation. Community involvement and active participation in the working of a juvenile court is a reasoned response . . . [currently] community members are not solicited for input or asked for their resourcefulness in assisting the system to meet public safety, treatment and sanctioning aspirations. (Diaz 1996)

But treatment and punishment models are not the only options for juvenile justice intervention. Increasingly, citizens and juvenile justice professionals are beginning to recognize that answering the questions who did it, what laws were broken, and what must be done to the offender fails to address the complex needs facing communities in the aftermath of a crime.

THE NEW LENS: RESTORATIVE
COMMUNITY JUSTICE

The problem of crime can no longer be simplified to the problem of the criminal.
—Leslie Wilkins (1991, 312)

While current criminal and juvenile justice responses are driven by questions of guilt, lawbreaking, and the response to the needs and risks of offenders, restorative justice views crime through a lens that suggests that much more is at stake (Zehr 1990). What is important about crime is that it causes harm to real people: crime injures individual victims, communities, offenders, and their families, and it damages relationships. If crime is more about peace breaking than lawbreaking, justice responses cannot focus simply on offender punishment or treatment. If crime can be viewed as a

TABLE 1
WHAT RESTORATIVE JUSTICE LOOKS LIKE

Crime victims
    Receive support, assistance, compensation, information, and services.
    Receive restitution and/or other reparation from the offender.
    Are involved and are encouraged to give input at all points in the system and direct input into how the offender will repair the harm done.
    Have the opportunity to face the offender and tell their story to the offender and others if they so desire.
    Feel satisfied with the justice process.
    Provide guidance and consultation to professionals on planning and advisory groups.
Offenders
    Complete restitution to their victims.
    Provide meaningful service to repay the debt to their communities.
    Must face the personal harm caused by their crimes by participating in victim-offender mediation, if the victim is willing, or through other victim awareness process.
    Complete work experience and active and productive tasks that increase skills and improve the community.
    Are, if young, monitored by community adults as well as juvenile justice providers and are supervised to the greatest extent possible in the community.
    Improve decision-making skills and have opportunities to help others.
Citizens, families, and community groups
    Are involved to the greatest extent possible in holding offenders accountable, in rehabilitation, and in community safety initiatives.
    Work with offenders on local community service projects.
    Provide support to victims and provide support to offenders as mentors, employers, and advocates.
    Provide work for offenders to pay restitution to victims and service opportunities, which provide skills and also allow offenders to make meaningful contributions to the quality of community life.
    Via community groups, assist families to support young offenders to repair the harm and increase competencies.
    Play an advisory role to courts and corrections and/or play an active role in disposition through one or more neighborhood sanctioning processes.

SOURCE: Balanced and Restorative Justice Project, Florida Atlantic University.

wound on the community, justice must focus on healing the wound (Van Ness and Strong 1997).

The restorative justice response to crime can be best described as a three-dimensional collaborative process. As Table 1 illustrates, the restorative vision is best understood by examining what justice might look like for victim, community, and offender as stakeholders and co-participants in this process. For the victim, restorative justice offers the hope of restitution or other forms of reparation, information about the case, the opportunity to be heard, and input into the case as well as expanded opportunities for involvement and influence. For the community, there is the promise of reduced fear and safer neighborhoods, a more accessible justice process, and accountability, as well as the obligation for involvement and participation in sanctioning crime, reintegrating offenders, and crime prevention and control. For the offender, restorative justice requires accountability in the form of obligations to repair the harm to individual victims and victimized communities, as well as the opportunity to develop new competencies and social skills and the capacity to avoid future crime.

Why restorative justice?

The principles and approaches now being referred to as restorative justice are certainly not new. In fact, historically, settlement based on dispute resolution and restitution, rather than punishment, was the dominant response in virtually all ancient societies (Weitekamp 1999). Restitution, community service, and, to a lesser extent, victim-offender mediation became widely popular as sentencing options in the 1970s and early 1980s and have been used since then with some regularity in U.S. criminal and juvenile courts. Often administered by probation and community diversion programs (Galaway and Hudson 1990; Schneider 1986; Umbreit 1994), in the 1990s these and other reparative sanctions and associated conflict resolution processes are again receiving a high level of interest as part of a broader restorative justice movement. Moreover, a wider menu of programs and decision-making processes, including family group conferencing, victim impact panels, and community sanctioning boards, have been added to the core restitution, community service, and victim-offender mediation options (see Table 2 for a description of restorative sanctioning practices).

There are no easy explanations for the rise in interest in restorative justice at a time when juvenile justice systems in most states appear to be embracing a punitive model. Despite divergent political and cultural influences, however, restorative justice seems to be uniting a growing number of community leaders and justice professionals around an emerging consensus that neither punitive nor rehabilitation-focused models are meeting the needs of communities, victims, and offenders. While restorative justice is clearly in the air in juvenile justice policy discussions throughout the world, restorative justice policies and practices are also on the ground in a more systemic manifestation in local communities, states, provinces, and even entire countries.[5]

Beyond the fork in the road:
  Restorative justice
  and systemic reform

How is restorative justice related to the future of the juvenile court? Is juvenile justice really a promising laboratory for implementing restorative justice, and will restorative justice help to strengthen and provisionally preserve the juvenile court? Currently, the open door that juvenile justice systems seem to be providing, at least to restorative ideas, may be part of a desperate search for legitimacy, motivated more by survival instinct than by commitment to the values of restorative justice. In this context, restorative justice could be viewed as another intervention approach that must compete in a very crowded field with boot camps and other dubious practices in an

TABLE 2

SOME RESTORATIVE SANCTIONING PRACTICES

Restitution to crime victims: It is important that payment be clearly linked to the victim, even if it is processed through the court, and that young offenders be provided opportunities to earn funds to repay victims (for example, through employment programs).

Victim-offender mediation: Offenders meet with victims and a third-party mediator to allow the victim to obtain information about the crime and express feelings to the offender, to develop a reparative agreement, and to increase the offender's awareness of the physical, emotional, and material impact of crime.

Direct service to victims: At the victim's request (usually through mediation or another process), offenders are required to perform direct service.

Service to surrogate victims: Offender work crews (crime repair crews) repair homes and businesses damaged by break-ins and vandalism.

Restorative community service: Offenders perform work that is valued by the community and that is often suggested by neighborhood groups or by crime victims; such service often helps the disadvantaged, promotes economic development, or improves the general quality of life.

Service chosen by the victim: Victims recommend service projects for offenders as part of a mediation agreement.

Payment to victims service fund: Offenders pay to support victims' services when restitution to their specific victim is not needed.

Victim impact statements: With approval from the victim, young offenders can read victims' impact statements or listen to and view audio/video statements that tell how the crime detrimentally affected the victim and his or her loved ones.

Victim awareness programs: Youthful offenders participate in programs that include an educational model that helps youthful offenders understand the impact their crimes have on their victims, their communities, their families, and themselves and that include crime victims as guest speakers.

SOURCE: Balanced and Restorative Justice Project, Florida Atlantic University.

organizational environment where new, trendy programs of the month vie for the attention of juvenile justice administrators. Alternatively, restorative justice could become just another buzzword in jurisdictions that adopt new mission statements and slogans while taking few actions to promote change in business as usual. Restorative reforms could be limited to special programs, new alternatives to formal court processing such as victim-offender mediation, or new job descriptions such as restorative justice coordinator, and they could easily be pigeonholed in one component of the system, such as diversion or corrections, or could become associated with one function, such as disposition, or one ancillary specialization, such as victim services.

On the other hand, opening up the closed setting of the juvenile court to citizen and victim input may begin to break down much of the distrust that citizens feel toward juvenile justice (Bazemore 1997) and may, in individual cases, increase understanding of and support for young offenders and their victims (Umbreit 1994; Young 1995). Moreover, the restorative approach to sanctioning and accountability may garner more credibility among citizens than the existing individual treatment approach and could provide some challenge to the retributive juggernaut that is now sweeping through juvenile justice systems internationally. But if it is to bring meaningful change, restorative justice reform cannot follow the course of prior piecemeal juvenile justice reform efforts. While usually well intended, these reforms have primarily helped to rationalize and improve the structure, process, and techniques by which offenders are treated and punished, without questioning why.

What is most new and different about restorative justice theory and practice, therefore, is its agenda for systemic reform that makes possible a fundamental questioning of basic values and assumptions about youth crime, as well as the ends and means of the response to it. Restorative justice begins with questions about the context of intervention: what values, principles, and assumptions define the essence of crime and what should be done about it; who the system should serve as clients; what stakeholders should be involved in the response to crime and in making decisions about intervention; and by what process these decisions should be made. Answers to these questions drive bottom-up change in the mission of juvenile justice agencies focused on the content of intervention: what goals and performance outcomes best reflect the needs of stakeholders or clients, what messages are to be communicated, and what changes are to be brought about as a result of intervention. Answers to these questions, in turn, help to

determine what programs and intervention practices can be best employed to accomplish these goals. While current juvenile justice policy is often structural and program driven, systemic reform would ensure that programs are selected and intervention priorities are established based on their capacity to accomplish mission outcomes and are therefore value driven. Finally, the choice of intervention priorities should then provide the blueprint for transforming the structure of the juvenile justice system and thus determine what staffing patterns, resources, and professional roles are required to carry out these interventions and accomplish system goals. Hence, while current policy and reform begin with the current structure and seek to make top-down changes in procedure and programs, systemic reform from the bottom up ends with questions about structure, after holistic change in content and context has been addressed (see Figure 1).

CHANGING THE INTERVENTION CONTEXT: VALUES, STAKEHOLDERS, AND DECISION MAKING

Crime [control and prevention] should never be the sole or even primary business of the State if *real differences* are sought in the well-being of individuals, families and communities. The structure, procedures, and evidentiary rules of the formal criminal justice process, coupled with most justice officials' lack of knowledge and connection to [the parties] affected by crime, preclude the state from acting alone to achieve transformative changes.

—Judge Barry Stuart (1995, 7)

FIGURE 1
NEW PARADIGMS AND SYSTEMIC REFORMS

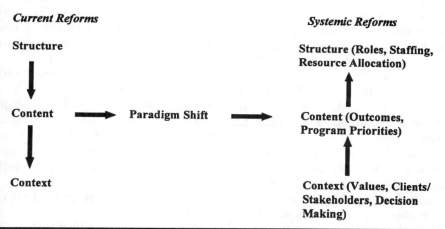

SOURCE: Balanced and Restorative Justice Project, Florida Atlantic University.

Victims frequently want longer time [in prison] for offenders because we have not given them anything else. Or because we don't ask, we don't *know* what they want. So [the system] gives them Door Number One or Two, when what they really want is behind Door Number 3 or 4.
—Mary Achilles, victim advocate (1996, 15)

Viewed through the restorative lens, crime is understood in a broader context than what is suggested by the questions of guilt and what should be done to punish or treat the offender. Howard Zehr (1990) argues that, in restorative justice, three very different questions receive primary emphasis. First, what is the nature of the harm resulting from the crime? Second, what needs to be done to make things right or repair the harm? Third, who is responsible for this repair?

New values

Professionals sitting in their offices cannot answer questions one and two, nor can policymakers standardize or legislate reparative approaches in isolation from those most affected by crime. Defining the harm and determining what should be done to repair are best accomplished with input from crime victims, citizens, and offenders in a decision-making process that maximizes their participation. The decision about who is responsible for the repair focuses attention on the future rather than the past and also sets up a different configuration of obligations in the response to crime (Zehr 1990). No longer simply the object of punishment, the offender is now primarily responsible for repairing the harm caused by his or her crime. A restorative juvenile court and justice system would, in turn, be responsible for ensuring that the offender is held accountable for the damage and suffering caused victims and victimized communities by supporting, facilitating, and enforcing reparative agreements. But, most important, crime victims and the community play critical roles in setting the terms of accountability and monitoring and supporting completion of obligations (Pranis 1997).

As the foregoing quotation from Judge Stuart illustrates, the need to engage communities in the response to crime is based on an implicit, and sometimes explicit, critique of the ability of the formal justice system (and the capacity of criminal justice professionals) to address the needs of those most adversely affected by crime. This assumed incompetence of the formal justice system, and the inherent limitations of current questions about guilt, lawbreaking, and punishment, suggest the need for a different value framework. As Zehr (1990) has proposed, restorative justice values about crime and justice contrast sharply with the values of the current retributive paradigm and provide a new set of principles that redefine crime and the reaction to it, the process that is most helpful in responding to crime, and the role of victim, offender, and community in this process (see Table 3).

New stakeholders:
Engaging crime victims

What is most unique about the restorative justice value base, and most difficult for many criminal justice professionals to accept, is its expansion of the role of crime victims in the justice process. Although victims' rights have received increased attention throughout the criminal justice systems in most states, victim needs (for example, for physical and material reparation and emotional healing) are often addressed only after the needs of police, judges, prosecutors, and corrections staff (for example, with respect to winning cases, processing offenders, or managing resources) have been considered.[6] These needs are especially likely to be overlooked unless victims are given a direct voice in decision making.

When actively engaged, victims often express unique concerns and interests, which are frequently unrelated to offender punishment or even the need for material reparation:

I can tell you that what most victims want most is quite unrelated to the law. It amounts more than anything else to three things: victims need to have people recognize how much trauma they've been through . . . they need to express that, and have it expressed to them; they want to find out what kind of person could have done such a thing, and why to them; and it really helps to hear that the offender is sorry—or that someone is sorry on his or her behalf. (Elaine Berzins, quoted in Stuart 1995, 12)

Although years of neglect has meant that juvenile justice professionals moving toward restorative justice are giving central emphasis to victim needs and the requirement that offenders are held accountable to victims, the restorative justice paradigm also responds to the "mu-

TABLE 3
PARADIGMS OF JUSTICE, OLD AND NEW

	Retributive Justice	Restorative Justice
Crime and reaction	Crime is an act against the state, a violation of a law, an abstract idea.	Crime is an act against another person or a community or both.
	Punishment is effective: the threat of punishment deters crime, and punishment changes behavior.	Punishment alone is not effective in changing behavior and is disruptive to community relationships.
	The criminal justice system controls crime.	Crime control lies primarily in the community.
Victims and the community	Victims are peripheral to the process.	Victims are central to the process.
	The community is on the sidelines, represented abstractly by the state.	The community is a facilitator in the restorative process.
	Pain is imposed to punish and deter.	Restitution is used as a means of restoring both parties; reconciliation is a desired outcome.
The offender	The offender is defined as taking punishment.	Offender accountability is defined as taking responsibility and taking action to repair harm.
	The offender is defined by deficits.	The offender is defined by the capacity to make reparation.
	Repentance and forgiveness are not encouraged.	Forgiveness is possible.

SOURCE: Adapted from Zehr 1990, 211-14.

tual powerlessness" of offenders and victims in the current system and assumes the need for communities to provide opportunities for offender repentance and forgiveness following appropriate sanctioning (Wright 1991; Zehr 1990). From a restorative justice perspective, the best response to crime is one that allows for active participation of victim, offender, and community in a decision-making process that is sensitive to and supportive of victim and citizen needs.

New decision-making processes

The following examples show a variety of responses to offenses committed by youths.

Case 1. After approximately two hours of at times heated and emotional dialogue, the mediator felt that the offender and victim had heard each other's story and had learned something important about the impact of the crime and about each other. They had agreed that the offender, a 14-year-old, would pay $200 in restitution to cover the cost of damage to the victim's home resulting from a break-in. In addition, he would be required to reimburse the victim for the cost of a videocassette recorder he had stolen, estimated at $150. A payment schedule would be worked out in the remaining time allowed for the meeting. The offender had also made several apologies to the victim and agreed to complete community service hours working in a food bank sponsored by the victim's church. The victim, a middle-aged neighbor of the offender, said that she felt less angry and fearful after learning more about the offender and the details of the crime and thanked the mediator for allowing the mediation to be held in her church basement.

Case 2. After the offender, his mother and grandfather, the victim, and the local police officer who had made the arrest had spoken about the offense and its impact, the youth justice coordinator asked for any additional input from other members of the group of about 10 citizens assembled in the local school (the group included two of the offender's teachers, two friends of the victim, and a few others). The coordinator then asked for input into what should be done by the offender to pay back the victim, a teacher who had been injured and had a set of glasses broken in an altercation with the offender, and pay back the community for the damage caused by his crime. In the remaining half hour of the approximately hourlong conference, the group suggested that restitution to the victim was in order to cover medical expenses and the costs of a new pair of glasses and that community service work on the school grounds would be appropriate.

Case 3. The victim was a middle-aged man whose parked car had been badly damaged when the offender, a 16-year-old, had crashed into his car and also damaged a police vehicle after joyriding in another vehicle. The victim talked about the emotional shock of seeing what had happened to his car and his costs to repair it (he was uninsured). Following this, an elder leader of the First Nations community where the circle sentencing session was being held, and an uncle of the offender, expressed his disappointment in and anger with the boy. The elder observed that this incident, along with several prior offenses, had brought shame to his family; he noted that, in the old days, he would have been required to pay the victim's family a substantial compensation as a result of such behavior. After he finished, the feather was passed to the next person in the circle, a young man who spoke about the contributions the offender had made to the community, the kindness he had shown toward the elders, and his willingness to help others with home repairs. Having heard all this, the judge asked the Crown Council (the prosecutor) and the public defender, who were also sitting in the circle, to make statements and then asked if anyone else in the circle wanted to speak. A Royal Canadian Mounted Police officer, whose police car had also been damaged, then took the feather and spoke on the offender's behalf, proposing to the judge that, in lieu of statutorily required jail time for the offense, the offender be allowed to meet with him on a regular basis for counseling and community service. After asking the victim and the prosecutor if either had any objections, the judge accepted this proposal. In addition he ordered restitution to the victim and asked the young adult who had spoken on the offender's behalf to serve as a mentor for the offender. After a prayer in which the entire group held hands, the circle disbanded and everyone retreated to the kitchen area of the community center for refreshments.

Case 4. The young offender, a 16-year-old caught driving with an open can of beer in his pickup truck, sat nervously awaiting the conclusion of a deliberation of the Reparative Board. He had been sentenced by a judge to reparative probation and did not know whether to expect something tougher or much easier than regular probation. About a half hour earlier, prior to retreating for their deliberation, the citizen members of the board had asked the offender several simple and straightforward questions. At the conclusion of the board's deliberations, the chairperson explained the four conditions of the offender's contract: (1) he had to begin work to pay off his traffic tickets; (2) he had to complete a state police defensive driving course; (3) he had to undergo an alcohol assessment; and (4) he had to write a three-page paper on how alcohol had negatively affected his life. After the offender had signed the contract, the chairperson adjourned the meeting.

The process of responding to youth crime illustrated by the foregoing case examples seems a far cry from current dispositional processes in juvenile court. These examples of a victim-offender mediation (Case 1), a family group conference (Case 2), a circle sentencing (Case 3), and a reparative board hearing (Case 4) also suggest that the limitations of formal court structures and procedural rules will necessitate broader reforms if more active involvement of community members in decision making is to be achieved. At the micro level, restorative justice reform has therefore focused on maximizing the use of less formal and informal sanctioning processes that allow for more meaningful participation of victims, offenders, and community members. Hence the most important change brought by restorative justice to the justice context is who is involved in decisions about the response to crime. The preceding case examples are only illustrations of selected restorative decision-making processes, and they by no means represent the diversity of sanctioning and rehabilitative practices, new policies, new victim services, and new agendas for community involvement ultimately required for systemic restorative justice reform (Bazemore 1997). Neither these processes nor the restorative agenda is without problems. Yet the promise of involvement of those most directly affected by crime is a necessary (if not sufficient) step on the road to systemic juvenile justice reform.

Addressing the questions of harm, what should be done to address it, and who is responsible for repair (rather than the questions of offender punishment and treatment) implies a change in the way juvenile justice professionals define and respond to each case. Most important, a case in restorative justice cannot be equated with the offender. Responding to each case as encompassing victim, offender, and community involves much more than adding new programs. Rather, this three-dimensional response would begin to transform the way in which the goals of public safety, sanctioning, rehabilitation, and victim healing are addressed throughout juvenile justice and thereby gradually change the content and structure of intervention.

CHANGING INTERVENTION
CONTENT AND STRUCTURE:
MEETING NEEDS,
RETHINKING ROLES

Support without accountability leads to moral weakness. Accountability without support is a form of cruelty.
—Steve Basler, Oklahoma Council of Churches (Quoted in Pranis and Bussler 1997, 7)

Worse still, we fear that even when something does work, it is seen to do so only in the eyes of certain professionals, while "outside" the system ordinary citizens are left without a role or voice in the criminal justice process.
—John Braithwaite and Stephen Mugford (1994, 34)

There is no way to put and keep all criminals in jail because, just as an untended garden keeps on producing weeds, our eroded communities sprout crop after crop of criminals. The punishment we mete out to any given offender, no matter how severe, has no more effect on his replacement than the fate one weed has on its successor.
—Ronald Earle, District Attorney, Austin, Texas (1996, 8)

The following examples reflect new thoughts on sanctioning:

1. In inner-city Pittsburgh, young offenders in an intensive day treatment program solicit input from community organizations about service projects the organizations would like to see completed in the neighborhood. The offenders then work with community residents on projects that include home repair and gardening for the elderly, voter registration drives, painting homes and public buildings, and planting and cultivating community gardens.

2. In cities and towns throughout Utah, young unemployed offenders pay restitution to their victims out of an hourly wage paid for public service work. In other jurisdictions, businesspeople provide job slots for youths, and probation departments operate youth businesses for offenders who owe restitution.

3. In Deschutes County, Oregon, offender work crews cut and deliver firewood to senior citizens and recently worked with local contractors and community volunteers to build a homeless shelter.

4. In more than 150 cities and towns throughout North America, victims and offenders meet with volunteer mediators in victim-offender mediation sessions or other victim-offender meetings to allow victims to express their feelings about the crime to the offenders, gain information about the offense, hear an apology from the offenders, and develop a restitution agreement.

5. In cities and towns in Pennsylvania, Montana, and Minnesota—as well as in Australia and New Zealand—offenders, victims, family members, and citizens acquainted with both the offenders and the victims gather to determine what should be done in response to the offense. These family group conferences are aimed at ensuring that offenders are made to hear community disapproval of their behavior and apologize to the victim and that an agreement for repairing the damages to victim and community is developed.

The following examples show new approaches to rehabilitation:

1. In South Florida, youthful offenders, sponsored by the Florida Department of Juvenile Justice and supervised by The 100 Black Men of Palm Beach County, Inc., plan and execute projects that serve a shelter for the care and treatment of abused, abandoned, and HIV-positive or AIDS-infected infants and children. Other work crews develop and carry out plans to restore a historic black cemetery in the town of Boynton Beach.

2. In several jurisdictions in Colorado and Florida, offenders work with skilled tradespersons and Habitat for Humanity under the sponsorship of the Homebuilders Institute to refurbish homes and restore public buildings while learning skilled trades, earning money, and completing classroom assignments.

3. In Cleveland, ex-offenders, mentoring participants in juvenile justice programs, work with churches and faith communities to provide shopping and support services for the homebound elderly.

4. In numerous jurisdictions in the United States, young people gain valuable and meaningful work experience, earn money, and repay victims as they work in crews developed by juvenile justice staff and supervised by public service workers and community members. These crews provide important services under contract with public agencies in environmental restoration, service to the elderly, transportation, and recreation.

5. In several Montana cities, college students and other young adult members of the Montana Conservation Corps supervise juvenile offenders in environmental restoration, trail building, and other community service projects and also serve as mentors to one or more of the young offenders.

6. In Portland, Oregon, office workers are trained in the use of the Internet by offenders and other young people with behavior problems in a youth development program who have acquired significant computer programming skills.

The following are examples of new ideas regarding public safety:

1. In Palm Beach County, Florida, and a number of other jurisdictions, probation officers are "out-posted" in neighborhoods to "walk the beat" in an effort to strengthen the ability of families, schools, churches, and community groups to monitor offenders under community supervision and develop local guardianship of neighborhoods.

2. In numerous jurisdictions in North America, school-based probation officers seek to mediate conflict between students and to work with school administrators. In other cities and towns, offenders trained in mediation and dispute resolution teach these skills to other young people in schools and community organizations.

3. Community police officers in Boston; Pompano Beach, Florida; and other jurisdictions work collaboratively with probation officers to

monitor youths on probation and under aftercare supervision during evening hours in high-risk neighborhoods. In the process, some officers develop their own mentoring and prevention programs.

4. In several Minnesota towns, juvenile police officers train school personnel in family group conferencing techniques for resolving school disputes without recourse to courts. In several Oregon towns, probation officers provide parenting classes in schools and train teachers in anger-management techniques.

5. In Tasmania, Australia, offenders and other young people work on planning and action teams with the elderly and other adults to reduce fear of victimization by young people in public spaces such as malls and bus stops.

If one asks what these examples have to do with juvenile justice— more specifically, with rehabilitation, sanctioning crime, or public safety—the answer would be, Very little, if the reference is to punishment strategies and public safety approaches based primarily on incarceration or the threat of it, or to most juvenile court treatment programs. While it is possible to find activities similar to those described in various locations around the country, many juvenile justice professionals view these interventions as sideshows rather than core features of the intervention agenda of most criminal and juvenile justice agencies.

Because juvenile justice interventions have seldom been informed by meaningful citizen input, most ignore the myriad justice needs of communities that have little or nothing to do with whether and how offenders are punished or treated. Citizens want to feel and be safe, and they want to see that there are tolerance limits and consequences for lawbreakers and opportunities to express disapproval of behavior that harms others and those who perpetuate such behavior. According to recent surveys, citizens also want to give most young offenders a second chance, and they want to ensure that those who are under the supervision of juvenile justice agencies return to their communities better prepared to function as productive community members. If the juvenile court is to survive, and if restorative justice is to develop into a fully fledged alternative for juvenile justice, its proponents must rethink the content of intervention and then design and institutionalize more meaningful responses to those needs.

As the examples suggest, a restorative response to the justice needs of communities is focused less on getting tough on crime by punishing offenders and more on holding offenders accountable to those they have harmed. It is focused less on achieving public safety by incarcerating individual offenders and more on reducing fear, building youth-adult relationships, and increasing the capacity of community groups and institutions to prevent crime and safely monitor offenders in the community. Finally, the new way of thinking about rehabilitation and reintegration is focused less on treating offenders in treatment programs and correctional facilities that isolate them from others and more on institutional reform to promote youth development; less on counseling to improve self-image and more on changing the public image of those in trouble after they have demonstrated that they have learned the consequences of their behavior and made things right with their victims and the community.

Generally, sanctioning, public safety, and reintegrative functions are best accomplished in this new way of thinking less by criminal justice experts in formal settings such as courts and programs and more by crime victims, other community members, community groups, and socializing institutions (such as schools and the workplace) through informal processes of relationship building and social control.

What could juvenile courts and justice systems do to begin to move toward a future based on a restorative community justice response to youth crime? What restructuring is necessary to achieve the goals of a new mission to meet community needs and expectations for safety, sanctioning, and offender reintegration, and what organizational framework and mandate for the court and juvenile justice are most appropriate given the changes in the context and content of intervention required by restorative justice?

Increased involvement by victims, other citizens, and offenders as active participants in a restorative justice process focused on repair of harm, as well as new intervention priorities aimed at addressing the needs of those stakeholders, would have significant systemic implications for resource allocation, job descriptions, and the roles of judges, prosecutors, probation officers, corrections workers, and other juvenile justice professionals. Moreover, restorative justice must necessarily reinvent and restore a revitalized role for citizens and community groups in the response to youth crime. This new role assumes even more macro-level changes in the government role, and it must be based on a realistic assessment of the capacities and weaknesses of communities and a strategic plan for changing the relationship between government and the community in this response.

*The decline of informal
    social control and the
    harm of formal intervention*

Government is responsible for preserving order; the community is responsible for preserving peace.
—Daniel Van Ness and
Karen H. Strong (1997, 35)

Children grow up in communities, not programs. Development is most strongly influenced by those with the most intensive, long-term contact with children and youth—family, informal networks, community organizations, churches, synagogues, temples, mosques and schools. Development is not achieved only through services, but also through supports, networks and opportunities.
—Halperin et al. (1995, 6)

Structural and cultural changes in the community's capacity to respond to crime and trouble, coupled with an expanding role for juvenile justice, have left many adults and the community institutions they once relied upon helpless and hapless in socializing young people. Although juvenile justice professionals have frequently blamed parents for youth crime, a more contextual analysis would emphasize a critical historical reality. The past 30 to 40 years represent the first period since humans formed communities that parents alone have been expected to socialize their children, without the support and reinforcement of other adults in the community. As Pranis and Bussler (1997) suggest, this unique state of affairs has two important implications:

Parents can't do that alone; it is an impossible job. The overwhelming nature of such an assignment contributes to the enormous stress experienced by families . . . the second implication relates to children. If adults, other than parents, do not informally intervene in response to the negative behaviors of children, then the message to children is that the expectations of their parents are not community norms, because other adults see them do these things and don't say anything. . . . If the only people who intervene in their lives besides family, are those who are paid—police, teachers, youth workers, probation officers, then children may interpret this to mean that others do not care about them, that they do not belong to the community, that they are unimportant to the community. (2)

As John McKnight has argued, when the role of the justice system is not defined in concert with the community's role, justice and social service programs are likely to overextend their reach and contribute to the isolation rather than the reintegration of people in trouble. The reasons for this state of affairs are complex. One is that, despite their unique professional mandate, what all juvenile justice and social service systems have in common is a deficit focus, emphasizing identification of needs and risks and the provision of services intended to correct presumed deficits and dysfunction. Unfortunately, those who end up in the programs of social service systems often find it difficult, as McKnight suggests, to transition back to the mainstream of conventional socialization networks such as those found in school, work, and the like:

A preliminary hypothesis is that services that are heavily focused on deficiency tend to be pathways out of community and into the exclusion of serviced life. We need a rigorous examination of public investments so that we can distinguish between services that lead people out of community and into dependency and those that support people in community life. (McKnight 1995, 20)

A second reason such systems can inadvertently cause harm is that, as David Moore (1994) has observed, government programs that "take sole responsibility for authoritarian control" may themselves be criminogenic because they "perpetuate the illusion that the state, rather than civil society, is ultimately responsible for social order" (10). Hence the very structures we have created to manage (not solve) the youth crime problem, despite our best efforts and intentions, may themselves be one part of the problem.

On the other hand, there is an important role for government, and specifically juvenile justice and youth-serving agencies, in response to the growing youth socialization crisis. But this function is best accomplished through a community-building agenda, which might seek to re-create new, indigenous social control and support structures. It is least effectively accomplished when juvenile justice systems, on a case-by-case basis, assume responsibility for socialization processes that can be meaningfully carried out only in communities. Such socialization needs are best met by caring adults who spend time with young people not because they are paid to do so but because they share a commitment to the idea that youth development is a community responsibility.[7]

Restorative justice and the new juvenile court mandate

Further expansion of the court's jurisdiction through early intervention to simply identify at-risk individuals (for example, developing centralized assessment or truancy centers) therefore seems counterproductive. Building and expanding an advocacy and leadership role for juvenile justice professionals in promoting community responses that strengthen neighborhood social control, however, could be an effective focus for juvenile court reform.

Such a facilitative, community-building focus would, as suggested, redirect juvenile justice resources and would begin to redefine the role of the intervention professional. For example, probation officers, rather than focusing on offender monitoring and casework, could also emphasize community problem solving and victim advocacy. Such officers might be assigned to develop neighborhood sanctioning and dispute resolution programs, hence intervening not

with individual youths directly, but with at-risk schools, families, and neighborhoods to ensure that young offenders are given opportunities for involvement in work, service, and other roles that facilitate conventional bonding (Pranis 1997; Bazemore and Schiff 1996). In a more naturalistic approach to offender rehabilitation (Bazemore 1999), juvenile justice professionals would no longer view themselves, or be viewed by their communities, as experts in providing service or treatment to change offender attitudes and behavior. Rather, they would function more as a catalyst for building relationships between young people, adults, and adult institutions, while facilitating change in the role and image of youths in trouble.

But more naturalistic intervention strategies do not occur naturally. Most advocates of holistic healing, for example, recognize that expanded use of these processes will not remove the occasional need for surgery. Similarly, most advocates of restorative community justice recognize that there is nothing magical about the community and that identifying and mobilizing citizens to allow for a greater community role in rehabilitation, sanctioning, safety, and peacemaking processes more reliant on nonexperts will change but not eliminate the role of experts (Bazemore 1997; Braithwaite and Parker 1999). As implied throughout this article, the problem with juvenile justice intervention has not been with government itself but with a failure to define a suitable role for government. The juvenile court's responsibility in sanctioning crime, ensuring public safety, rehabilitating offenders, and socializing children has become far too broad, while the community's role in these tasks is now almost invisible.

Paradoxically, a court designed with regard for the principles of restorative and community justice would assume less responsibility for tasks best accomplished by others, while at the same time adopting a broader mandate and vision. The broader mandate, but circumscribed responsibility, for the court itself in the context of an expanded community role would have several implications that could be played out especially in the dispositional arena. Specifically, as illustrated most explicitly by the recent reforms in New Zealand (for example, McElrae 1994), the court could seek to cede much greater decision-making power to the community in determining the nature of sanctioning responses to youth crime. Once guilt has been admitted or determined, in the majority of cases, community panels or conferences, with facilitative support from the court, could make these decisions in a way more sensitive to the needs of crime victims, offenders, and their families. The future court would thus be more free to focus primary attention on legal and advocacy functions including adjudicating, fact-finding, ensuring that the rights of offenders (and victims) are protected, and providing an important enforcement and backup role in dispositional obligations. Because the need for secure facilities and other restrictions on freedom is likely to remain, the need for a vigorous safeguarding of

individual rights will not go away. In addition, Braithwaite and Parker (1999) suggest that, in a restorative juvenile justice system, the court should maintain a review and oversight role to protect against possible "tyranny of the community" and unfairness to offenders and victims, if and when these emerge in the informal setting of community sanctioning conferences.

A second type of advocacy role for the court would focus court authority and leadership on protecting and defending the rights of young people, regardless of their involvement in crime and delinquency. Freed from a large part of its dispositional responsibilities, the court's authority, both formal and informal, could be extended to influence school policy, housing practices, and access to employment and recreational activities. From a restorative perspective, the formal and informal advocacy role of the court must also extend to crime victims. Judicial and court leadership is the primary vehicle by which courts and community justice processes can be opened up to crime victims, and judges can ensure (and insist) that the attention of communities and justice agencies is focused on victim needs and services at all points in the justice process and that the input of victims and their advocates as community members is valued.

If the community is to be empowered as a partner in the response to crime, a redefinition of the role of government from crime control expert to facilitator of community justice and community-building processes is required. The community's role must also change from one viewed by justice professionals as "nuisance," allowed occasional but superficial input, to one of full partner and even "driver" in the response to youth crime (Pranis 1997). This new relationship will be an evolving one. It goes almost without saying that justice systems are not currently set up to support or enhance the kind of community collaboration effort advocated here.

CONCLUSION

Thirty or more years of rising public expectations that the juvenile court can solve the problems of at-risk young people and reduce and control youth crime will make the task of returning authority to the community a difficult one. The juvenile court has been pushed to respond to an increased demand that it solve problems it cannot solve, and it has overreached in a way that has rendered it increasingly less effective.

But while crises such as the one occurring in juvenile justice today are uncomfortable and disruptive, an emerging paradigm shift appears to be removing the blinders imposed by the treatment and punishment paradigms, thus making systemic reform possible. As this occurs, a belief that solutions lie in the community and that the court can both empower neighborhood groups and build their capacity to respond effectively to youth crime is gaining a foothold. Moreover, currently this belief may require less of a leap of faith than the once widespread belief in the expertise of court professionals to

solve the problems of young people in trouble.

The restorative justice change from a focus on individual offenders to an equal emphasis on meeting the needs of victims and communities and involving them in the process will not be easy. If prior reform efforts provide any indication, there are certainly many ways in which restorative reforms could fail to deliver the kind of change hoped for by many advocates. Juvenile justice systems have proven that they are capable of absorbing a variety of new concepts and new policies, and, too often, they have done so while making few real changes and, in some cases, expanding the reach and responsibility of the dominant formal system. Most juvenile justice professionals now sense that some change is inevitable, and juvenile justice systems are currently quite open to change of a certain superficial kind. Although many juvenile justice professionals appear to be working harder today than at any time in the history of the court, perhaps the greatest obstacle to restructuring the juvenile court around a restorative community justice model will be the culture of juvenile justice systems. Over the decades an intense resistance to change has stifled numerous reform efforts. Too often, this resistant culture takes the form of reasons why anything new will not work.

Many legitimate questions can be raised about restorative and community justice. However, many of the most commonly cited obstacles are spurious ones, and, indeed, rationales for opposing the approach are often the best reasons that it is necessary to change focus. For example, if victims seem angry and offenders appear to lack skills and empathy, a primary objective should be to develop interventions that facilitate changes in offender empathy and competency and that attempt to meet the needs of victims and ask for their input. If citizens seem apathetic, a primary objective should be to work toward reducing community apathy and noninvolvement and toward strengthening neighborhoods by changing the nature of current practices and decision-making processes. Finally, if staff do not have time or skills to work with communities, now may be the moment to reexamine and consider changing hiring practices and/or enhancing staff competencies, while restructuring priorities and incentives. The proposed restorative justice model must rise or fall based on empirical outcomes rather than rhetoric. Although restorative justice research and practice are in their infancy, there is now a growing body of encouraging empirical evidence and practical experience with these interventions. Among the most promising findings are those that suggest that citizens in at least some jurisdictions are willing to get involved, under appropriate terms of involvement (Dooley 1995; Barajas 1995; Bazemore and Day 1996).

Ultimately, however, any movement of the court toward a capacity-building role that places communities at the center of justice intervention will not be based solely on research evidence but also on a commitment to certain principles and values. Key among these values is the belief that while the state, as represented by the juvenile justice system, is the source of legal authority, the community is the source of moral authority (Pranis 1997). If the juvenile court is to survive as an independent structure for responding to youth crime, those professionals who will shape its future will be committed to this change in the relationship between juvenile justice and the community, will view apparent obstacles as challenges, and will work with the input and advice of community groups and citizens.

Notes

1. While only a few states have come close to outright abolition of the court, the just-deserts framework on which the abolitionist position is based has had surprising influence in the past two decades. For example, court purpose clauses have been rewritten to give priority to punishment and remove the traditional concern with the "best interests of the child," and mandatory minimum sentences are now increasingly common (Feld 1990). Other court abolitionists seem more aligned with traditional crime control movements and are far less concerned with proportionality, individual rights, and due process than are just-deserts advocates. Another libertarian movement in juvenile justice has generally favored preserving a juvenile court, but one with less sweeping powers over young people—especially the power to detain and incarcerate (Guarino-Ghezzi and Loughren 1995; Schwartz 1987).

2. I will use the terms "restorative justice" and "restorative community justice" (Young 1995; Bazemore and Schiff 1996) somewhat interchangeably to describe the proposed intervention model, although its designation is not fixed. "Community justice" refers generally to a preference for more accessible and less formal justice services (U.S. Department of Justice 1996) that shift the locus of the justice response to those most affected by crime and redefine the role of justice agencies as one

aimed at strengthening the capacity of citizens and community groups to carry out justice responsibilities and supporting them in doing so. While there are many variations in restorative justice intervention, the common focus is on policies, practices, and processes that involve victims, offenders, and other citizens in an effort to repair the harm that crime causes (Galaway and Hudson 1996; Bazemore and Umbreit 1995).

3. The role of the private sector in developing special programs for youths diagnosed with a variety of problems (for example, mental illness, drug use, or simple insubordination) is also well documented (for example, Schwartz 1987).

4. Indeed, modern criminal and juvenile justice ideologies—conservative, liberal, libertarian, just-deserts—can be easily grouped into general categories based on different views of how this fourth question should be addressed.

5. In some cases, such as New Zealand, where disposition of all delinquency cases with the exception of murder and rape are handled in family group conferences (informal meetings between offenders and victims, along with family or other supporters of both, facilitated by a coordinator), and the state of Vermont, where most nonviolent felons and misdemeanants are sentenced to make reparation to the victims by community boards, restorative justice plays a dominant and systemic role in juvenile justice policy (Belgrave 1995; Dooley 1995). Although, in most of the United States, implementation of restorative justice principles is primarily limited to small local experiments, significant state impact can also be seen, for example, in Minnesota, Missouri, Ohio, Pennsylvania, and other states that have adopted restorative justice principles in policy or statute as the mission for juvenile or adult corrections departments. Modern restorative justice appears to have emerged during a unique period of convergence between diverse justice philosophies and political, social, and cultural movements that continue to influence its current development; these philosophies and movements include the victims' rights movement and an expanded role for victims in a community justice process (Young 1995); the community and problem-oriented policing philosophy and movement (Sparrow,

Moore, and Kennedy 1990); renewed interest in indigenous dispute resolution, settlement process, and associated political efforts (especially in Canada) to devolve criminal justice responsibilities to local communities (Griffiths and Hamilton 1996); the women's movement and feminist critique of patriarchal justice (Harris 1990); and the growing critique of both just-deserts and rights-based, adversarial perspectives, as well as of social welfare models, in criminal and juvenile justice (Braithwaite and Petit 1990; Bazemore and Umbreit 1995; Walgrave 1995).

6. Despite frequent complaints about the inability of offenders to pay victim restitution, for example, many jurisdictions that do a poor job of enforcing restitution orders have been highly successful in the collection of offender fines and fees. Indeed, in many probation and parole agencies, victim compensation and restitution have taken a back seat to the collection of moneys used to support criminal justice agency functions (Hillsman and Greene 1992). Moreover, while prosecutors appear to spare no expense and effort to gain victim input for efforts to increase the probability of conviction and length of sentence, time and resources for providing victim services, mediation, and reparative programs seem always in short supply.

7. This attempt to refocus justice intervention and social control on the community is not without a theoretical and empirical basis. While restorative justice is not associated with specific etiologic theories of crime (and indeed, is not focused simply on the offender and individual motivation), emerging intervention theories of restorative rehabilitation and reintegration are consistent with several traditions in criminological theory (Karp 1997; Bazemore 1996, 1999). For example, social control perspectives emphasize the importance of the bond that individuals have to conventional groups (Hirschi 1969; Polk and Kobrin 1972). This bond can in turn be viewed as culturally and structurally fixed in the roles individuals assume in the context of community groups and socializing institutions (such as family, work, school), which presume networks of relationships that provide informal constraints on deviant behavior based on affective ties to significant others (teachers, parents). At a more intermediate, interactional

level of analysis, consistent with social learning theories such as differential association, the restorative justice response to crime seeks to mobilize intimates and "communities of concern" (Stuart 1995) around the offender to promote settlement, restitution, or other informal resolution in the aftermath of a crime (Braithwaite and Mugford 1994; Retzinger and Scheff 1996). At a more macro-community level, the restorative effort to build and strengthen relationships by increasing the quality of participation in problem solving and the response to crime and conflict is grounded in social ecological and disorganization theories of crime and community, which sensitize us to the relationship between structure, culture, and community "collective efficacy" in utilizing informal controls to limit deviant behavior (Sampson and Groves 1989; Sampson, Roedenbush, and Earls 1997; Karp 1997).

References

Achilles, Mary. 1996. Crime Victims and Restorative Justice. Paper presented at the international conference of the Society for Professionals in Dispute Resolution, Oct., Anaheim, CA.

Barajas, Eduardo, Jr. 1995. Moving Toward Community Justice. *Topics in Community Corrections* (National Institute of Corrections).

Bazemore, Gordon. 1996. Three Paradigms for Juvenile Justice. In *Restorative Justice: International Perspectives*, ed. Burt Galaway and Joe Hudson. Monsey, NY: Criminal Justice Press.

———. 1997. The "Community" in Community Justice: Issues, Themes and Questions for the New Neighborhood Sanctioning Models. *Justice System Journal* 19(2):193-228.

———. 1999. After Shaming, Whither Reintegration: Restorative Justice and Relational Rehabilitation. In *Restorative Juvenile Justice: Repairing the Harm of Youth Crime*, ed. Gordon Bazemore and Lode Walgrave. Monsey, NY: Criminal Justice Press.

Bazemore, Gordon and Susan Day. 1996. Restoring the Balance: Juvenile and Community Justice. *Juvenile Justice* 3(1):3-14.

Bazemore, Gordon and Mara Schiff. 1996. Community Justice/Restorative Justice: Prospects for a New Social Ecology for Community Corrections. *International Journal of Comparative and Applied Criminal Justice* 20(1):311-35.

Bazemore, Gordon and Mark Umbreit. 1995. Rethinking the Sanctioning Function in Juvenile Court: Retributive or Restorative Responses to Youth Crime. *Crime & Delinquency* 41(3):296-316.

Belgrave, John. 1995. *Restorative Justice: A Discussion Paper*. Wellington, New Zealand: Ministry of Justice.

Braithwaite, John. 1994. Thinking Harder About Democratizing Social Control. In *Family Conferencing and Juvenile Justice*, ed. C. Alder and J. Wundersitz. Canberra: Australian Institute of Criminology.

Braithwaite, John and Stephen Mugford. 1994. Conditions of Successful Reintegration Ceremonies: Dealing with Juvenile Offenders. *British Journal of Criminology* 34(2):139-71.

Braithwaite, John and C. Parker. 1999. Restorative Justice Is Republican Justice. In *Restorative Juvenile Justice: Repairing the Harm of Youth Crime*, ed. Gordon Bazemore and Lode Walgrave. Monsey, NY: Criminal Justice Press.

Braithwaite, John and Philip Petit. 1990. *Not Just Deserts: A Republican Theory of Criminal Justice*. Oxford: Clarendon Press.

Crouch, Ben M. 1993. Is Incarceration Really Worse? Analysis of Offenders' Preferences for Prison over Probation. *Justice Quarterly* 10(1):67-88.

Diaz, Jesus. 1996. Pinal County Department of Juvenile Court Services, Florence, AZ. Mission statement.

Dooley, Michael J. 1995. Reparative Probation Program. Vermont Department of Corrections. Monograph.

Earle, Ronald. 1996. Community Justice: The Austin Experience. *Texas Probation* 11(1):6-11.

Ezell, M. 1992. Juvenile Diversion: The Ongoing Search for Alternatives. In *Juvenile Justice and Public Policy*, ed. Ira M. Schwartz. New York: Lexington Books.

Feld, Barry. 1990. The Punitive Juvenile Court and the Quality of Procedural Justice: Distinctions Between Rhetoric and Reality. *Crime & Delinquency* 36(4):443-46.

Galaway, Burt and Joe Hudson, eds. 1990. *Criminal Justice, Restitution and Reconciliation*. Monsey, NY: Criminal Justice Press.

————. 1996. *Restorative Justice: International Perspectives*. Monsey, NY: Criminal Justice Press.

Griffiths, Curt T. and Ron Hamilton. 1996. Spiritual Renewal, Community Revitalization and Healing: Experience in Traditional Aboriginal Justice in Canada. *International Journal of Comparative and Applied Criminal Justice* 20(1):285-310.

Guarino-Ghezzi, Susan and Edward Loughren. 1995. *Balancing Juvenile Justice*. Thousand Oaks, CA: Sage.

Halperin, Samuel, John Cusack, Robert O'Brien, Gordon Raley, and John Wills, eds. 1995. *Contract with America's Youth: Toward a National Youth Development Agenda*. Washington, DC: American Youth Policy Forum.

Harris, M. Kay. 1990. Moving into the New Millennium: Toward a Feminist Vision of Justice. In *Criminology as Peacemaking*, ed. H. Pepinsky and R. Quinney. Bloomington: Indiana University Press.

Hillsman, Sally and Judith Greene. 1992. The Use of Fines as an Intermediate Sanction. In *Smart Sentencing*, ed. J. M. Byrne, A. Lurigio, and J. Petersilia. Newbury Park, CA: Sage.

Hirschi, Travis. 1969. *Causes of Delinquency*. Berkeley: University of California Press.

Karp, David. 1997. "Community Justice," research seminar on community, crime, and justice. George Washington University and U.S. Department of Justice, National Institute of Justice.

Krisberg, Barry. 1988. *The Juvenile Court: Reclaiming the Vision*. San Francisco: National Council on Crime and Delinquency.

McElrae, Fredrick W. M. 1994. Justice in the Community: The New Zealand Experience. In *Relational Justice: Repairing the Breach*, ed. Jonathan Burnside and Nicola Baker. Winchester, UK: Waterside Press.

McKnight, John. 1995. *The Careless Society: Community and Its Counterfeits*. New York: Basic Books.

Moore, David B. 1994. Illegal Action—Official Reaction. Australian Institute of Criminology. Manuscript.

Moore, David B. and Terrance O'Connell. 1994. Family Conferencing in Wagga Wagga: A Communitarian Model of Justice. In *Family Group Conferencing and Juvenile Justice: The Way Forward or Misplaced Optimism?* ed. C. Adler and J. Wundersitz. Canberra: Australian Institute of Criminology.

Palmer, Ted. 1992. *The Re-invention of Correctional Intervention*. Newbury Park, CA: Sage.

Polk, Kenneth. 1984. When Less Means More. *Crime & Delinquency* 30(3):462-80.

Polk, Kenneth and S. Kobrin. 1972. *Delinquency Prevention Through Youth Development*. Washington, DC: Department of Health, Education and Welfare, Office of Youth Development.

Pranis, Kay. 1997. From Vision to Action: Some Principles of Restorative Justice. *Church and Society Presbyterian Church Journal* 87(4):32-42.

Pranis, Kay and Darrol Bussler. 1997. *Achieving Social Control: Beyond Paying!* St. Paul: Minnesota Department of Corrections.

Retzinger, Susan and Thomas Scheff. 1996. Strategy for Community Conference: Emotions and Social Bonds. In *Restorative Justice: International Perspectives*, ed. Burt Galaway and Joe Hudson. Monsey, NY: Criminal Justice Press.

Sampson, Robert J. and W. B. Groves. 1989. Community Structure and Crime: Testing Social-Disorganization Theory. *American Journal of Sociology* 94:774-802.

Sampson, Robert J., Steven Roedenbush, and Felton Earls. 1997. Neighborhoods and Violent Crime: A Multi-Level Study of Collective Efficacy. *Science Magazine* 277:918-24.

Schneider, Ann. 1986. Restitution and Recidivism Rates of Juvenile Offenders: Results from Four Experimental Studies. *Criminology* 24(3):533-52.

Schur, Edwin. 1972. *Radical Nonintervention: Rethinking the Delinquency Problem*. Berkeley: University of California Press.

Schwartz, Ira M. 1987. *Injustice for Juveniles*. Lexington, MA: Lexington Books.

Sparrow, M., Michael Moore, and David Kennedy. 1990. *Beyond 911*. New York: Basic Books.

Stuart, Barry. 1995. Sentencing Circles: Making "Real" Differences. Territorial Court of the Yukon. Manuscript.

Umbreit, Mark. 1994. *Victim Meets Offender: The Impact of Restorative Justice and Mediation*. Monsey, NY: Criminal Justice Press.

U.S. Department of Justice. National Institute of Justice. 1996. *Communities Mobilizing Against Crime: Making Partnerships Work*. Washington, DC: Department of Justice, National Institute of Justice.

Van Ness, Daniel and Karen H. Strong. 1997. *Restoring Justice*. Cincinnati, OH: Anderson.

Walgrave, Lode. 1995. The Restorative Proportionality of Community Service for Juveniles: Just a Technique or a Fully-Fledged Alternative? *Howard Journal of Criminal Justice* 34(3):228-49.

Weitekamp, Elmar G. 1999. The History of Restorative Justice. In *Restorative Juvenile Justice: Repairing the Harm of Youth Crime*, ed. Gordon Bazemore and Lode Walgrave. Monsey, NY: Criminal Justice Press.

Wilkins, Leslie. 1991. *Punishment, Crime and Market Forces*. Brookfield, VT: Dartmouth.

Wilson, James Q. 1967. *Varieties of Police Behavior: The Management of Law and Order in Eight Communities*. Cambridge, MA: Harvard University Press.

Wright, Martin. 1991. *Justice for Victims and Offenders*. Buckingham, England: Open University Press.

Young, Marlene. 1995. *Restorative Community Justice: A Call to Action*. Washington, DC: National Organization for Victim Assistance.

Zehr, Howard. 1990. *Changing Lenses: A New Focus for Crime and Justice*. Scottsdale, PA: Herald Press.

ANNALS, *AAPSS*, **564**, July 1999

(Un)equal Justice: Juvenile Court Abolition and African Americans

By JOHN JOHNSON KERBS

ABSTRACT: Many academics now call for the abolition of juvenile court jurisdiction over delinquency adjudications. This article examines Barry Feld's assumptions behind his call for juvenile court abolition and the potentially adverse impact of the criminal court alternative in the lives of young African Americans. Three assumptions are examined: (1) criminal courts can provide the same or greater substantive and procedural protections compared to the current juvenile court; (2) criminal courts can provide shorter sentences for reduced culpability, with fractional reductions of adult sentences in the form of an explicit youth discount; and (3) treatment strategies are of dubious efficacy, and the possibility of effective treatment is inadequate to justify an entirely separate justice system. This article finds that these assumptions are erroneous and that the juvenile court's abolition may very well be harmful to young African Americans due to false assumptions concerning both juvenile and criminal courts.

John Kerbs is a Ph.D. candidate in social work and sociology at the University of Michigan, where he conducts research on juvenile and criminal justice issues. He has a master's degree in social welfare from the University of California at Berkeley and a master's degree in sociology from the University of Michigan.

NOTE: The writing of this article was supported by the National Institute of Aging, Training Grant T32-AG0017. The author would like to thank Dr. Ruth Dunkle, Dr. Jeffrey Fagan, Dr. Sheila Feld, Dr. Richard Lempert, Kimberly Osborne, Dean Ira Schwartz, Dr. Thomas Reed, and Dr. Patricial Welch for their support in the development of this article.

INTRODUCTION

In 1999, the juvenile court commemorates its hundredth birthday. While many will celebrate, others will view this event as symbolic of the nation's historical failure to provide children with a rights-based jurisprudence. We should pause and reflect upon the juvenile court's legacy of second-rate justice. We should also reflect as respected and well-intentioned academics call for the abolition of juvenile court jurisdiction over delinquency adjudications. These calls began early in the juvenile court's history (Onley 1938) and continue today via published statements by well-known figures such as Barry Feld (1993a, 1993b) and others (for example, see Ainsworth 1991).

One academic, Martin Guggenheim (1978), who once supported abolition, now denounces it (Rosenberg 1993). Like Guggenheim, I, too, once supported juvenile court abolition; however, I have reversed my opinion because I feel that most arguments in favor of juvenile court abolition are based upon false assumptions, which can lead to unequal and second-rate justice for minority children, particularly African American children facing criminal courts. This article reviews these assumptions in relation to advancing a rights-based jurisprudence for all children. Barry Feld is the best-known proponent of juvenile court abolition, and, because I respect and agree with most (but not all) of his depictions of juvenile court deficiencies, I will critique his call for abolition. His position is ill advised because of potentially harmful consequences that may arise for young African Americans due to false assumptions concerning both juvenile and criminal courts. This article explores his assumptions about due process, sentencing, and treatment.

Assumption #1: Criminal courts can provide the same or greater substantive and procedural protections compared to those provided by the current juvenile court (Feld 1993a)

Feld has clearly asserted that criminal courts should provide juveniles with full procedural parity in criminal courts, and additional protections that recognize their developmental differences in competence, maturity, and vulnerability. Feld (1993a) calls this approach a "dual maximal strategy" that provides children with enhanced protections that he envisions as follows:

The right to counsel would attach as soon as a juvenile is taken into custody and would be self-invoking. . . . It would not require a juvenile to affirmatively request counsel as is the case for adults (*Moran* v. *Burbine* [475 U.S. 412 (1986)]). . . . The presence and availability of counsel throughout the process would assure that juveniles' rights are respected and implemented. (291)

Feld's comments sound authoritative, but I am not confident we can "assure" the presence and availability of counsel for juveniles that guarantees their rights are "respected and implemented." Feld's statement implicitly assumes that available and effective counsel respects and implements the rights of adult defendants. Here, Feld wants to augment the base package of procedural safeguards accorded adults by automatically providing juveniles with the right to counsel. Still, we must first examine the quality of criminal court representation to determine if augmenting the base package will improve how juveniles, particularly young African Americans, experience substantive and procedural justice in criminal courts.

Clearly, the quality of representation in criminal courts depends, in large part, upon the defendants' economic position, since this may determine whether they retain private counsel or indigent defense representation. Since African American children disproportionately live in poverty, one can assume that more young African American defendants (compared to young white defendants) will rely upon indigent defense systems, just as they do in juvenile courts (Feld 1993a). Recent research has indicated that 16 percent of all white children under age 18 lived below the poverty line in March of 1996; this statistic stands in stark contrast to the 41 percent of all African American children under age 18 in this position (Children's Defense Fund 1997).

For practical purposes, this discussion will start with the U.S. Supreme Court's 1962 decision in *Gideon* v. *Wainwright* (372 U.S. 335 [1963]), which determined that indigent defendants facing felony prosecutions were entitled to counsel. This decision was congruent with the Sixth Amendment of the Constitution, which states, "In all criminal prosecutions, the accused shall enjoy the right to have the Assistance of Counsel for his defense." Since 1963, right to counsel has been extended, theoretically, to cover delinquency adjudications via *In re Gault* (387 U.S. 1 [1967]) and many misdemeanors (Worden 1991).

Unfortunately, rhetoric and reality regarding counsel in juvenile and criminal courts differ. Juvenile courts often fail to live up to the promise of *In re Gault* since a high proportion of children never receive counsel during delinquency adjudications (Feld 1988, 1990). Moreover, urban public-defender caseloads in delinquency courtrooms often range between 250 and 550 cases, despite standards set by the National Advisory Commission on Criminal Justice Standards and Goals that call for a maximum of 200 cases per year (American Bar Association 1995) to ensure the effective assistance of counsel.

While these findings demonstrate profound problems concerning access to counsel and the quality of representation in delinquency proceedings, the adult system is equally problematic. Many adult indigent defendants have been forced to accept substandard representation because of limitations in the mechanisms designed to provide indigent counsel—that is to say, representation via assigned counsel, public defenders, and contracted representation (Worden 1991).

Generally speaking, these three indigent-defense systems are overloaded and underfunded, and recent research indicates that almost every assigned counsel program in the country is inadequately funded

(Klein 1993). Low pay and excessive, unworkable caseloads have been problems for years, but the situation is qualitatively worse than in the past. Klein (1993) noted that the "number of indigents charged with crimes has increased, in part due to expanded funding for *police and prosecutors* to fight the national and local 'war on drugs' " (363). No similar increase in funding has been forthcoming for indigent defense systems (Marcus 1994), causing serious repercussions, since (by coincidence, consequence, or design) most national, state, and local governments have primarily focused the war on drugs against the poor (Tonry 1994). Between 70 and 90 percent of defendants charged with drug or drug-related offenses are deemed indigent and require appointed counsel (Murphy 1991).

Still, all levels of government have largely failed to fund indigent counsel systems. Gross funding disparities exist between prosecutorial and indigent defense budgets (White 1988), and indigent defense funding for court-appointed counsel and public defenders has decreased in several localities (Klein 1993). The best available evidence (see Marcus 1994) to date demonstrates a 324 percent differential between the amounts allocated by federal, state, local, county, and municipal governments to prosecution in 1990 ($5.5 billion) and the amounts allocated to indigent defense ($1.7 billion).

Poorly funded indigent defense systems are not adequately prepared to guarantee the constitutionally mandated effective assistance of counsel (Klein 1993). As in juvenile courts, public defenders in criminal courts carry caseloads that are, generally speaking, twice the national standard said to ensure adequate representation (Marcus 1994). Fiscal constraints have also blocked lawyers' access to the computers, experts, investigators, and support staff needed to properly represent indigent defendants (Sevilla 1997). Consequently, many indigents are "being represented all too often by walking violations of the Sixth Amendment" (White 1988, 239-40). Mounts (1986) denounces this situation as indicative of a system of "non-representation." Child advocates, juvenile justice professionals, and policymakers alike should be concerned about the constitutional issues here because, as White (1988) noted, the Sixth Amendment implicitly assumes that a counsel's assistance will be effective, though all major studies of indigent defense representation have found that the right to counsel remains largely unfulfilled and in crisis.

Not surprisingly, defendants with private counsel obtain more favorable results than those using court-appointed counsel. One study, for example, revealed that a higher percentage of those with court-appointed counsel (70 percent), as compared to those with private counsel (22 percent), ended up in pretrial detention (Bodensteiner, Bork, and Moskowitz 1983). Conviction rates were also higher for those with appointed counsel, and they received prison sentences twice as often.

Such differential outcomes are, in part, due to the inappropriate use of plea bargaining. Like health maintenance organizations that cap doctors' reimbursements, some states cap the maximum reimbursements lawyers can receive for each indigent case (regardless of time constraints). The reimbursement structure creates a clear incentive for lawyers to plead clients guilty. Moreover, "some lawyers will accept a court-appointed case only if it is apparent that the defendant will plead guilty" (Klein 1993, 374). The pressure to plea-bargain indigent cases will increase as caseloads rise and funding languishes. Not surprisingly, over 90 percent of all criminal convictions result from plea bargaining instead of trials (Champion and Mays 1991). This de facto denial of access to jury trials in criminal courts resembles the de jure denial of jury trials in juvenile courts as per *McKeiver* v. *Pennsylvania* (403 U.S. 528 [1971]), the court decision that found that a jury is not required in juvenile proceedings.

Many committed public defenders believe they cannot provide effective or adequate counsel under such adverse conditions, and concerns arise about their inability to comply with constitutional mandates. For example, the Fourteenth Amendment states, ". . . nor shall any state deprive any person of life, liberty, or property without due process of law; nor deny to any person within its jurisdiction the equal protection of the laws." Every time an individual has to accept the services of ineffective indigent defense systems, that person, to be sure, is denied the "equal protection of the laws."

To the extent that the poor and racial minorities are dispropor-tionately dependent upon ineffective public defense systems, they are systematically denied access to rights provided by the Sixth and Fourteenth Amendments. In outlining the juvenile court's failure to provide effective counsel, abolitionists such as Feld nevertheless fail to devote equal attention to corresponding constitutional concerns in criminal court. Feld's relative silence on the criminal court's constitutional deficiencies weakens his argument.

To paraphrase, because due process is expensive, quality representation is often denied to poor defendants, despite safeguards to guarantee or ensure some degree of equal access. These defendants disproportionately include young African Americans. The scales of justice balance procedural justice for indigents inadequately. Thus, the unfulfilled promise of *In re Gault* is little different from the unfulfilled promise of *Gideon* v. *Wainwright*; consequently, the right to counsel is effectually denied the poor in both juvenile and criminal courts.

Clearly, then, Feld's abolition argument floats on the assumption that criminal courts can provide the same substantive and procedural (that is, due process) protections as the current juvenile court or protections that are greater. This assumption appears valid for those affluent enough to pay for due process protections such as the right to counsel in criminal court. His assumption is highly suspect when applied to poor children because it masks the social injustice of criminal courts for children in poverty. Feld's dual maximal protections, despite their apparent availability to all, will result primarily in a system of illusory rights for young African Americans and other poor defendants who will have trouble accessing these rights (Lempert and Sanders 1986).

Assumption #2: "Criminal courts can provide shorter sentences for reduced culpability with fractional reductions of adult sentences in the form of an explicit 'youth discount' " (Feld 1993a, 418)

Feld's second assumption is that adult courts can provide shorter sentences for convicted young persons. This assumption rests on the will of politicians to pass state legislative sentencing policies permitting the implementation of age-related sentence reductions in criminal courts. Unfortunately, politicians and the public seem reluctant to move in this direction. The current political slogan is "adult crime/adult time" (Kiernan 1995), not "reduced time for adult crimes." The era is characterized by successful efforts to pass legislation that makes it easier to try children in adult courts (Forst and Blomquist 1991) and sentence them to jail and prison (Schwartz 1992). Since 1980, over 80 percent of all states have passed legislation subjecting juveniles to the full force of criminal court sanctions, including prison terms (Fagan 1990; Hamparian et al. 1982), leading, not surprisingly, to an increased number of persons under age 18 now serving time in jails and prisons (U.S. Department of Justice 1994, 1996).

Both the political rhetoric of the day and public opinion polls over the past decade have emphasized just-desert strategies, namely, punishment over treatment and rehabilitation. Whereas waiver and "adult crime/adult time" legislation are not hard to find, the current political climate makes it hard to find examples of explicit "youth discount" legislation, most likely because just-desert strategies for juveniles reflect punitive public desires (Schwartz 1992).

For example, a 1994 survey by *USA Today*, CNN, and Gallup found that a clear majority of the U.S. public (60 percent) supported the death penalty for juveniles convicted of murder (Edmonds 1994). Half supported giving juveniles the same sentence as adults for their first conviction, and 83 percent supported using the same sentence as adults for second and third convictions. Punitive attitudes like these are problematic; while abolitionists like Feld conceptually separate the adult judicial and correctional systems (keeping the former and bypassing the latter), the general public and politicians voting on legislation see no reason to do so.

None of this bodes well for the concept of youth discounts, but serious issues arise for African American children facing criminal sanctions linked to drug convictions without concomitant sentence reductions. Clearly, the so-called war on drugs differentially affects African Americans. Even though young African Americans between 12 and 25 years of age are less likely to use illegal drugs than are young whites (Mosher and Yanagisako 1991), research indicates that they are more likely than white youths to face delinquency adjudications for drug arrests (Butts 1996). The delinquency drug-case rates for African American juveniles rose drastically, by 215 percent between 1985 (3.4 per 100,000) and 1994 (10.7 per 100,000), while the corresponding rates for white juveniles increased only 22 percent, from 2.7 per 100,000 in 1985 to 3.3 per 100,000 in 1994 (Butts 1996). Some scholars (Federle and Chesney-Lind 1992; Snyder 1990) have suggested that increased drug law adjudications and racism have led to the overrepresentation of African American juveniles in secure forms of detention.

As adult crime/adult time sanctions increase, a disproportionate number of African American youths will find themselves in criminal courts, mirroring the experience of African American adults, who are also overrepresented at the point of arrest, in criminal courts, and in prison populations (Daly 1994). An often quoted statistic reveals that, as of 31 December 1994, African American adults represented around 50 percent of all state and federal inmates combined (U.S. Department of Justice 1996), despite representing only about 12 percent of the U.S. population. The rising rate of imprisonment for African American men and women appears to be traceable to the increased enforcement of more severe punishment for drug offenses (Daly 1994). Nolan (1997) noted that we should consider the following: although African Americans constitute 12.1 percent of the U.S. population and 13.0 percent of drug users,

35.0 percent of all drug arrests involve African Americans. Furthermore, 55.0 percent of all drug-possession convictions involve African Americans, and 74.0 percent of all adults imprisoned as a result of drug possession are African American. While these statistics are not conclusive evidence of systemic racism, they do make for compelling prima facie evidence.

Differential treatment is, perhaps, most visible at the point of sentencing; here, criminal courts use capital and noncapital sentencing systems "rife with racial bias" to mete out harsher sanctions to minority defendants (Developments in the Law 1988, 1627). Tonry (1994) noted that "purveyors of crack cocaine, a drug used primarily by poor urban blacks and Hispanics, are punished far more severely than are purveyors of powder cocaine, a pharmacologically indistinguishable drug used primarily by middle-class whites" (488). While differential sentencing occurs at all levels (federal, state, and county), the federal courts are, perhaps, the worst offenders. Federal sentencing practices equate 5 grams of crack with 500 grams of powder, and both weights result in a minimum five-year sentence (Nolan 1997; Tonry 1994). As a result, African Americans in federal prisons serve 40 percent more time on average than comparable whites (McDonald and Carlson 1993).

I am not confident that, in this get-tough era, young African Americans processed for drug offenses will receive sentencing discounts in criminal courts. Rather, they will probably face the same statutes that led to the overrepresentation in prison of their adult counterparts. If anything, I believe that existing sentencing statutes for crack cocaine appear to provide African Americans with sentence enhancements while whites get a relative discount for powder cocaine. Feld does not examine the criminal court along these racial and class lines, yet the differential treatment of African Americans convicted of drug offenses suggests that youth discounts would not be uniformly applied. One cannot assume that young African Americans will receive a youth discount if convicted under adult sentencing statutes since African American adults already receive differentially harsher sanctions for capital and noncapital convictions (Developments in the Law 1988), especially drug convictions (Tonry 1994).

Juvenile courts are no less biased than criminal courts in their treatment of juveniles. Feld's own research has indicated that African Americans in juvenile court generally receive harsher dispositions than white juveniles when controlling for present offense and prior record (Feld 1993a). Sampson and Lauritsen (1997) argue that juvenile courts may be more racist than criminal courts because the former system is relatively informal, thus permitting discrimination to operate more freely there. Nonetheless, since racial biases exist in both courts, I find it disconcerting that Feld fails to examine the relative danger of biased treatment in the criminal court alternative, with its more severe array of sanctions.

Moreover, I think we must consider that it is increasingly difficult to redress racially disparate processing in criminal courts, since the U.S. Supreme Court will not accept statistical evidence of disparate treatment as presumptive evidence of discrimination. In *McCleskey* v. *Kemp* (481 U.S. 279 [1987]), an African American defendant sought to overturn his death sentence for the murder of a white police officer. The defense used the Baldus study, which, via statistical analyses, clearly demonstrated that African American defendants "in Georgia were disproportionately more likely to receive the death penalty for killing a white person than white defendants were for killing a black person" (Marcus 1994, 245). The U.S. Supreme Court, however, held that statistical evidence alone was not sufficient to prove a violation of the Fourteenth Amendment's equal protection of the laws. Instead, proof of discriminatory purpose or intention was required.

Experts have shown that this intention standard is nearly impossible to prove and essentially halts efforts to address discrimination even though statistical disparities have been accepted historically as indicative of presumptive discrimination in civil rights struggles surrounding school desegregation, employment discrimination, and voting rights (Lempert and Sanders 1986). By refusing to accept such evidence as sufficient, the Supreme Court is in essence refusing to address the criminal court's institutionalized discrimination, unless intention can be shown (a near impossibility).

More disturbing, this situation raises serious doubt as to whether the racism of juvenile courts is actually less intense than that found in adult criminal courts. Feld's criminal court alternative for all juveniles appears to be particularly problematic for young African Americans, who may well experience a more intense level of differential treatment, particularly since criminal courts appear to openly tolerate disparate outcomes involving the severest sanction—the death penalty—which is applicable to 16- and 17-year-old adolescents as per *Stanford v. Kentucky* (109 S.Ct. 2969 [1989]) and *Wilkins* v. *Missouri* (109 S.Ct. 2969 [1989]).

Of course, many juveniles also face the potentially disparate application of prison sentences in criminal court. Mauer (1997) found that the average national ratio of African American to white incarceration was 7.66:1 in 1994; "twelve states and the District of Columbia incarcerate [African Americans] at a rate more than ten times that of whites" (Mauer 1997, 1). Between-state variation ranged from a low of 3.43:1 in Idaho to a shocking high of 22.77:1 in Minnesota.

Are these get-tough sentencing statutes effectively reducing crime rates? No. Therefore, it is unconscionable that get-tough policies continue unabated despite evidence indicating that punitive measures have few, if any, effects on crime rates (Tonry 1994). Indeed, widespread consensus indicates that longer and harsher sentences do not significantly enhance public safety via general deterrent effects (Tonry

1994). Not surprisingly, legislative waivers for serious juvenile crimes have not reduced violent juvenile crime rates (Jensen and Metsger 1994; Singer and McDowall 1988).

Still, politicians continue promoting adult crime/adult time legislation even though it has deleterious effects on juveniles. For example, juvenile robbers subjected to either probation or incarceration in adult facilities were more likely to recidivate than similar children with juvenile dispositions (Fagan 1995). Research also shows that juvenile offenders are at greatest risk of being the victim of sexual assault in prison (Dumond 1990); juveniles in adult jails and prisons are also more likely to be otherwise victimized and commit suicide than juveniles in age-segregated facilities (Forst, Fagan, and Vivona 1989; Flaherty 1983; Library Information Specialists 1983; Memory 1989). While this is problematic for all juveniles, it is especially problematic for minority youths, who are more likely to end up in adult facilities and spend more time in them than their white counterparts (Fagan 1990; Fagan, Slaughter, and Hartstone 1987; Federle and Chesney-Lind 1992).

Assumption #3: Since treatment strategies are of "dubious efficacy," the "possibility of effective treatment" cannot justify "an entire[ly] separate justice system" (Feld 1993b, 411)

If Feld (1993a) is correct to say that the juvenile court's treatment strategies are of "dubious efficacy," then I agree that the possibility of effective treatment is inadequate to justify the existence of juvenile courts. If Feld is wrong in these assertions, then there are concerns for juveniles in general, and young African Americans in particular, who may lose the benefit of treatment and rehabilitation offered through the juvenile courts and face the punitive orientations of the criminal courts, which mete out differentially harsher sentences along racial lines (Developments in the Law 1988; Tonry 1994). Of course, even juvenile courts have become less rehabilitative and more punitive in recent years (Feld 1993b). This move toward punitive strategies concerned LeFlore (1987), who said the current just-desert approach to juveniles would ultimately hurt young African Americans by blocking their potential benefit from the juvenile court's rehabilitation-oriented strategies. If we abolished juvenile courts and then were to find that the juvenile court and juvenile justice system outperformed criminal courts at reducing recidivism, then LeFlore's fears would be correct.

Feld's assumption about treatment efficacy cuts to the philosophical foundation of juvenile courts. According to Feld (1993b, 404-5), Progressive reformers (also known as the child savers) originally envisioned the juvenile court as a "welfare agency in which an expert judge, assisted by social workers and probation officers, made individualized dispositions in a child's best interests." In stark contrast to criminal courts, juvenile courts were to rely on assessment, diagnosis, and interventions as the means through which

treatment and rehabilitation were realized for juveniles.

While I agree that juvenile courts have done less than stellar jobs at achieving their stated goals, I do not believe that all treatment strategies are of dubious efficacy. Indeed, I believe treatment can be highly effective; I also believe that the rehabilitative doctrine remains an adequate justification for a separate court system for juveniles. Certainly, treatment will not be uniformly successful, but this standard is not required to justify a separate juvenile court system. The bottom line is that all that juvenile courts must do is produce statistically significant reductions in recidivism.

Numerous studies and literature reviews from the last two decades show that treatment programs result in "demonstrable reductions in recidivism" (Frazier, Bishop, and Lanza-Kaduce 1997, 13). In addition, recent meta-analytic research has found sound evidence of the effectiveness of behavioral interventions (Lipsey 1997), cognitive interventions (Izzo and Ross 1990), cognitive-behavioral interventions, and residential interventions (Garrett 1985). Contrary to Feld's assertions that treatment strategies are of "dubious efficacy," these studies suggest that many treatment strategies are statistically effective. To be fair, studies have also revealed strategies that fail to reduce recidivism (Lab and Whitehead 1988, 1990; Whitehead and Lab 1989; Martinson 1979), which suggests that we must be careful not to replicate ineffective modalities. Due to the space constraints of this article, I cannot exhaustively review the extant literature on juvenile rehabilitation, but it is important to indicate that there is support for the validity of the child savers' rehabilitative vision.

Most damaging to Feld's position regarding treatment efficacy is the recent and methodologically advanced research that finds that juvenile courts outperform criminal courts at reducing recidivism for comparable juveniles in both cross- and within-jurisdictional studies. Cross-jurisdictional studies compare the same type of offenders across two jurisdictions: one that typically retains juveniles in criminal courts and one that typically retains similar juvenile offenders in juvenile court. Within-jurisdictional studies carefully match and compare juveniles within the same jurisdiction who are either transferred to criminal courts or retained by the juvenile court.

In a review of cross-jurisdictional research (Fagan 1995) and within-jurisdictional research (Frazier et al. 1997), Frazier, Bishop, and Lanza-Kaduce (1997) found that "transfer is more likely to aggravate recidivism than to prevent it" (28). Cross-jurisdictional research by Fagan (1996) examined 800 15- and 16-year-old adolescents charged with burglary and robbery; the findings indicated that incarceration rates were higher for adolescents processed through criminal courts and that "recidivism rates were significantly lower for adolescents sentenced in the juvenile court, regardless of sentence type or severity" (77). Because criminal court processing exacerbated recidivism rates, Fagan concluded that "there is no support

for legislative efforts to eliminate the special jurisprudence for adolescent crimes or the separate jurisdiction for juvenile offenders" (77). Such conclusions were also supported by within-jurisdictional research using survival analyses that found that transferred juveniles were rearrested faster and more times on average than comparable cases processed in juvenile court (Winner et al. 1997).

The child savers were correct in their assumption that a rehabilitative juvenile court would ensure better outcomes. If young African Americans are adjudicated as delinquent, they should have the option to benefit from the juvenile justice system. Relative to criminal courts, juvenile courts have (1) a belief that juveniles can change; (2) a greater propensity to use community-based options, options that produce lower recidivism rates than incarceration; (3) a tendency to rely on smaller facilities such as camps, group homes, half-way houses, and more humane residential facilities than the large-scale correctional facilities found in the criminal justice system; and (4) age-segregated facilities (Frazier, Bishop, and Lanza-Kaduce 1997).

CONCLUSION

Engraved in a piece of marble over the entrance of the U.S. Supreme Court is the phrase "Equal Justice Under Law" (Higginbotham 1996). Certainly, the U.S. Supreme Court has made some effort to reform juvenile and criminal courts so that defendants can experience the laudable goal of equal justice. But the

Supreme Court has largely failed in its efforts to transform both juvenile and criminal courts, which still dispense second-rate justice with differentially adverse outcomes for minority children. The juvenile court is essentially wedded to a model of due process as deficient as the criminal court's failed version. If juvenile courts become extinct, there is little reason to believe that criminal courts will provide any silver-bullet solution leading to a rights-based jurisprudence for all children. Indeed, the criminal court alternative will probably continue to do what it does now: subject juveniles to a severe array of sanctions while providing the poor with illusory rights and unequal justice under law.

The standard of justice produced by both courts is flawed to the extent that equal justice under the law represents little more than an elusive goal for many, especially poor African American children and adults. Both courts need restructuring, and they need it now. I suggest that juvenile court abolitionists step back from efforts to fold juvenile courts—lest we end up with the sole option of a procedurally deficient and racially biased criminal court that metes out sentences known to exacerbate juvenile recidivism rates. Instead, let us restructure both courts to advance the quality of due process, justice, treatment, and rehabilitation for all. Both young and old deserve access to available and effective assistance of counsel; jury trials—rather than plea bargaining—where appropriate; and humane and rehabilitative treatment strategies. Indeed, everyone should receive equal justice under the law, without worrying that the scales of justice are weighed against them as a result of age, class, race, or social position.

Unfortunately, the Supreme Court has made it difficult to take corrective action to redress the biased scales of justice. The courts refuse to recognize statistical disparities as sufficient evidence of racial discrimination, as evidenced by *McCleskey* v. *Kemp*. As this article has shown, racial sentencing disparities are graphic at the national and state levels, and efforts must be made to eliminate such disparities. To this end, statistical evidence needs to be viewed as sufficient to prove a violation of the Fourteenth Amendment's equal protection of the laws. If the present standard of discriminatory purpose or intention is allowed to remain as the required proof of discrimination, then future corrective measures will be stalled because intention is almost impossible to prove. Child advocates, juvenile justice professionals, and policymakers should promote the use of statistical findings as indicative of presumptive discrimination in both juvenile and criminal courts.

As for public safety, recidivism rates indicate that criminal courts and adult correctional venues do relatively poor jobs of treatment, rehabilitation, and reducing recidivism. This suggests that we should conceptually detach and safeguard the juvenile system of age-segregated dispositional options, which keep children away from adult sentencing statutes and related correctional options, especially jails and prisons. Significantly, 22 states do this with reverse waivers, which allow criminal courts to transfer children back to juvenile court for adjudication and/or disposition (U.S. Department of Justice 1997). Unfortunately, more work is needed here because the number of juveniles in jails and prisons rises each year, a fact that does not bode well since adolescents "behind the walls" face an increased risk of victimization and potential suicide.

Moreover, concerns arise because criminal court convictions can mortgage the life course and long-term well-being of youths convicted of felonies. Sampson and Laub (1993, 248) noted that juvenile and adult incarcerations "had negative effects on later job stability which in turn was negatively related to crime over the life course." In economic terms, Johnson and Farrell (1998) noted that African Americans with criminal records made far less pretax income in 1992 ($13,371) than African Americans without criminal records ($21,471), whites with criminal records ($27,595), and whites without criminal records ($30,043). These differentials are probably related to employer attitudes and preferences for applicants without criminal records; research has shown that only a minority of employers (around 33 percent) "would hire someone with a criminal record" (Holzer 1996, 58).

Unfortunately, the social disadvantage of criminal court convictions does not end in mere economic terms. Voting rights are also affected by felony convictions and criminal justice incarcerations. While all but 4 states deny prisoners the right to vote, 31 states deny this right to those on probation and parole, and 13 states deny most felons this right for life (Mauer 1997).

Finally, child advocates, juvenile justice professionals, and policymakers must consider the adverse consequences that appear to be associated with any effort to abolish juvenile court jurisdiction over delinquency adjudications. The criminal court alternative, at a minimum, promises higher recidivism rates for juveniles; compromised due process for the poor; adult crime/adult time sentences to jails and prisons, which place juveniles at risk of victimization and suicide; and unstable employment histories, with associated reductions in the incomes and earning potentials of convicted juveniles. Hence, the assumptions underlying Feld's analysis appear erroneous, and juvenile court abolition may very well be harmful to young African Americans due to false assumptions concerning both juvenile and criminal courts. The debate on the abolition of the juvenile court will probably continue until this country commits itself to overhauling both courts, which perpetrate unequal justice under law, leaving little more than a jurisprudence of illusory rights and discrimination for the poor.

References

Ainsworth, Janet E. 1991. Re-imagining Childhood and Reconstructing the Legal Order: The Case for Abolishing the Juvenile Court. *North Carolina Law Review* 69(June):1083-133.

American Bar Association. 1995. *A Call for Justice: An Assessment of Access to Counsel and Quality of Representa-*

tion in Delinquency Proceedings. Washington, DC: American Bar Association, Juvenile Justice Center.

Bodensteiner, Ivan E., Jeffrey S. Bork, and Seymour H. Moskowitz. 1983. Unequal Justice Under Law: An Analysis of Indigents in the Criminal Justice System: The Indiana Experience. *Western New England Law Review* 6(Fall):263-332.

Butts, Jeffrey A. 1996. Offenders in Juvenile Court, 1994. *OJJDP Juvenile Justice Bulletin* (U.S. Department of Justice).

Champion, Dean J. and G. Larry Mays. 1991. *Transferring Juveniles to Criminal Courts: Trends and Implications for Criminal Justice*. New York: Praeger.

Children's Defense Fund. 1997. *The State of America's Children: Yearbook 1997*. Washington, DC: Children's Defense Fund.

Daly, Kathleen. 1994. Criminal Law and Justice System Practices as Racist, White, and Racialized. *Washington and Lee Law Review* 51(Spring):431-64.

Developments in the Law: Race and Criminal Process. 1988. *Harvard Law Review* 101(May):1472-641.

Dumond, R. W. 1990. *Sexual Assault of Male Inmates in a Prison Setting*. NCJRS pub. no. 125721. Rockville, MD: Department of Justice, National Institute of Justice.

Edmonds, Patricia. 1994. To Some, Ultimate Penalty Is Ageless. *USA Today*, 28 Sept., final ed.

Fagan, Jeffrey. 1990. Social and Legal Policy Dimensions of Violent Juvenile Crime. *Criminal Justice & Behavior* 17(Mar.):93-103.

———. 1995. Separating the Men from the Boys: The Comparative Advantage of Juvenile Versus Criminal Court Sanctions on Recidivism Among Adolescent Felony Offenders. In *A Sourcebook: Serious, Violent and Chronic Juvenile Offenders*, ed. James Howell, Barry Krisberg, J. David Hawkins, and John J. Wilson. Thousand Oaks, CA: Sage.

———. 1996. The Comparative Advantage of Juvenile Versus Criminal Court Sanctions on Recidivism Among Adolescent Felony Offenders. *Law & Policy* 18(Jan.-Apr.):77-112.

Fagan, Jeffrey, E. Slaughter, and E. Hartstone. 1987. Blind Justice? Racial Disparities in Juvenile Justice Processing. *Crime & Delinquency* 33(Apr.):224-28.

Federle, Katherine H. and Meda Chesney-Lind. 1992. Special Issues in Juvenile Justice: Gender, Race, and Ethnicity. In *Juvenile Justice and Public Policy: Toward a National Agenda*, ed. Ira M. Schwartz. New York: Lexington Books.

Feld, Barry C. 1988. *In re Gault* Revisited: A Cross-State Comparison of the Right to Counsel in Juvenile Court. *Crime & Delinquency* 34(Oct.):393-424.

———. 1990. The Punitive Juvenile Court and the Quality of Procedural Justice: Disjunctions Between Rhetoric and Reality. *Crime & Delinquency* 36(Oct.):443-66.

———. 1993a. *Justice for Children: The Right to Counsel and the Juvenile Courts*. Boston: Northeastern University Press.

———. 1993b. Juvenile (In)justice and the Criminal Court Alternative. *Crime & Delinquency* 39(Oct.):403-24.

Flaherty, Michael G. 1983. The National Incidence of Juvenile Suicide in Adult Jails and Juvenile Detention Centers. *Suicide and Life Threatening Behavior* 13(Summer):85-94.

Forst, Martin, Jeffrey Fagan, and T. Scott Vivona. 1989. Youth in Prisons and Training Schools: Perceptions and Consequences of the Treatment-Custody Dichotomy. *Juvenile and*

Family Court Journal 40(Winter):1-14.

Forst, Martin L. and Martha-Elin Blomquist. 1991. Cracking Down on Juveniles: The Changing Ideology of Youth Corrections. *Notre Dame Journal of Law, Ethics & Public Policy* 5:323-76.

Frazier, Charles E., Donna M. Bishop, and Lonn Lanza-Kaduce. 1997. "Get Tough" Juvenile Reforms: Does "Adultification" Make Matters Worse? Paper presented at the Symposium on the Future of the Juvenile Court, University of Pennsylvania, Philadelphia.

Frazier, Charles E., Donna M. Bishop, Lonn Lanza-Kaduce, and Lawrence Winner. 1997. The Transfer of Juveniles to Criminal Court: Does It Make a Difference? *Crime & Delinquency* 42(Apr.):171-91.

Garrett, Carol J. 1985. Effects of Residential Treatment on Adjudicated Delinquents: A Meta-Analysis. *Journal of Research in Crime and Delinquency* 22(Nov.):287-308.

Guggenheim, Martin. 1978. A Call to Abolish the Juvenile Justice System. *Children's Rights Reporter* 1:3.

Hamparian, Donna, Linda Estep, Susan Muntean, Ramon Priestino, Robert Swisher, Paul Wallace, and Joseph White. 1982. *Youth in Adult Court: Between Two Worlds*. Washington, DC: Department of Justice, Office of Juvenile Justice and Delinquency Prevention.

Higginbotham, A. Leon. 1996. *Shades of Freedom: Racial Politics and Presumptions of the American Legal Process*. New York: Oxford University Press.

Holzer, Harry J. 1996. *What Employers Want: Job Prospects for Less-Educated Workers*. New York: Russell Sage Foundation.

Izzo, Rhena L. and Robert R. Ross. 1990. Meta-Analysis of Rehabilitation Programs for Juvenile Delinquents: A

Brief Report. *Criminal Justice & Behavior* 17(Mar.):134-42.

Jensen, Eric L. and Linda K. Metsger. 1994. A Test of the Deterrent of Legislative Waiver on Violent Juvenile Crime. *Crime & Delinquency* 40(Jan.):96-104.

Johnson, James H., Jr. and Walter C. Farrell, Jr. 1998. Growing Income Inequality in American Society: A Political Economy Perspective. In *The Inequality Paradox: Growth of Income Disparity*, ed. James A. Auerbach and Richard S. Belous. Washington, DC: National Policy Association.

Kiernan, L. 1995. Despite Setbacks, Massachusetts Is Beacon in Juvenile Reform. *Chicago Tribune*, 17 Apr.

Klein, Richard. 1993. The Eleventh Commandment: Thou Shalt Not Be Compelled to Render the Ineffective Assistance of Counsel. *Indiana Law Journal* 68(Spring):363-433.

Lab, Steven P. and John T. Whitehead. 1988. An Analysis of Juvenile Correctional Treatment. *Crime & Delinquency* 34(Aug.):60-85.

———. 1990. From "Nothing Works" to "the Appropriate Works": The Latest Stop on the Search for the Secular Grail. *Criminology* 28(Aug.):405-17.

LeFlore, Larry. 1987. The Just Desert Philosophy and Its Impact on Child Saving: From the Perspective of Black Children. *Free Inquiry in Creative Sociology* 15(Nov.):145-50.

Lempert, Richard and Joseph Sanders. 1986. *An Invitation to Law and Social Science*. New York: Longman.

Library Information Specialists. 1983. *Suicides in Jail*. Corrections Information Series. Boulder, CO: National Institute of Corrections.

Lipsey, Mark W. 1997. Can Intervention Rehabilitate Serious Delinquents? Research on a Central Premise of the Juvenile Justice System. Paper presented at the Symposium on the Future of the Juvenile Court, University of Pennsylvania, Philadelphia.

Marcus, R. 1994. Racism in Our Courts: The Underfunding of Public Defenders and Its Disproportionate Impact Upon Racial Minorities. *Hastings Constitutional Law Quarterly* 22:219-67.

Martinson, Robert. 1979. New Findings; New Views: A Note of Caution Regarding Sentencing Reform. *Hofstra Law Review* 7(Winter):243-58.

Mauer, Marc. 1997. *Intended and Unintended Consequences: State Racial Disparities in Imprisonment.* Washington, DC: Sentencing Project.

McDonald, Douglas and Kenneth Carlson. 1993. *Sentencing in the Federal Courts: Does Race Matter?* Washington, DC: U.S. Department of Justice, Bureau of Justice Statistics.

Memory, John M. 1989. Juvenile Suicides in Secure Detention Facilities: Correction of Published Rates. *Death Studies* 13(Sept.-Oct.):455-63.

Mosher, J. F. and K. Yanagisako. 1991. Public Health, Not Social Welfare: A Public Health Approach to Illegal Drug Policy. *Journal of Public Health Policy* 12:278-323.

Mounts, Suzanne E. 1986. The Right to Counsel and the Indigent Defense System. *Review of Law & Social Change* 14(Winter):221-41.

Murphy, Timothy R. 1991. Indigent Defense and the U.S. War on Drugs: The Public Defender's Losing Battle. *Criminal Justice* 6(Fall):14-20.

Nolan, Thomas J. 1997. Racism in the Criminal Justice System: Problems and Suggestions. *Harvard Journal of Law and Public Policy* 20(Winter):417-21.

Onley, J. 1938. The Juvenile Courts—Abolish Them. *State Bar Journal of the State Bar of California* 13:1-6.

Rosenberg, Irene M. 1993. Leaving Bad Enough Alone: A Response to the Ju-

venile Court Abolitionists. *Wisconsin Law Review* (Jan.-Feb.):163-85.

Sampson, Robert and John Laub. 1993. *Crime in the Making: Pathways and Turning Points Through Life.* Cambridge, MA: Harvard University Press.

Sampson, Robert J. and Janet L. Lauritsen. 1997. Racial and Ethnic Disparities in Crime and Criminal Justice in the United States. *Crime and Justice: A Review of Research* 21:311-74.

Schwartz, Ira M. 1992. Juvenile Crime-Fighting Policies: What the Public Really Wants. In *Juvenile Justice and Public Policy: Toward a National Agenda*, ed. Ira M. Schwartz. New York: Lexington Books.

Sevilla, Charles M. 1997. Criminal Defense Lawyers and the Search for Truth. *Harvard Journal of Law and Public Policy* 20(Winter):519-27.

Singer, Simon and David McDowall. 1988. Criminalizing Delinquency: The Deterrent Effects of the New York Juvenile Offender Law. *Law & Society Review* 22(Aug.):521-35.

Snyder, Howard. 1990. *OJJDP Update on Statistics: Growth in Minority Detentions Attributed to Drug Law Violators.* Washington, DC: Department of Justice.

Tonry, Michael. 1994. Racial Politics, Racial Disparities, and the War on Crime. *Crime & Delinquency* 40(Oct.):475-94.

U.S. Department of Justice. 1994. *Bureau of Justice Statistics Sourcebook of Criminal Justice Statistics—1993.* Washington, DC: Department of Justice, Office of Justice Programs, Bureau of Justice Statistics.

———. 1996. *Bureau of Justice Statistics Sourcebook of Criminal Justice Statistics—1995.* Washington, DC: Department of Justice, Office of Justice Programs, Bureau of Justice Statistics.

———. 1997. *Bureau of Justice Statistics (Select Findings): National Survey of Prosecutors, 1994—Juvenile Prosecution in State Criminal Courts*. Washington, DC: Department of Justice, Office of Justice Programs, Bureau of Justice Statistics.

White, Penny J. 1988. A Noble Idea Whose Time Has Come. *Memphis State University Law Review* 18(Winter):223-65.

Whitehead, John T. and Steven P. Lab. 1989. A Meta-Analysis of Juvenile Correctional Treatment. *Journal of Research in Crime and Delinquency* 26:276-95.

Winner, Lawrence, Lonn Lanza-Kaduce, Donna M. Bishop, and Charles E. Frazier. 1997. The Transfer of Juveniles to Criminal Court: Reexamining Recidivism over the Long Term. *Crime & Delinquency* 43(Oct.):548-63.

Worden, Allisa Pollitz. 1991. Privatizing Due Process: Issues in the Comparison of Assigned Counsel, Public Defender, and Contracted Indigent Defense Systems. *Justice System Journal* 14(Winter-Spring):390-418.

ANNALS, *AAPSS*, **564**, July 1999

Myopic Justice?
The Juvenile Court
and Child Welfare Systems

By IRA M. SCHWARTZ, NEIL ALAN WEINER, and GUY ENOSH

ABSTRACT: The two major institutions set up to assist at-risk youths—the juvenile court and the child welfare system—have failed at their common historical mission to treat, supervise, rehabilitate, protect, and care for youths. Institutional survival has almost always taken precedence over this core mission. The result has been the unintended but not unexpected victimization of their vulnerable, often already victimized young clientele. There are profound political, social, and institutional forces in tense balance surrounding the two systems. Some of these forces keep the two institutions from coming apart and crumbling. Others keep them from pursuing the basic required changes that would presage meaningful institutional reform and, perhaps, revival. Despite these obstacles to change, there are still possibilities for embarking upon a politically and socially sound process of change. This process might enable the juvenile court and the child welfare system to better fulfill their mission.

Ira M. Schwartz is dean of the School of Social Work at the University of Pennsylvania and former administrator of the Office of Juvenile Justice and Delinquency Prevention at the U.S. Department of Justice.

Neil Alan Weiner is a senior research associate at the Center for the Study of Youth Policy at the University of Pennsylvania.

Guy Enosh is a student in the Ph.D. program in social welfare at the University of Pennsylvania. His research concerns youth and family violence.

THE pervasiveness of the blindness and myopia, both inside and outside the juvenile court, is eye opening. Too many, whether inside the court or outside, whether critics or supporters, suffer from one or another kind of visionary impairment. Within the juvenile court, faulty vision is forcefully and widely illustrated by the court's continuing unwavering commitment to relying heavily upon reports and judgments of caseworkers or the opinions of judges as to the best interests of the child. The long- and deeply ingrained commitment, which at first blush seems to be noncontroversial, has been turned into a vacuous slogan precisely because, upon close inspection, it raises grave legal and practical concerns and obstacles. Once holding great promise for saving vulnerable children and their families, the concept of the best interests of the child has become tied up in knots. Its legal and practical evisceration coupled with the mixed and lukewarm institutional and political support for it that still lingers has prompted many to advocate the abolition of the juvenile court precisely because the best interests of the child are not being served.

The source of the call for abolition is the tension between the treatment-supervision-rehabilitation triad and punishment (Krisberg and Austin 1993; Schwartz, Weiner, and Enosh 1998; Singer 1996). Abolitionists regard the juvenile court as both a failed experiment in rehabilitation and an ineffective dispenser of punishment. Furthermore, abolitionists are particularly critical of the juvenile court's failure to provide young people with the basic due process and procedural protections accorded adults accused of crimes and who thereby face the loss of their liberty (Feld 1988a, 1988b, 1993). This court-reform posture is myopic because it overlooks and, consequently, fails to consider other critical issues, for example, the role of the court in handling cases of child abuse and neglect and its controversial role in addressing the recurring issue of status offenders.

When reformers focus on one group or class of juveniles who fall under the juvenile court's jurisdiction, such as status offenders, they tend to overlook the fluid connections between these and the many other kinds of youths who may also be subject to the court's jurisdiction. For example, today's status offender can become tomorrow's dependent or delinquent youth. The current system criminalizes and, in practice if not in intent, punishes status offenders and dependent youths, many of whom are victims of familial and other hardships. Abolition of the juvenile court would neither preserve nor advance the rights of any of these groups. In fact, it would probably leave these children and their families, often urgently in need of protection, care, and services, with these urgent needs unmet.

THE MISSION OF
THE JUVENILE COURT

The juvenile court is founded upon a cluster of beliefs, attitudes, and sentiments fundamental to the contemporary, Western European orientation toward children. This cluster engenders the following core ideas: children are dependent upon adults; children are in the midst of developing emotionally, morally, and cognitively and, therefore, are psychologically impressionable and behaviorally malleable; children have different, less competent levels of understanding and collateral mental functioning than adults; and, accordingly, unlike adults, children should not be held fully accountable for their behavior. A corollary is that when parents are unable to care for or discipline a child, it becomes the state's duty to intervene on the child's behalf. This is the time-honored prerogative of political society to supersede civil society, called *parens patriae* (Alper 1941; Stevenson et al. 1996).

The juvenile court is expected to fulfill the complicated dual roles of societal disciplinarian that can punish and of parental substitute that can treat, supervise, and rehabilitate. Although these two roles may jockey with respect to which one will become the court's prevailing function at a particular time and, therefore, be invoked in applications to individual cases under consideration, they nonetheless are an integral if not inherent part of the foundation upon which the court's capacity to survive has depended, does depend now, and will surely depend. Another factor playing a pivotal role in the juvenile court's ability to survive, and one that is too often overlooked, is the simple fact that the court faces few limits regarding the kinds of youthful behavior over which it can exercise control. In other words, the juvenile court has virtually unrestricted authority to define new groups of clients. Few agencies or institutions can match this capacity to create a client base by pure fiat.

Historically, the juvenile court has dealt with three different types of clients: delinquents, status offenders, and dependents (due to abuse and neglect) (Alper 1941; Fox 1996; Stevenson et al. 1996). This diversity has been at the heart of the court's capacity to manufacture a core, long-term clientele as well as clienteles that fit its marginal, short-term needs. This diversity also dovetails seamlessly with the court's tripartite, but tightly interlocked, overarching mandate to care for, to discipline, and to rehabilitate, treat, and supervise. The combination of a broad mandate and an equally broad client base is the lifeline that has made the juvenile court the immovable institution it has been vis-à-vis the many irresistible forces it has confronted and successfully countered over the course of its 100-year existence.

THE CALL FOR ABOLITION

Over the last 30 years, the juvenile court has weathered many blistering attacks. Those attacks have had multiple goals: the diversion of delinquents (Blomberg 1977; Ezell 1989; Paternoster et al. 1979); the decriminalization of specific kinds of behavior (Krisberg and Austin 1993; Singer 1996); the introduction of broader and stricter due process and procedural protections (Feld 1988a, 1988b, 1990; Stevenson et al., 1996);

and, most potentially far-reaching in its implication, the call for complete abolition (Feld 1993; Guggenheim 1976).

These attacks have had several common features. On the one hand, those advocates who have viewed delinquents and status offenders as the juvenile court's main clients have claimed that the court has not served these offenders' best interests. Moreover, it has also been claimed that the court's loose judicial procedures have undercut these youths' legal rights, unduly exposing them to one or another kind of pre- and post-dispositional punishment. On the other hand, those who have viewed society as the juvenile court's client have claimed that the court has failed in its mission to protect society from some of its most troublesome and possibly troubled youngsters, those who are violent. As a result of these emotionally persuasive claims, virtually all states have adopted policies and procedures by which violent, chronic, and other serious juvenile offenders can be tried in the adult criminal courts and receive adult sentences (Singer 1996).

When considered from a historical perspective, one can understand more fully the motives and theories behind calls for change. It has been shown that reforms of juvenile court procedures and legislation have typically come in waves (Singer 1996; Bernard 1992). Like actual waves, changes seem to advance and then retreat. The ebb and flow is, we think, between the two types of social and correctional philosophies mentioned earlier: rehabilitation and punishment. Whenever the social climate focuses on the real or perceived increase in the crime rate, a more punitive approach is pushed by the media, politicians, and policy analysts. After some time, attention is redirected toward the plight of juveniles in the justice system, and the call for rehabilitation or alternative approaches is once again heard. Some researchers have applied theories of social change and vested interests, such as moral panics, in order to understand and explain the ebb and flow or cyclical dynamic (Bernard 1992; Jacobs 1990). Singer (1996) argues that explanations entailing single-source waves of change are too simplistic to fit the historical record. Rather, he thinks that a more complex process is at work. For example, whatever the main content might be of a particular wave of policy change, an alternative is always retained as a potential fallback position.

THE JUVENILE COURT AND CHILD WELFARE

Almost everyone knows that the juvenile court is heavily involved in delinquency and young-adult crime issues. Juvenile delinquency, particularly serious and violent offenses, receives more than its fair share of coverage by the media. The public knows that juveniles who are arrested must appear in juvenile court unless they do something so heinous that they deserve to be tried and sentenced as adults.

In stark contrast, the juvenile court's role in child welfare is hardly understood at all. In fact, with the possible exception of adoption procedures, the public probably does not know that the juvenile court plays much, if any, role in child welfare. Although child welfare atrocities, mainly related to abuse and neglect, routinely appear in newspapers and on television, the only agency or institution that is portrayed as being connected to these issues is the state or local public child welfare authority. The juvenile court is rarely, if ever, mentioned. Nor does the juvenile court step forward and accept commensurate responsibility for responding to these issues.

All states have enacted legislation mandating the reporting, to child welfare or law enforcement agencies, of child abuse and neglect by specific professional groups that routinely serve children and families as part of their occupational mission (Barth 1996). Once a report is received by a statutorily designated agency, two procedural pathways are available; either the case is closed as unfounded or inappropriate for the agency to investigate, or it is investigated through a phone call or one or more home visits. The results of investigated reports are classified in one of three ways: substantiated, unsubstantiated, or indicated (that is, there is some evidence but not enough to indicate child abuse or neglect) (Barth 1996).

According to the Third National Incidence Study of Child Abuse and Neglect (Sedlak and Broadhurst 1996), the number of children reported under each category of abuse and neglect greatly increased between 1986 and 1993; nationally, child protective services investigated

44 percent of the reported cases in 1986 but only 28 percent in 1993. This is a substantial decrease. However, the raw numbers of children investigated in the two years were nearly the same. As Sedlak and Broadhurst (1996) have suggested, the child welfare system seems headed toward the limits of its capacity to handle abuse and neglect cases, at least as long as it operates in its current and relatively ineffective way.

Each year, however, despite the lower recent rate of case investigations, hundreds of thousands of children are still taken away from their birth parents and placed in foster care due to abuse and neglect. Most people still do not know that the decision to take children away from their parents, place them in foster care, and keep them there must generally be approved by the juvenile court. Federal and state laws typically mandate that such a decision not be made unless "reasonable" efforts have been made to keep children and their parents together if at all possible (Adoption Assistance and Child Welfare Act of 1980; Schwartz and Fishman 1999). In addition, federal and state laws require the juvenile court periodically to review each and every case where a public child welfare agency believes that a child must continue to stay in foster care beyond the court-specified period of time (Schwartz and Fishman 1999; Gelles 1996).

Although the juvenile court's role in handling child welfare cases may seem to be relatively straightforward, this is far from true. Child abuse and neglect cases are complicated and often quite contentious.

The court is in the unenviable position of having to sort through the evidence about whether abuse or neglect occurred. If it did, the court must then determine whether the potential danger to the child is such that it warrants removal from the home. At the same time, the court must determine if "reasonable efforts" have been implemented to keep the family together. If the child is allowed to stay with the birth parents, then the court must approve a plan to provide supervision and, if necessary, other services to ensure the child's safety and to provide support and other assistance to the family. If the child must be removed from home, then the court must turn the custody of the child over to a child welfare agency and approve an appropriate placement. The assumption is that the child welfare authority will provide a loving, stable, caring, and, above all, safe environment for the child.

In most instances, the child welfare agency that conducts the child protective service investigations, presents the evidence in court, and recommends to the judge what the disposition of the cases should be is the very agency that manages and oversees the foster care system. Although there has been little, if any, systematic research in this area, it is hard to imagine how child protective service investigations can be completely impartial and objective under these circumstances. This is particularly likely to be the case when child welfare agencies may be under various kinds of policy, fiscal, administrative, or even media pressures. For example, the public child welfare agency in Montgomery County (Day-

ton), Ohio, experienced a sudden and significant increase in the number of children entering foster care. The agency's foster care budget increased accordingly. Discussions with agency officials, local elected public officials, and others revealed that the increases were largely driven by a small number of highly publicized deaths of young children who died at the hands of their parents. These were cases of children left in the care of their birth parents despite the fact that the risk of doing so was well known to the child welfare authorities (Center for the Study of Youth Policy 1997). In Michigan, child welfare authorities were routinely placing abused and neglected children with relatives instead of in foster homes. This was done, in part, because of fiscal pressures and in order to avoid paying for the costs of care with the foster care budget (Schwartz and Fishman 1999; Schwartz forthcoming).

There are also other problems, many of which are deeply embedded in the very ideological and procedural infrastructure of the child protective service agencies. For instance, in many litigation cases, the pressing issue most often cited is the extensive power wielded by child protective services. Many judges accept the recommendations and attendant decisions of the protective service agency without appropriate checks and balances (National Center for Youth Law 1998). There is little meaningful opportunity to challenge and critically appraise agency judgments. Court-appointed or -attached professionals, such as child psychologists, who are supposed to inform the court based on their independent, professional judgment, are not always used and, in some instances, have been known to subvert their own judgment by uncritically embracing the position of the child protective agency (National Center for Youth Law 1998; Schwartz and Fishman 1999). This erosion of professional independence is not mainly based upon fear, although sometimes it may be, but upon a clear-headed rational assessment of bureaucratic reality: a professional who fails to comply with agency expectations and support the "professional" opinions and judgments of the staff may find that his or her well-compensated services may no longer be needed (Schwartz and Fishman 1999).

These conflicts of interest, while serious, pale when compared to the myriad of other problems confronting child welfare. For example, more than half the states have been successfully sued by public interest attorneys for having abusive, mismanaged, and scandal-ridden child welfare systems (National Center for Youth Law 1998; Schwartz and Fishman 1999). The same is true for dozens of county- and city-administered systems. Many of these agencies are operating under federal court orders or detailed settlement agreements with independent monitors charged with the responsibility of tracking and evaluating progress and performance. In a few instances, such as in Washington, D.C., the responsibility for managing these agencies has been put in the hands of a court-appointed master (Schwartz and Fishman 1999). Despite these horrific conditions and the fact that abused and vulnerable children are being removed from dangerous and, in some instances, life-threatening home situations, they are being placed in potentially dangerous and abusive substitute living arrangements by the people charged with ensuring their safety and well-being. Moreover, this is being done with the full blessing of the juvenile court.

THE ROLE OF DEPENDENCY
ISSUES IN THE JUVENILE COURT

The extent and duration of the malfunctioning of the child welfare system should, by all reasonable measures, trigger a thorough, critical rethinking and revision of the system. At the very least, there should be firmer, more consistent, and more accountable case control and surveillance mechanisms. It is certainly possible that such oversight can be provided by the juvenile court, which is mandated to foster the well-being of children, although its own record of achievement as a champion of children—whether delinquent or dependent—has been wanting. Asking the juvenile court to become a champion of change may be too fanciful a strategy on which to pin one's hopes. However, there may be no other alternative on the immediate horizon.

Child placement functions (for example, family reunification and adoption) fall under the authority of the juvenile court. The juvenile court is statutorily entrusted with sorting out dependency issues, oftentimes related to abusive and neglectful treatment. Unfortunately, there are no reliable data that show how many cases of child abuse and neglect, which are thought to account for a large segment of dependency placements, handled by child protective services are then passed on to the juvenile court (Barth 1996). There is some indication that, nationwide, abuse and neglect cases take up about 16 percent of the juvenile court's caseload (Stevenson et al. 1996). While this is a substantial proportion, it does not shed light on the proportion of caseworker time that these cases consume, which some researchers have estimated to be much larger than their percentage representation in the numerical caseload (Stevenson et al. 1996). When child protective service cases are combined with status offender cases (such as truancy and runaways), the noncriminal caseload facing the court constitutes approximately 27 percent of the total caseload (Ostrom and Kauder 1997). Other estimates are that the total noncriminal caseload is as high as 50 percent (Lindsey 1994).

The Adoption Assistance and Child Welfare Act of 1980 formally changed the relationship between the juvenile court and child protective services. Until this act was passed, the court's role had been minimal; it had conducted one hearing per case in order to verify the allegations of child abuse or neglect and to rule on custody if the allegations were confirmed. Since then, federal law has demanded that the juvenile court take responsibility for overseeing a case after the child is removed from home and for ensuring that the child is placed in a legally permanent and stable setting (Hardin 1996).

When a child is removed from the home, several procedures are triggered. All state child welfare agencies convene an emergency placement hearing within a few days of the removal of the child. This hearing was originally designed to protect the legal rights and civil liberties of the parents but is now used to identify safe placement alternatives and, when circumstances permit, alternatives to placement. Once the emergency placement hearing has taken place, the next procedural step is the trial (adjudication), which assesses and then makes a finding about whether the child was actually abused or neglected. Federal law requires that there be a six-month review of this finding, which can be conducted either by the court or by an administrative agency (Hardin 1996). The review is intended to determine the appropriateness of the placement, the progress of the case, and the degree of compliance with the case plan. Unfortunately, in many states, the court has no actual power to enforce its recommendations and findings. Worse still, in some states, the court is merely a rubber stamp for the child protection agency's decisions (Hardin 1996; Schwartz and Fishman 1999).

The juvenile court and child welfare agencies form a "loosely coupled system" (Hagan, Hewitt, and Alwin 1979). The idea of a coupled system was imported into organizational theory from biology (Capra 1996; Maturana and Varela 1980). The term refers to the symbiotic, synergistic relationship between two or more entities within the same environmental setting. Loosely coupled systems tend to operate with rules that are not consistently followed, can be violated, or can be ignored. Consequently, the decision-making process is vague, the capacity to achieve outcomes is by no means certain, and there are few clear standards to guide or monitor the operational quality of the linked systems (Meyer and Rowan 1977). Despite the fact that the juvenile court has the legal power today to monitor the operation of the child welfare system in most states, in practice, the court is mostly dependent upon and manipulated by representatives of the very system whose operation it is expected to monitor.

The consequences of such porous, sporadic oversight can be disastrous for child clients because of their developmental, political, and legal vulnerabilities. Perhaps the greatest conundrum of this kind of loosely coupled system is that both the child welfare and child protection system, on the one hand, and the juvenile court, on the other, need greater monitoring. The requisite checks and balances would need to entail, at the very minimum, clearer procedural rules, more consensus regarding evidence-based decision making, greater independence of the recommendations by professionals who are outside the system, and greater consideration of such independent recommendations.

Such changes do not appear to be on the immediate horizon. Their introduction would be difficult under the best of circumstances. The existence of a loosely coupled system in tandem with "dynamic conserva-tism" (which will be discussed later), which is at the heart of the juvenile court, makes for a gloomy prognosis. We now focus on the juvenile court and try to account for why it has not delivered on what had been its great historical promise in alleviating the societal distresses of delinquency and dependency. Elsewhere, we have argued that, despite the juvenile court's many detractors, it will not roll over and die (Schwartz, Weiner, and Enosh 1998). Loosely coupled systems that have both internal and external loci of support do not present clear targets for extinction or massive change. Just as such institutions are lined up in the crosshairs, they step out of range.

JUVENILE COURT: DESTINED FOR EXTINCTION OR JUST TEMPORARILY STUCK?

There is no shortage of thinking about why institutions like the juvenile court persist rather than roll over and die. One variation of such thought is the well-known notion of "dynamic conservatism" (Schon 1971). The juvenile court, like many other public and private institutions, engenders a basic resistance to change. Such resistance is more virulent than common inertia: it entails the "tendency to fight to remain the same" (Schon 1971, 32). As we have argued elsewhere (Schwartz, Weiner, and Enosh 1998), but somewhat less specifically and systematically than here, the juvenile court is poised at virtually every turn to wage just such a fight. It is so poised (1) in its structure of hierarchical roles and statuses, which entails complexes of conservative norms, values, attitudes, beliefs, and opinions supporting ties to past practices, unless an imminent threat compels otherwise; (2) in its theory, or organizational philosophy, which justifies judicial and concomitant managerial decisions based upon supportable precedents that create dogged ties to old ways of doing things; and (3) in its technology, which engenders a repertoire of tools for communicating, crystallizing, and concretizing its conservative, precedental structure and theory.

Broadly speaking, the juvenile court's structure, theory, and technology operate to straitjacket and ossify current practices, so that what might otherwise be dynamic momentum is transformed into dynamic inertia. They operate in this fashion as well as they do because each institutional feature is heavily layered, so that only the most peripheral elements of structure, theory, and technology are visible, and, consequently, only the most peripheral elements are vulnerable to being targeted for change. The layering, common to all institutions but especially those, like the court, that are most deeply steeped in history, politics, and law, provides a protective shield, absorbing blows to the system by dispersing the force of impact in ways described elsewhere (Schwartz, Weiner, and Enosh 1998). For example, potential structural, theoretical, and technological changes are muted or entirely neutralized by acts of appropriation; agents of potential change are taken over, worked over,

and, thereby, controlled through their septic conversion. This is what we had in mind when we referred to the juvenile court as an institutional chameleon (Schwartz, Weiner, and Enosh 1998). The locus of change is at the surface, not at the core. The court simply looks as if it has fundamentally changed in its structure, theory, or technology.

How might this diluting or nullifying appropriation of the agents of change take place? Some of the better-known ways that entail clients involve (1) controlling who one's clients are (input filtering), (2) stipulating how long one handles these clients (output queuing and timing), (3) expanding those aspects of one's clients' lives that are controlled (input net-widening), and (4) increasing one's organizational investment and, thereby, the radius of the lives of the clients whom one controls (structural, theoretical, and technological widening).

Some recent developments in juvenile justice are surfacing that provide an almost textbook example of these dynamics. These developments pertain to the anticipated repositioning of the status offender to a more central place, if not center stage, in juvenile justice debates. The status offender is a peculiar legalistic hybrid. Such a youth is treated as an offender for acts that would fail to constitute an offense if committed by an adult. These acts include, among others, school truancy, ingesting intoxicants (mainly alcoholic beverages), and the inability to be controlled by parents (Hardin 1996).

Through the 1970s, status offenders were processed like other delinquents or even adult criminals; they could be sent to state institutions or jailed in adult prisons. After the 1970s, federal legislation intervened to change these practices. Status offenders began to be processed differently from other delinquents. However, if a status offender continued to engage in status offenses after having been processed by the court, the offender was in technical violation of a court order and, consequently, could be apprehended and processed like any other delinquent. The status offender is, therefore, one of the juvenile court's most malleable client types because it is so easily switched from the dependency role, which triggers the court's child protection function, to the societal-menace role, which triggers the societal protection function.

Current national statistics show a rise in the number of status offenders being handled by the juvenile court (Ostrom and Kauder 1997; Sickmund 1997). Two concurrent developments may amplify the role that the status offender is likely to play in the juvenile court, especially with respect to the court's survival strategies. The first development is the snowballing crusade against smoking tobacco, especially smoking by adolescents. In the aftermath of the U.S. surgeon general's recommendation to make juvenile smoking a delinquent offense in order to deter it (U.S. Department of Education 1994), several states are considering just such an approach (Merker-Rosenberg 1998). In view of the fact that smoking is addictive and,

moreover, strongly influenced by a youth's peers, the chances of realizing a meaningful deterrent effect are slim to nil. The more likely outcome is that an entirely new class of status offenders will be created and, by virtue of the procedural sequence outlined earlier, many of these offenders will make the transition to delinquency (Merker-Rosenberg 1998; Schwartz and Wong 1998).

Another concurrent development can be detected in a recent spate of publications from the Office of Juvenile Justice and Delinquency Prevention. These publications underscore the growing number of status offenders, their tendency to become delinquents or criminals, and, most critically, the case for their more severe handling (Garry 1998; Sickmund 1997). It is quite possible that not only will juvenile smokers become status offenders and then delinquents but that they will be disposed of more harshly to boot.

The juvenile court's close connection with other agencies that serve children (for example, educational and mental health agencies) has enabled it to acquire or divest itself of children served by those agencies, almost as if, if one did not know better, a quid pro quo arrangement were operating. With the advent of the smoker status offender, the juvenile court will have added still another set of agencies to its list of loosely coupled actors: public health agencies.

The juvenile court has repeatedly made the appropriative gambit work to its benefit, if not always that of its clients. That is what makes this somewhat abstract discussion so disturbing. Many institutions are characterized by dynamic conservatism. Our point is that such a posture has been especially imprudent and counterproductive within the specific context of the juvenile court.

The juvenile court seems to have championed its institutional agenda at the expense of its clients. This is what sets off the juvenile court from the many other agencies that attempt to protect themselves from perceived adverse outcomes. The court seems to have placed a higher priority on itself than on its legally and politically vulnerable clients. Also, unlike other institutions, which cease to exist when they fail to serve clients and other customers or constituents as well as they might, the juvenile court can protect itself in the ways described previously and survive despite its adverse impacts because it can always recast itself in a societally and politically viable way. Few among us have the moral coinage to attack an institution that can claim, in one breath, to protect children from themselves as well as from adults and to protect adults from children. The politics of children effectively insulates the juvenile court from meaningful criticism, fortifying still more the already formidable institutional bulwark described earlier.

It is as though the juvenile court has been deliberately blind to important new trends in organizational structure. Perspectives on what makes for a successful, leading-edge institution have undergone major revision and refinement over the last decade. There has been a movement away from large, inflexible, rule-based bureaucracies toward more customer-responsive, performance-driven organizational structures. These new structures emphasize greater decentralization and competition in service delivery. Survival is based upon greater accountability, enhanced performance, and customer service. These goals seem to have been and to remain foreign to the juvenile court.

Despite its many shortcomings, however, the juvenile court is not a dinosaur slated for extinction. It has many bolstering life supports, in addition to those described earlier: insularity; great social and cultural currency; stubborn and strong political protection; perpetual governmental economic subsidy; a virtually unlimited reservoir of clients; and statutory flexibility in setting its own mission and agenda. Although the juvenile court may occasionally be stuck in its tracks, with neither visionaries, paragons, nor elder statespersons as its champions, it nevertheless seems destined for repeated extraction from the tarry mires of its own making by the very traction of its own peculiar brand of dynamic conservatism.

CONCLUSION

It is clear that juvenile court justice is not blind justice. This applies in equal measure to juvenile delinquent and child welfare cases under the juvenile court's jurisdiction. The juvenile court and child welfare systems have vision problems: sometimes blindness, sometimes myopia. Not surprisingly, this combination makes aspirations toward achieving blind justice empty rhetoric, a mere slogan. Although, due to the court's shortcomings and weaknesses, it is unlikely that full vision can be restored, we nonetheless believe that it is possible to fit the court with corrective lenses. These lenses can assist in restoring enough vision that blind justice is a meaningful aspiration. Some corrective activities and mechanisms are discussed next.

The debates surrounding the future of the juvenile court tend to focus mostly on the court's procedural convergence with the adult criminal courts and the issues relating to violent offenders. This discourse overlooks the vital, sometimes salutary role of the juvenile court in the lives of those children and youths who most need society's protection. Because today's dependent child may become tomorrow's status offender or delinquent, the juvenile court is especially well placed, if there were applicable theory and practice, which is not so at the present time, to intervene in these undesirable transitions. The definitional ambiguities of "dependency," "status offending," and "delinquency," in conjunction with their fluid, often interchangeable, application, are well documented. In this article, we have emphasized the societal and moral implications for policy of these ambiguities and fluidities. The loose statutory definitions and day-to-day practices of the child welfare system and the juvenile court result in the secondary victimization by these agencies of many of the very children and youths whom they are mandated to serve. Several about-faces are needed to change these change-resistant agencies.

Curb the misconduct

Perhaps first and foremost, the child welfare system must clean up its act. Simply stated, it must reduce its misconduct. This can be accomplished by adhering to its own best child protection practices; by limiting its goals to, for example, stability, permanency, reunification, and adoption; and, equally important, by subjecting the goals and best practices to careful scientific and evaluative scrutiny. Also, the role of the status offender should be thoroughly rethought and revised. The idea of the status offender is an offshoot and holdover from a peculiarly American legal tradition that does not have many counterparts worldwide. Status offenses are frequently the result of primary victimization in the youths' homes or closely surrounding environment. Whether a youngster has run away from home, school, or a foster home, one often observes a common underlying motivational element: a physically harmful or otherwise hurtful environment. Criminalizing the youth's self-protective attempt at withdrawal results in other attendant harms, what some professionals call secondary and tertiary victimization. Rather than trying to undo a harm, the child welfare and juvenile justice systems, with the best of intentions, penalize the victim for having been victimized.

Recast the roles of the juvenile court and child welfare agencies

The central role of a judicial system is to promote a context in which informed and impartial judgments are made. Historically, the juvenile court has delegated this function to outside experts without really questioning their expertise or monitoring them or holding them accountable for their recommendations. This has been especially so for child welfare cases. To make matters worse, these experts often tailor their judgments to what they think the court expects or is willing to hear.

*Promote rigorous national
and international research*

To help correct these institutional abnormalities, an encompassing perspective is needed that recasts the relationship between the child welfare system and the juvenile court. This broadened perspective should be informed by rigorous research instead of the knee-jerk reactions and armchair theorizing that have characterized these agencies. This perspective could benefit from studying the juvenile justice and welfare systems in other countries.

*Convene a national
blue-ribbon commission*

In the past, academic, practitioner, and policy debates have mainly focused on the relationship between juvenile delinquency and the juvenile court rather than the relationship between child welfare and the juvenile court. This imbalance needs to be redressed. In order to achieve more than cosmetic changes in this area, a national blue-ribbon commission should be convened similar to the IJA-ABA Joint Commission on Juvenile Justice Standards (1980) that was created in the 1970s. This commission should give thorough consideration to the operation of the child welfare system, the proper involvement of the juvenile court in dependency cases, and the standards for operating and monitoring the operations of the court and the child welfare agencies. The commission's mandate should include, among other things, drafting standards for solid procedures to govern child placements and their continued monitoring by the juvenile court; creating clear standards for child protective services to make decisions about whether to remove a child from home; shortening adoption procedures; and determining when a placement should be permanent.

In order to achieve those goals, the commission should broaden and extend the prevailing thinking that has historically guided the legislature and the judicial and welfare systems. It is not enough to experiment with minor changes within the systems. That has been done, and the tinkering has not paid off.

The commission should also launch several other initiatives. First, it should examine the approaches to coupling child welfare agencies and juvenile and family courts that have been implemented in other countries. Second, it should rethink the role of legislative constructions like the status offender. Third, it should propose how to protect the rights of children and parents who are victimized by the very systems designed to serve and protect them. Fourth, it should promulgate standards that would govern child welfare investigations. Fifth, it should develop standard rules of evidence that would be used by child protective service and judicial fact finders and decision makers. Sixth, it should set the standards of training that would be required of all professionals who make decisions related to the lives of children and their families. Finally, it should draft a set of standards for tightening the coupling between the juvenile justice and child welfare systems in ways that facilitate and ensure better monitoring of each system's quality of performance.

References

Adoption Assistance and Child Welfare Act of 1980. 94 Stat. 500.

Alper, Benedict S. 1941. Forty Years of the Juvenile Court. *American Sociological Review* 6(2):230-40.

Barth, Richard P. 1996. The Juvenile Court and Dependency Cases. *The Future of Children* 6(3):100-110.

Bernard, Thomas J. 1992. *The Cycle of Juvenile Justice*. New York: Oxford University Press.

Blomberg, Thomas G. 1977. Diversion and Accelerated Social Control. *Journal of Criminal Law & Criminology* 68(2):274-82.

Capra, Fritjof. 1996. *The Web of Life: A New Scientific Understanding of Living Systems*. New York: Anchor Books.

Center for the Study of Youth Policy. 1997. *Needs Analysis for Children in Out-of-Home Care in Montgomery County*. Philadelphia: University of Pennsylvania, School of Social Work, Center for the Study of Youth Policy.

Ezell, Mark. 1989. Juvenile Arbitration: Net Widening and Other Unintended Consequences. *Journal of Research in Crime and Delinquency* 26(4):358-77.

Feld, Barry C. 1988a. *In re Gault* Revisited: A Cross-State Comparison of the Right to Counsel in Juvenile Court. *Crime & Delinquency* 34(4):393-424.

———. 1988b. The Juvenile Court Meets the Principle of the Offense: Punishment, Treatment and the Difference It Makes. *Boston Law Review* 68: 821-915.

———. 1990. The Punitive Juvenile Court and the Quality of Procedural Justice: Disjunctions Between Rhetoric and Reality. *Crime & Delinquency* 36(4):443-66.

———. 1993. Juvenile (In)justice and the Criminal Court Alternative. *Crime & Delinquency* 39(4):403-24.

Fox, Sanford J. 1996. The Early History of the Court. *The Future of Children* 6(3):29-39.

Garry, Eileen M. 1998. *Truancy: First Step to a Lifetime of Problems*. Washington, DC: Department of Justice, Office of Justice Programs, Office of Juvenile Justice and Delinquency Prevention. Available: http://www.ncrj.org/txtfiles/truancy.txt.

Gelles, Richard J. 1996. *The Book of David*. New York: Basic Books.

Guggenheim, Martin. 1976. Juvenile Justice and the "Violent Juvenile Offender." *New York State Bar Journal* 48:550-55.

Hagan, John, John D. Hewitt, and Duane F. Alwin. 1979. Ceremonial Justice: Crime and Punishment in a Loosely Coupled System. *Social Forces* 58:367-97.

Hardin, Mark. 1996. Responsibilities and Effectiveness of the Juvenile Court in Handling Delinquency Cases. *The Future of Children* 6(3):111-25.

IJA-ABA Joint Commission on Juvenile Justice Standards. 1980. *Juvenile Justice Standards*. Cambridge, MA: Ballinger.

Jacobs, Mark D. 1990. *Screening the System and Making It Work*. Chicago: University of Chicago Press.

Krisberg, Barry and James F. Austin. 1993. *Reinventing Juvenile Justice*. Newbury Park, CA: Sage.

Lindsey, Duncan. 1994. *The Welfare of Children*. New York: Oxford University Press.

Maturana, Humberto R. and Francisco G. Varela. 1980. *Autopoiesis and Cognition: The Realization of the Living*. Boston: Reidel.

Merker-Rosenberg, Irene. 1998. Using the Juvenile Courts to Stop Smoking. Center for Study of Youth Policy, School of Social Work, University of Pennsylvania. Typescript.

Meyer, John W. and Brian Rowan. 1977. Institutionalized Organizations: Formal Structure as Myth and Ceremony. *American Journal of Sociology* 83:340-63.

National Center for Youth Law. 1998. *Foster Care Reform Litigation Docket*. San Francisco: National Center for Youth Law.

Ostrom, Brian J. and Neal B. Kauder. 1997. *Examining the Work of the State Courts, 1996: A National Perspective from the Courts Statistics Project*. Pittsburgh, PA: National Center for State Courts.

Paternoster, Raymond, Gordon P. Waldo, Theodare G. Chiricos, and Linda S. Anderson. 1979. The Stigma of Diversion: Labeling in the Juvenile Justice System. In *Courts and Diversion: Policy and Operations Studies*, ed. P. L. Brantingham and T. G. Blomberg. Thousand Oaks, CA: Sage.

Schon, Donald A. 1971. *Beyond the Stable State*. New York: Norton.

Schwartz, Ira M. Forthcoming. Michigan's Child Welfare System: A Dynamic Perspective. In *Toward a Child-Centered, Neighborhood-Based Child Protection System*, ed. Garry Melton.

Schwartz, Ira M. and Gideon Fishman. 1999. *Kids Raised by the Government*. Westport, CT: Praeger.

Schwartz, Ira M., Neil A. Weiner, and Guy Enosh. 1998. Nine Lives and Then Some: Why the Juvenile Court Does Not Roll Over and Die. *Wake Forest Law Review* 33:533-52.

Schwartz, Ira M. and Caroline Wong. 1998. Preventing and Stopping Children from Smoking and Using Tobacco Products: Promising Policies and Strategies. Center for the Study of Youth Policy, School of Social Work, University of Pennsylvania. Typescript.

Sedlak, Andrea J. and Diane D. Broadhurst. 1996. *Executive Summary of the Third National Incidence Study of Child Abuse and Neglect*. Washington, DC: Department of Health and Human Services, Administration for Children and Families, Administration on Children, Youth and Families, National Center on Child Abuse and Neglect.

Sickmund, Melissa. 1997. Offenders in Juvenile Court, 1995. *OJJDP-Juvenile Justice Bulletin* (U.S. Department of Justice).

Singer, S. I. 1996. *Recriminalizing Delinquency: Violent Juvenile Crimes and Juvenile Justice Reform*. New York: Cambridge University Press.

Stevenson, Carol S., Carol S. Larson, Lucy S. Carter, Deanna S. Gomby, Donna L. Termon, and Richard E. Behrman. 1996. The Juvenile Court: Analysis and Recommendations. *The Future of Children* 6(3):4-28.

U.S. Department of Education. 1994. *Youth and Tobacco: Preventing Tobacco Use Among People*. A Report of the Surgeon General. Washington, DC: Government Printing Office.

Can Intervention Rehabilitate
Serious Delinquents?

By MARK W. LIPSEY

ABSTRACT: Much contemporary discussion of the future of the juvenile court revolves around the balance between rehabilitation and punishment, especially with regard to the most serious juvenile offenders. Political forces increasingly press in the direction of punitive approaches, while the historical orientation of the court has been rehabilitative. This article addresses the question of whether rehabilitative treatment can be effective for the most serious offenders. Meta-analysis techniques were used to synthesize the large body of empirical research on the effects of rehabilitative programs in community and institutional settings. The results show that well-designed rehabilitative strategies do reduce recidivism for such offenders and cannot be dismissed on the grounds that they are ineffective.

Mark W. Lipsey is professor of public policy at Vanderbilt University's Peabody College, where he serves as co-director of the Center for Evaluation Research and Methodology at the Vanderbilt Institute for Public Policy Studies. His research interests are in the areas of public policy, program evaluation research, and research synthesis. The foci of his recent research have been risk and intervention for juvenile delinquency and issues of methodological quality in program evaluation research.

NOTE: The research reported in this article was supported in part by grants from the National Institute of Mental Health (MH42694 and MH39958) and the Russell Sage Foundation.

THE primary rationale for maintaining a separate juvenile justice system is the belief that juvenile offenders should be treated differently from adult offenders. Most important, perhaps, is the notion that, for juveniles, greater emphasis should be placed upon rehabilitation than upon punishment. Juveniles, by definition, are immature and may warrant more latitude to make a mistake than adults and more help to recover from it. In addition, their habits and propensities may be relatively malleable so that rehabilitative intervention may be effective in changing the trajectory of their antisocial behavior. Moreover, their youth means that, if that trajectory is not changed, they potentially have long and destructive criminal careers in front of them.

In this context, the presumption that rehabilitative intervention can be effective in reducing subsequent offense rates is central. If it were to be demonstrated that the rehabilitative programs currently available were universally ineffective, a key premise of the juvenile justice system would be undermined. A related issue has to do with which juveniles respond to rehabilitative efforts. The increased use of waivers to criminal court for juveniles committing serious offenses, for instance, is supported in part by the view that such offenders are hardened and thus not amenable to rehabilitation.

Questions about the effectiveness of rehabilitation are most convincingly answered by empirical research on the behavioral changes induced among offenders by various program or treatment regimens.

Fortunately for this purpose, a rather sizable quantity of research has been conducted and reported over the last 50 years. Unfortunately, the experts who have reviewed this research have presented conflicting interpretations of what it reveals about rehabilitative programs.

The most notable controversy has swirled around the massive review conducted by Lipton, Martinson, and Wilks in the mid-1970s (Lipton, Martinson, and Wilks 1975). Though the published report identified some promising programs, the overall conclusion was that most did not show consistent evidence of effectiveness. This conclusion was sufficiently provocative for the National Academy of Sciences to commission further study of the issue in the early 1980s (Martin, Sechrest, and Redner 1981; Sechrest, White, and Brown 1979). That endeavor largely supported the original conclusion by Lipton, Martinson, and Wilks, and other reviews during that era reached similar conclusions (for example, Greenberg 1977; Lundman, McFarlane, and Scarpitti 1976; Romig 1978; Wright and Dixon 1977).

The view that rehabilitation is generally ineffective, however, has not gone uncontested. Early critics argued variously that available research was flawed and its conclusions invalid, that there was convincing evidence that some programs were effective, and that negative conclusions had more to do with ideology than evidence (for example, Cullen and Gilbert 1982; Gendreau and Ross 1979; Gottfredson 1979; Palmer 1975, 1983). More recently, a vigorous reinterpretation of research on rehabilitation has resulted from application of meta-analysis, a quantitative technique for analyzing and summarizing research evidence (Palmer 1992, 1994). Though initially controversial, meta-analysis is now widely (though not universally) accepted as a sophisticated way to extract, analyze, and summarize the substantive results from a collection of related research studies (Cooper and Hedges 1994; Durlak and Lipsey 1991; Glass, McGaw, and Smith 1981; Hunter and Schmidt 1990; Rosenthal 1991).

The purpose of this article is to provide a relatively nontechnical summary of the results of a comprehensive meta-analysis of research on the effectiveness of rehabilitative programs for reducing the likelihood that young offenders will reoffend. Since the greatest challenge to the rehabilitative premise is the case of serious offenders, who are increasingly viewed as beyond rehabilitation, the analysis will focus upon intervention with them.

INTERVENTION AND RECIDIVISM OF SERIOUS JUVENILE OFFENDERS

The extensive meta-analysis of the effects of intervention on delinquency upon which the present review is based (Lipsey 1992, 1995; Lipsey and Wilson 1997) involved an exceptionally thorough bibliographic search employing multiple sources and procedures to identify published and unpublished studies that met the following criteria:

1. Juveniles aged 12-21 received an intervention, broadly defined, that could have some positive effect on their subsequent delinquency.

2. Quantitative results were reported for a comparison between a treatment condition and a control condition for at least one delinquency outcome measure. In addition, the assignment of juveniles to conditions was random or, if not, pretreatment group differences were reported by means of, for example, a pretest on the dependent variable, demographic comparisons, matching, or the like.

3. The study was conducted between 1950 and 1995 in an English-speaking country and reported in English.

More than 500 studies meeting these criteria were retrieved. They were coded by trained personnel on more than 150 items describing study methods and procedures, subject characteristics, treatment and program characteristics, outcome effect sizes, and related matters. For the review reported here, studies were selected from this larger database if they involved intervention with serious offenders. While few studies were found that focused exclusively on serious offenders, many studies included such offenders within a more diverse sample of delinquents. Certain of the items coded on the studies in the database were therefore used to select studies with samples that included a relatively high proportion of serious offenders, though that proportion was rarely 100 percent. In particular, studies were selected with the following characteristics:

1. The great majority of all of the juveniles were reported to be adjudicated delinquents. In addition, most or all of the juveniles had a record of prior offenses that involved person or property crimes, or an aggregate of all offenses, but not primarily substance abuse, status offenses, traffic offenses, or the like.

2. The referral to the intervention program was made by a juvenile justice source (not schools, parents, or the like) or the juveniles were recruited directly by the researcher.

3. If studies were not otherwise selected due to the foregoing criteria, they were added if most or all of the juveniles in them were reported to have a history of violent behavior.

This selection resulted in 200 studies judged to involve serious juvenile offenders to some degree. To examine the effects of intervention on the recidivism of those offenders, the primary recidivism outcome measure from each study was selected for analysis. Police contact or arrest recidivism was used if it was available (since this was the most common outcome measure), and, if not, the outcome most comparable to police arrest was used, such as recorded contact with the juvenile court. To represent the magnitude of the estimated intervention effect on recidivism for each study, an effect size index was computed as the mean difference between the treatment group and the control group on the selected recidivism measure divided

by the pooled standard deviation (Cooper and Hedges 1994). This effect size index can be read as a statement of how much better the recidivism was for juveniles receiving intervention than for those in the control group, measured in standard deviation units.[1] Thus an effect size of 0.25 means that the recidivism for treated juveniles was one-fourth of a standard deviation lower than that for untreated juveniles. While this effect size index has advantageous statistical properties for meta-analysis, it is not very intuitive. At appropriate points in the discussion, therefore, summary results in this metric will be translated into the equivalent difference in recidivism rates, which are generally more interpretable.

For the 200 effect sizes representing intervention effects for the entire set of studies selected for relevance to serious offenders, the overall mean recidivism value for treated juveniles was 0.12 standard deviation units lower than that for the control groups with which they were compared (a statistically significant difference). A mean effect size of 0.12 is equivalent to the difference between a 44 percent recidivism rate for treated juveniles and a 50 percent rate for the untreated control group. This six percentage-point difference represents a 12 percent decrease in recidivism (6/50), which does not seem trivial but is certainly relatively modest. This simple overall result gives some answer to the question of whether intervention, generally, can reduce recidivism rates for serious juvenile offenders. The grand mean effect size over 200 studies of intervention with the more serious end of the spectrum of juvenile offenders is positive, statistically significant, and, though modest, not trivial.

The most important finding of the preliminary analysis, however, was that the heterogeneity between the 200 effect sizes was very large. This indicates that the effect sizes varied substantially around the overall mean of 0.12, with some considerably larger and others considerably smaller. Such variability between studies in their estimates of the effect of intervention on recidivism might stem from many different sources. One relatively uninteresting source, for present purposes, is methodological and procedural differences between the studies. It is likely, however, that effects also vary because some interventions are more effective than others. This prospect motivates further analysis in order to identify the characteristics of those interventions that have the largest effects on recidivism.

In order to get a clean look at the differences between interventions that are related to differences in recidivism effects, however, we must first identify the variability in effect sizes that can plausibly be attributed to differences between studies due to their methods and procedures, and then statistically remove that variability from the effect size distribution. If this is not done, comparison of the effect sizes observed in various studies may be quite misleading. Differences that may appear to indicate that one intervention is more effective than another may, in actuality, only reflect the fact that the studies

used different methods. The desired statistical adjustment can be accomplished by using multiple regression analysis to predict effect size solely from the methodological and procedural features of the studies, then subtracting the predicted values from the observed values. The residual values represent the portions of the effect sizes that cannot be accounted for by differences in study methods. All the meta-analytic results reported in the remainder of this article are based on these method-adjusted effect sizes, that is, observed study-level effect size estimates from which variation attributable to between-study differences in method and procedure have been statistically removed.

At this point in the analysis, studies of intervention with noninstitutionalized juveniles ($N = 117$) were separated from those with institutionalized juveniles ($N = 83$). These two situations involve quite different circumstances of intervention, and the nature and response of the juveniles who receive intervention may differ as well. The characteristics of effective intervention might thus also be distinct for each of these circumstances.

*Intervention with
   noninstitutionalized
   juvenile offenders*

The samples of noninstitutionalized offenders represented in the 117 studies that met the selection criteria were quite diverse. The majority consisted of juveniles on probation or parole, with the remainder comparable in terms of their delinquency but selected from other contexts; for example, they were recruited directly by the researcher or identified as participants in intervention programs based in schools, mental health agencies, or other such community organizations. In brief, their profile is as follows:

1. The vast majority of eligible studies were conducted in the United States and involved samples of juveniles that were mostly or all males, predominantly of Anglo or mixed ethnicity, and with an average age in the 13-16 range.

2. As required by the selection criteria, most or all of the juveniles in each study sample had prior offenses, generally mixed offenses, although about one-third were property offenses. For three-fourths of the samples, at least some of the juveniles were identified as having a history involving aggressive behavior.

3. The majority of studies involved juveniles under juvenile justice authority at the time of intervention and whose participation in the program was mandatory, not voluntary.

4. The service providers were about evenly divided between juvenile justice personnel, mental health and other professional counselors, and laypersons and miscellaneous others. The types of programs were diverse, with counseling the most frequent, followed by skill-oriented programs (academic, employment, interpersonal skills) and those involving multiple services.

5. The typical program lasted 10-30 weeks, involved 1-4 contacts per week with the juveniles, and provided 10 or fewer hours per week of total contact time.

To identify the characteristics of the intervention circumstances for noninstitutionalized offenders that were associated with the greatest recidivism reductions, four distinct categories of variables were examined: (1) the characteristics of the juvenile offenders, for example, the proportion with prior offense records, the proportion with indications of prior aggressive behavior, gender mix, mean age, and ethnic mix; (2) general program characteristics, for example, the age of the program, who provided the service (criminal justice, mental health, or other personnel), and whether the juveniles were under juvenile justice authority while in the program; (3) type of intervention, for example, restitution, counseling, behavioral programs, and multiple services; and (4) the amount of service provided during the intervention, for example, average number of weeks from first to last intervention event, frequency of contact with the program, and coders' rating of integrity of program implementation. The most important of the findings are as follows:

1. More than half of the variation between method-adjusted effect sizes across studies is systematically related to variables in the four clusters. Given that the remaining variance includes sampling error and measurement unreliability, this indicates that between-study differences in effect size should be largely understandable in terms of the study characteristics represented in the four clusters. Furthermore, each of the clusters showed some independent relationship to effect size; none

appears to be redundant or irrelevant in accounting for differences between studies in the size of the intervention effects reported.

2. The cluster of variables characterizing the juveniles who participated in the respective intervention programs showed the strongest relationship to effect size. This indicates that some subpopulations of juveniles show larger recidivism effects from intervention than others. In particular, samples in which all the juveniles had a prior history of offenses (in contrast to most of the juveniles) and those in which the prior offenses included a mix of person and property offenses (rather than mostly property) showed larger recidivism reductions. To the extent that there is a relationship between offender severity and program effectiveness among noninstitutionalized juveniles, therefore, the effects seem to be larger for the more serious offenders than for the less serious.

3. The cluster of variables identifying specific types of intervention showed the next largest relationship to effect size, followed closely by the cluster representing the amount of service delivered. Type of intervention is analyzed more fully later in this article. Regarding amount of service, three variables showed strong, independent, but somewhat contradictory relationships with effect size. Duration of service (total number of weeks; median = 23) was positively associated with effect size, while the mean number of hours per week of service was negatively correlated; that is, contact hours below the median (5-10 hours per week) were associated with somewhat larger

effects than those above the median. Also, difficulties in program delivery (indications that not all juveniles received the intended intervention protocol) were associated with smaller effects, as would be expected.

4. The cluster of general program characteristics showed the smallest relationship with effect size but was not negligible. The one variable in this group making a significant, independent contribution to effect size was the researcher's role in the intervention. The less involved the researcher was in the design, planning, and delivery of intervention, the smaller the effect size. This variable appears to distinguish those projects carefully constructed by the researcher for demonstration or research purposes from ongoing real-world programs with which the researcher is involved primarily as an evaluator.

In some regards, it is of equal interest to identify those characteristics of the program circumstances that were reported and coded but that did not prove to be related to the size of the effects on recidivism. For instance, there were no differential effects according to the gender mix, ethnic mix, or mean age of the juveniles in the samples, though it must be remembered that a rather circumscribed range on some of these characteristics was represented, especially for gender. Similarly, program effects on recidivism did not vary appreciably with whether the juveniles' participation was mandatory or voluntary or whether they were under juvenile justice authority (such as probation or parole) at the time.

Type of intervention and effects on recidivism

The issue of which types of intervention show the largest and smallest effects on the recidivism of noninstitutionalized offenders is of especial importance for practice and policy. For this reason, additional analysis was conducted on this matter to ensure that any findings were not excessively biased by the statistical assumptions used to make the effect size estimates. In brief, we computed and compared three different mean effect size estimates for the studies in each of the categories we used to represent type of intervention program. One was simply the original effect size computed from the statistics presented in each study, that is, the observed effect size. The other was the method-adjusted effect size described earlier and used to control for between-study differences in method and procedure. A third we called the equated effect size. This estimate adjusted for differences in method and procedure and for between-study differences in the characteristics of the juveniles receiving intervention, in the amount of service, and the other variables previously described that were shown to relate to effect size. This latter effect size estimate, therefore, represents an attempt to compare intervention types when all other significant aspects of the studies are statistically equated.

Each of these different estimates has advantages and disadvantages. In order to ensure a sound basis for any conclusions about differential intervention effects, we examined all three to determine their consistency along various dimensions. When the three estimates are consistent, what they indicate about intervention effects should be trustworthier than when they are inconsistent. To assess consistency, we looked first at the magnitude of the mean effect for each intervention type according to each estimate, aided by statistical significance testing. Second, we examined the variance around each of those means for the respective effect estimates from the individual studies contributing to the mean. The third consideration was the extent of agreement across the three different effect size estimates to check whether the different statistical controls associated with the different estimates made little enough difference to indicate that the effect size findings were relatively robust to irrelevant between-study differences.

Table 1 presents the results of this procedure. The number of studies for each type of intervention is in parentheses as a reminder that, in many cases, there were relatively few studies of the effects of that particular intervention with noninstitutionalized serious offenders. The different interventions are then grouped according to the pattern of findings across the effect size estimates.

The top group consists of those interventions that showed consistent positive effects. All the means for all the estimates were statistically significant and notably larger than the mean across all interventions. Moreover, the effect sizes averaged into each of those means were homogeneous, indicating no statistically significant variation across studies.

TABLE 1

MOST AND LEAST EFFECTIVE TYPES OF INTERVENTION WITH NONINSTITUTIONALIZED AND ESTIMATED EFFECTS ON RECIDIVISM

Intervention Type (N)	Estimated Effect Size	Treatment/ Control Recidivism Contrast*
Positive effects, consistent evidence		
Individual counseling (8)	.46	.28/.50
Interpersonal skills (3)	.44	.29/.50
Behavioral programs (7)	.42	.30/.50
Positive effects, less consistent evidence		
Multiple services (17)	.29	.36/.50
Restitution, probation/ parole (10)	.15	.43/.50
Mixed but generally positive effects, inconsistent evidence		
Employment related (4)	.22	.39/.50
Academic programs (2)	.20	.40/.50
Advocacy or casework (6)	.19	.41/.50
Family counseling (8)	.19	.41/.50
Group counseling (9)	.10	.45/.50
Weak or no effects, inconsistent evidence		
Reduced caseload probation/parole (12)	−.04	.52/.50
Weak or no effects, consistent evidence		
Wilderness or challenge (4)	.12	.44/.50
Early release, probation/parole (2)	.03	.48/.50
Deterrence programs (6)	−.06	.53/.50
Vocational programs (4)	−.18	.59/.50

*Recidivism of intervention group in comparison to assumed control group recidivism of .50.

These are the interventions showing the strongest evidence of effectiveness. Ranked according to the midpoint of the three effect size estimates, the intervention types in this top group were individual counseling, interpersonal skill training (only three studies), and behavioral programs.

Close behind this top group was a second tier of interventions for which the evidence was also rather convincing. Each showed statistically significant mean effects on all the effect size estimates, but not all those means were based on homogeneous sets of individual effect sizes. The two intervention types represented in this tier are multiple services (for example, service brokerage, multimodal service) and restitution programs for juveniles on probation or parole.

The bottom group in Table 1 consists of those intervention types with means based on homogeneous effect size estimates that were not significantly different from zero (except one case that was significantly negative). These interventions showed the strongest and most consistent evidence that they were not effective in reducing the recidivism of noninstitutionalized juvenile offenders. This group included wilderness or challenge programs, early release from probation or parole (only two studies), deterrence programs (mostly shock incarceration), and vocational programs. We should note that vocational programs are distinct from employment-related programs in this categorization. Programs that provided vocational training, career counseling, job search, interview skills, and the like were classified as vocational. Only those that actually involved paid employment were classified as employment.

The next to last tier in the groupings in Table 1 includes only one intervention type, reduced caseload programs for juveniles on probation or parole. The different effect size estimates agreed in finding no significant positive mean effects for these programs (but one significant negative effect). However, the individual effect sizes averaged into these means were not homogeneous, indicating that some of the studies showed significantly larger effects than others.

In the middle of Table 1 is a group of interventions that presented mixed or ambiguous evidence. While some of their effect size means were statistically significant and some were homogeneous, there was inconsistency across the various estimation procedures. This indicates that the statistical adjustments being applied by the different effect size estimation procedures were relatively large and, therefore, differences between these interventions are confounded with differences in study method or other characteristics of the intervention, such as amount of service or characteristics of the juvenile recipients. Without a better accounting of the source of the differences in the various estimates of mean effect sizes, it is uncertain whether the mean effects shown for intervention types in this group represent actual intervention effects or artifacts.

Given an identification of the interventions that appear to produce the largest positive effects on the recidivism rates of noninstitutionalized offenders, it is relevant to ask just how large those effects are in practical terms. As Table 1 summarizes, the standardized mean difference effect size index that was the statistical indicator of effect size used in this meta-analysis was found to have average values of around 0.40 for the most effective types of intervention. These values are more readily interpretable if they are transformed into equivalent recidivism rate values. For this purpose, we assumed that the untreated control groups in these studies had a police contact or arrest reoffense rate of 50 percent during the first year after intervention. In fact, the actual value was very near this for the subset of studies reporting police contact or arrest as proportions. With this baseline, the reoffense rate of the intervention group could be determined as the proportion that, when contrasted with 50 percent, yields the mean effect size value actually found for the intervention of interest.

As is evident, the magnitude of the effects of recidivism for the best interventions was appreciable when viewed in terms of relative reoffense rates. We estimated that with the most effective interventions, recidivism would drop from 50 percent to about 30 percent. Clearly this is a rather substantial decrease; indeed, the rate is nearly cut in half. If we proportion the 20-percentage point decrease against the 50 percent baseline (20/50), we find that these interventions reduced recidivism by about 40 percent. Given that the juveniles involved were on the upper end of the severity continuum, this is a rather impressive effect.

To show more detail about the nature of the intervention programs represented in the top group in Table 1, we have pulled a selection of the contributing reports from our files and summarized the authors' descriptions of the intervention (see Table 2).

TABLE 2
PROGRAM DESCRIPTIONS FROM STUDY REPORTS FOR THE BEST TYPES
OF INTERVENTION WITH NONINSTITUTIONALIZED JUVENILE OFFENDERS

Individual counseling

A program for juvenile probationers that used citizen volunteers in conjunction with regular probationary supervision to counsel offenders on a one-to-one basis. The volunteers were screened and matched with offenders based on sex, ethnicity, educational background, intellectual level, vocational aspirations, and recreational interests (Moore 1987).

Reality therapy counseling was given in weekly hourlong sessions for 12 weeks by two female graduate students enrolled in post-master's-level counseling courses. The reality therapy involved recycling eight steps until clients learned to take charge of their lives in a constructive manner: involvement/goal setting, behavior assessment, behavior evaluation, concrete plans of action, commitment to action plans, no excuses, no punishments, and no giving up with resistant clients (Bean 1988).

Juvenile sexual offenders were treated under multisystemic therapy. Each youth or family received 21 to 49 hours of therapy in which doctoral students in clinical psychology attempted to ameliorate deficits in the adolescents' cognitive processes (denial, empathy, distortions), family relations (family cohesion, parental supervision), peer relations, and school performance (Borduin et al. 1990).

Interpersonal skills

An experimental training program used drama and the making of video films as vehicles for helping delinquent juveniles see themselves from the perspective of others and as remedial training in deficient role-taking skills. There were 10 training sessions, occurring once a week for three hours each, at a neighborhood storefront. Sessions were run by three graduate students who facilitated the efforts of the participants while enforcing certain ground rules: (1) the skits must be about real situations involving people of the participants' ages, (2) everyone gets a part, (3) everyone gets a chance to play every role, and (4) the video recordings are viewed to see how they could be improved (Chandler 1973).

An intensive 10-day course in a large group camp or church retreat facility for juveniles. The course included lecture and discussion; group demonstrations and learning processes; daily exercise; challenging outdoor activities; discussion of responsible behavior in the context of the group setting; and opportunities for voluntary group service and leadership. The follow-up phase involved a commitment to one or more personal and community projects. For a 12-month period, the youths participated in monthly meetings, personal counseling, tutoring, sponsored social events, job skills training, involvement in production of future courses, and special workshops (Delinquency Research Group 1986).

Behavioral programs

Adjudicated delinquents were court-ordered to the Family Counseling Program as a condition of probation. The therapy program was divided into three phases: the assessment phase, in which problem behavior within the family was identified through interview and observation; the therapy phase, in which family members' intentions were relabeled to render them benign or positive; and the education phase, in which parenting skills and family living skills were taught in a structured manner (Gordon, Graves, and Arbuthnot 1987).

(continued)

TABLE 2 Continued

Probationers were included in a contingency contracting program as a method of behavior therapy. The average treatment was based on an agreement worked out between the parole officer and the juvenile to modify specific problem behaviors. Contracts usually provided some sort of monetary reward for exhibiting desired behavior or refraining from unwanted behavior. When applicable, parents and teachers were included in deciding upon and carrying out the terms of the contract (Jesness et al. 1975).

Multiple services

A probation program offered 24 different treatment techniques, with no juvenile receiving more than 12 or fewer than 4. The core procedure, used with almost 50 percent of the youths, trained responsible citizens from the community to act as unofficial counselors, friends, and role models. Other treatments included group counseling, work crews, alcohol awareness, and vocational training (Morris 1970).

Project New Pride provided three months of intensive services to probationed youths, followed by approximately nine months of follow-up services. The primary services included educational testing and remediation, disability testing and remediation, employment counseling, prevocational training, job development and placement, personal counseling, cultural education, recreation, and client advocacy (Browne 1975).

Youths were placed under intensive case management and received an array of services to meet their particular needs. Some categories of treatment were recreation, after-school programs, inpatient therapy, outpatient child therapy, outpatient family therapy, supervised group and independent living services, and vocational placement (Weisz et al. 1990).

Program profiles associated with the largest effects on recidivism

While the particular type of intervention is a significant determinant of the effectiveness of a program in reducing recidivism, as shown in Table 1, it is important to keep in mind that the analyses previously reported identified other program characteristics that were important. In particular, thorough implementation of the program so that each juvenile receives a full dose of the intended intervention was shown to be a significant factor in relation to recidivism effects. Similarly, programs of more than six months' duration were found to be notably more effective than those of shorter length. The analysis model used to identify the independent contribution of each program characteristic to recidivism effect size made it possible to estimate the add-on benefit as the various critical program features are combined. Figure 1 displays the combinations of program features most related to recidivism and the estimated effectiveness of each.

To provide a basis for comparison, Figure 1 first shows the recidivism rate of 50 percent that approximates what was found in the control groups of the studies reviewed here. These juveniles typically received routine probation or other treatment-as-usual services without whatever enhancement or special program was under study in the research. Figure 1

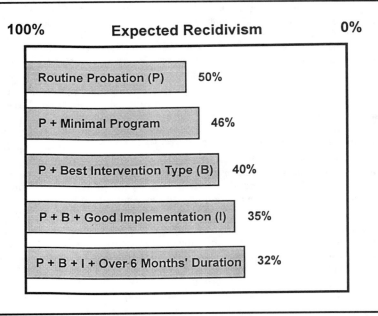

FIGURE 1
EXPECTED RECIDIVISM WITH VARIOUS INTERVENTION
CHARACTERISTICS FOR NONINSTITUTIONALIZED OFFENDERS

NOTE: Minimal programs are characterized by suboptimal intervention type, incomplete implementation, and less than six months' program duration.

then shows the successive decreases in recidivism rates expected if a minimal program is added to routine services, then if that minimal program is upgraded with one of the better intervention types (as shown in Table 1), with a strong implementation, and with a longer duration. As can be seen, the most effective programs not only use the better intervention types but also attain almost equal impact by implementing them well and continuing them for a longer period of time. It is when all these program elements are combined that the maximal effects on recidivism are attained. Moreover, degradation of any one of the critical components reduces the program impact by a significant increment.

Intervention with institutionalized juvenile offenders

Of the 200 studies investigating intervention with serious juvenile offenders, 83 dealt with programs for institutionalized youths. Of those, 74 studied programs in juvenile justice institutions and 9 involved residential facilities under private or mental health administration. The typical study in this group compared a control group participating in the usual institutional program with an experimental group participating in that program and receiving some additional service that was the intervention of interest in the research.

The general characteristics of the samples of institutional juveniles represented in these studies and of the programs they received are as follows:

1. All but about a dozen of the eligible studies were conducted in the United States. Three-fourths of the samples of juvenile offenders consisted entirely of males, and nearly half were identified as involving predominantly juveniles of Anglo ethnicity, with most of the rest being mixed. The average age of the juveniles in the study samples ranged primarily from 13 to 18, with the largest concentration in the 15-16 range.

2. In the vast majority of studies, virtually all the juveniles in the study sample had prior offenses, and most of those were reported as mixed types of offenses, with the remainder identified as involving mostly property offenses. For more than 80 percent of the samples, at least some of the juveniles were described as having a history of aggressive behavior.

3. Participation in the intervention program was mandatory for nearly three-fourths of the juvenile samples, and almost 90 percent of them were under juvenile justice authority, such as a correctional institution, when they participated in the program.

4. The service providers for the programs were juvenile justice personnel in over 40 percent of the studies, with mental health personnel, non-mental-health counselors, and laypersons next most frequent. The types of interventions were diverse, with the largest category representing various forms of counseling. Skill-oriented programs (academic, employment, interpersonal skills), community residential programs, and guided group or milieu therapy programs were also involved in a number of studies. The typical program was 2-30 weeks in duration, although more than a third were longer. A majority of the programs maintained virtually continuous contact with the participating juveniles, and the remainder required distinct sessions, ranging from 1-2 per week to daily program contact. Correspondingly, a majority of the programs were involved with the participating juveniles for more than 40 hours per week, but a sizable minority involved 10 or fewer hours per week of contact.

The same analysis procedures were used for these studies as those described earlier for studies involving noninstitutionalized juvenile offenders. The first step was to determine the strength of the relationship between the method-adjusted effect sizes and the four clusters of variables describing the characteristics of the juvenile offenders, the general program characteristics, the type of intervention, and the amount of service provided during the intervention. The major findings of this analysis for studies of the effects of intervention on the recidivism of institutionalized offenders were as follows:

1. As with the corresponding analysis earlier, a large proportion of the variation between method-adjusted effect sizes across studies was systematically related to variables in the four clusters. Thus between-study differences in effect size should be largely understandable in terms of the study characteristics represented in those clusters.

2. None of the variables describing the characteristics of the juveniles was significantly related to effect size. This was in marked contrast to the results for intervention with non-institutionalized juveniles, where this cluster showed the strongest relationship. The implication of this finding is that the effects for institutionalized offenders are much the same for a given intervention whatever the age, gender and ethnic mix, and history of prior offenses of the juveniles.

3. The cluster of general program characteristics showed the strongest overall relationship with effect size. Again, this stands in sharp contrast with the results for intervention with noninstitutionalized juveniles, where this cluster was the weakest. Among general program characteristics, the largest intervention effects were found for relatively well-established programs (two years or older) and those in which the services were not provided by juvenile justice personnel. This latter finding is quite striking considering that most of these juveniles were being treated in juvenile justice institutional settings. The alternative in most of these cases was services provided by mental health personnel, though these were not necessarily from the public mental health agencies.

4. The cluster of variables identifying specific types of intervention was in the middle with regard to its relationship to effect size and was very similar in magnitude to that found for noninstitutionalized juveniles. The amount of service delivered showed a similar middling relationship with duration of service longer than the median of 24 weeks associated with larger effects. Furthermore, intervention effects were larger when there was attention to the integrity of the program implementation, for example, systematic monitoring to ensure that the intended juveniles receive the intended service. Similar factors were also related to the effects of intervention with noninstitutionalized offenders, as summarized earlier.

Once again, it is informative to recognize the variables that were not importantly related to program effects on recidivism. As mentioned previously, there were no significant differences associated with the age or ethnic mix of the juveniles participating in the program. The same was true of the gender mix of the juveniles, but the samples were so heavily male that there was little opportunity for this variable to be active. Similarly, within the relatively narrow range of variation represented, there were no differences in recidivism effects associated with the extent or predominant type of prior offenses or with the extent of aggressive history. In addition, program effects were generally comparable for juveniles mandated to treatment and those who volunteered, and they were comparable for those under the authority of the juvenile justice system at the time of treatment and those who were not.

Type of intervention and effects on recidivism

As in the earlier case, an especially probing analysis was made to convincingly identify the types of intervention that had the largest and smallest effects on recidivism. Estimates of the effect sizes that would be expected for each intervention under uniform intervention conditions studied with uniform methodology were constructed to compare with method-adjusted effect sizes and the original observed effect sizes. The different types of intervention with institutionalized offenders were grouped according to the magnitude of the mean effect sizes on these estimates and the consistency of the estimates within and between those averaged values, as shown in Table 3. It is worth emphasizing once again the small number of studies upon which many of these estimates were based; more studies of intervention with institutionalized offenders will be needed before conclusive results can be achieved.

The interventions in the top group in Table 3 are distinguished by relatively large, statistically significant mean effect sizes based on homogeneous sets of individual effect sizes that are consistent across all the estimation procedures. The two types of

TABLE 3

MOST AND LEAST EFFECTIVE TYPES OF INTERVENTION WITH INSTITUTIONALIZED OFFENDERS AND ESTIMATED EFFECTS ON RECIDIVISM

Intervention Type (N)	Estimated Effect Size	Treatment/ Control Recidivism Contrast*
Positive effects, consistent evidence		
Interpersonal skills (3)	.39	.31/.50
Teaching family home (6)	.34	.33/.50
Positive effects, less consistent evidence		
Behavioral programs (2)	.33	.34/.50
Community residential programs (8)	.28	.36/.50
Multiple services (6)	.20	.40/.50
Mixed but generally positive effects, inconsistent evidence		
Individual counseling (8)	.15	.43/.50
Guided group counseling (7)	.09	.45/.50
Group counseling (9)	.05	.47/.50
Weak or no effects, inconsistent evidence		
Employment related (2)	.15	.43/.50
Drug abstinence (5)	.08	.46/.50
Wilderness or challenge (5)	.07	.46/.50
Weak or no effects, consistent evidence		
Milieu therapy (3)	.08	.46/.50

*Recidivism of intervention group in comparison to assumed control group recidivism of .50.

intervention in this group were interpersonal skill programs and the teaching family home. Interpersonal skill training, it should be recalled, was also one of the stronger interventions for noninstitutionalized juveniles (see Table 1). In the next tier were intervention types with consistently significant mean effects for all the estimation procedures, but with significant heterogeneity between the individual effect sizes that were averaged into the mean for at least one estimate. While these, too, represent very favorable results, the heterogeneity across studies indicates that different studies of this intervention found significantly different results, some larger and some smaller than the mean values shown. The types of intervention in this grouping were multiple service programs, community residential programs (mostly other than juvenile justice programs), and the miscellaneous category for other interventions that could not be classified elsewhere.

At the bottom of Table 3 is one intervention that showed consistent null effects (milieu therapy) and, in the tier above, three types of intervention that did not show statistically significant mean effects but had means based on heterogeneous distributions. Thus some studies of these interventions found effects significantly larger than the mean values shown, while others found significantly smaller effects. This grouping includes drug abstinence programs, wilderness or challenge programs, and employment-related programs (which showed notably larger effects for the noninstitutionalized offenders).

The middle tiers of intervention types in Table 3 showed mixed evidence. Some mean effect sizes were statistically significant, some were averaged over homogeneous findings from the contributing studies, and some were consistent across the three estimation procedures. None,

however, met all of these criteria. Therefore, the evidence was ambiguous for these groups of interventions. In the case of behavioral programs, the problem may simply be too few studies (2) because, other than the failure of the relatively high effect size means to reach statistical significance in two instances, the positive evidence was generally consistent. For the three counseling varieties (individual, group, and guided group), however, the effect size estimates were quite inconsistent. Some were positive and statistically significant, some near zero; none were consistent across the estimation procedures; and only one was based on a homogeneous set of individual effect sizes. Observed effects in the studies in these groups appear to be confounded with other study characteristics so that it is difficult to disentangle the actual intervention effects.

Table 3 also summarizes the results for each intervention type on the recidivism rate differentials that corresponded to the effect size differences. The most effective interventions had an impact on recidivism that was equivalent to reducing a control group with 50 percent recidivism to around 30-35 percent. This is a considerable decrease, especially in light of the fact that it applies to institutionalized offenders who can be assumed to be relatively serious delinquents.

To furnish additional details about the nature of the intervention programs represented in the top groups in Table 3 for institutionalized offenders, the authors' descriptions of the intervention program have been summarized in Table 4 for a selection of the research reports represented in the five interventions in the two highest groups.

Program profiles associated with the largest effects on recidivism

As with intervention for noninstitutionalized juveniles, the analysis of research on the intervention with institutionalized juveniles revealed that a number of critical program characteristics made independent, add-on contributions to overall effectiveness. Thus the programs with the largest effects on recidivism were those that involved the most favorable combination of these characteristics, and effectiveness was compromised if any critical feature was absent in a given program. Figure 2 displays the various combinations and their estimated relationship to reducing recidivism. A minimal program configuration is used as a baseline for comparison and is assumed to result in a recidivism rate of 50 percent, approximately the value actually found for the control groups in the research studies reviewed. Successively lower expected recidivism results if the minimal program is upgraded with the various critical features.

In particular, Figure 2 shows that the reduction in recidivism is progressively greater with application of one of the better types of intervention (from Table 3), a program of more than six months' duration, service providers who are not juvenile justice personnel, a strong program implementation so that all juveniles receive the intended treatment, and a program that has been established for two years or more. Moreover, each of the program characteristics is associated with about the same additional decrement in recidivism, in the 5-8 percentage-point range. Thus, while optimal results are associated with all of these conditions combined, any one of them can enhance program effectiveness by a significant increment.

THE PREMISE AND PROMISE OF EFFECTIVE REHABILITATION FOR JUVENILE OFFENDERS

There is no ready substitute for systematic research on intervention with juvenile offenders as a way to credibly determine which, if any, program approaches are effective in reducing subsequent rates of reoffense. But any given research study, at best, provides an estimate of the effects observed for one particular set of circumstances and is subject to various biases and errors that are inherent in the research process, especially under the uncontrolled field conditions within which real programs must be studied. Practice and policy, therefore, are best guided by a cumulation of research evidence sufficient to balance the idiosyncrasies of individual studies and support more robust conclusions than any single study can provide. Actually implementing this bit of simple practical wisdom, however, requires that some valid procedure be used to assemble, combine, analyze, and interpret the body of relevant research evidence. For empirical studies yielding evidence on

TABLE 4

**PROGRAM DESCRIPTIONS FROM STUDY REPORTS FOR THE BEST TYPES
OF INTERVENTION WITH INSTITUTIONALIZED JUVENILE OFFENDERS**

Interpersonal skills

Adolescent boys living in a community home school participated in 12 one-hour sessions of social skills training over a six-week period. Training was carried out in groups of four and involved the use of instructions, discussion, modeling, role-played practice, video-taped feedback, social reinforcement, and homework tasks (Spence and Marzillier 1981).

Adolescent boys at the Youth Center participated in Aggression Replacement Training, a multimodal, psychoeducational intervention. The intervention was made up of three components: structured learning training, anger control training, and moral education. There were 30 sessions over a 10-week period (Glick and Goldstein 1987).

The Social Interactional Skills Program was a structured didactic program that encouraged youths to recall problematic past experiences and identify the aversive social stimulus in their social interaction. This was followed by systematic desensitization using imagery techniques and cognitive reappraisal and enhancement of their behavior repertoire by experimenting with new behaviors (Shivrattan 1988).

Teaching family home

Achievement Place was a community-based, family-style, behavior-modification group home for six to eight delinquents. This program was administered by a couple, referred to as "teaching parents," who developed positive teaching relationships with the youths to impart needed behavioral skills, assumed responsibility for the youths, and acted as advocates for them in the community. The youths were able to return to their own homes on the weekend and remain in their local schools (Kirigin et al. 1982).

Adjudicated delinquents went to a community-based, family-style, behavior-modification group home where teaching parents utilized a token economy while closely monitoring the youths' progress in school and working individually to counsel the youths on difficulties they had in their lives (Wolf, Phillips, and Fixson 1974).

Behavioral programs

Incarcerated male and female adolescents participated in a 12-week cognitive mediation training program involving small discussion groups ranging in size from 10 to 14 youths. The program focused on remediating, through instruction and structured discussion, those social problem-solving skill deficits and modifying those beliefs that supported the use of aggression (Guerra and Slaby 1990).

Institutionalized male delinquents participated in a stress inoculation training program that included defining anger, analyzing recent anger episodes, reviewing self-monitoring data, and constructing an individualized six-item anger hierarchy. Specific coping skills taught were self-instructions, relaxation, backward counting, pleasant imagery, assertive responding, and self-reinforcement. Role playing and modeling were also used (Schlicter and Horan 1981).

Girls in a correctional institution were trained in reinforcement therapy principles and acted as peer counselors for newer incoming wards. As the newer girls progressed, they were exposed to the techniques through their peer counselors and by the staff, eventually achieving the role of peer counselor themselves (Ross and McKay 1976).

(continued)

TABLE 4 Continued

Community residential programs

The treatment center was a community-based all-girls group home. Residents were provided advocacy, counseling, educational support, and vocational support (Minnesota Governor's Commission on Crime Prevention and Control 1973).

Institutionalized youths were placed in a 32-bed therapeutic community setting in an inner-city neighborhood where they received individual and group counseling, remedial education services, vocational assessment and training, and other needed services (Auerbach 1978).

A community-based residential treatment center for adjudicated youths utilized extensive group discussion as a therapeutic community and emphasized progressive assumption of responsibility (Allen-Hagen 1975).

Multiple services

Camp Fenner was an experimental program of the Probation Department. Its distinctive aspects were the provision of supportive services, including vocational training, skill-oriented education, and job placement by a private contractor; cottage living; and enriched probation department staffing (Kawaguchi 1975).

Institutionalized boys were treated in a multifaceted program to overcome academic, vocational, and psychological deficits. Various therapeutic methods were available to meet their particular needs, as well as education, training, work opportunities, and supervision from a community volunteer upon release (Thambidurai 1980).

The Planned Re-Entry Program was a short-term 52-bed living unit that included cottage living, counseling, education, and recreational activities. The counseling component consisted of individual and small-group counseling. The educational component taught everyday survival skills such as basic reading and math, consumer education, problem solving, and job getting and keeping. The recreational program was designed to enhance the youths' use of leisure time. The program emphasized time management, interpersonal relationships, personal responsibility, and rule conformity (Seckel and Turner 1985).

comparable situations, formal meta-analytic techniques provide a systematic, detailed, and analytically powerful procedure for accomplishing this.

The presumption that rehabilitative intervention can be effective with juvenile offenders is central to the juvenile justice system. While a number of reasons can be advanced for processing juvenile offenders separately from adult offenders, one of the most compelling is that it best provides the opportunity to administer sanctions and programs that are tailored to youthful offenders and capable of redirecting their behavior. If the cumulative research were to demonstrate that rehabilitative programs were categorically ineffective in reducing subsequent offending, an interpretation made of some prior reviews, it would undermine the concept of separate proceedings for juveniles. Whether the available research evidence indicates that there are rehabilitative programs that are effective in reducing

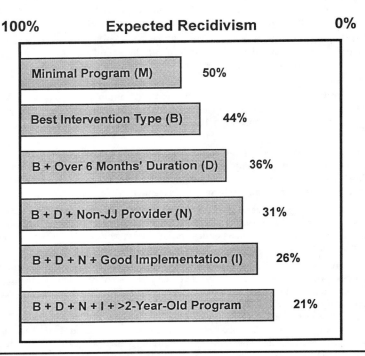

FIGURE 2
EXPECTED RECIDIVISM WITH VARIOUS INTERVENTION
CHARACTERISTICS FOR INSTITUTIONALIZED OFFENDERS

NOTE: A Minimal program is characterized by suboptimal intervention type, less than six months' program duration, juvenile justice providers, intermediate implementation, and a program less than two years old. "JJ" stands for "juvenile justice."

recidivism and whether that evidence is sufficient to be definitive, therefore, are critical questions with both practical and philosophical implications for the juvenile justice system.

In this context, the meta-analytic review summarized here provides pertinent findings. Since it was deliberately restricted to intervention with serious offenders, it addresses the more difficult end of the spectrum of cases that come before the juvenile courts and must be handled with probation, institutional, and aftercare programs. Furthermore, as part of a comprehensive meta-analysis, this particular review includes wide coverage of relevant research studies and involves an extensive coding and analysis of their characteristics and results. The result is a rather complete statement of currently available research evidence about the effects of rehabilitative intervention on the recidivism of serious juvenile offenders. Though numbering 200 studies, however, this body of research nonetheless has many gaps and omissions. When subdivided into studies with noninstitutionalized and institutionalized offenders, different types of intervention, and other such central characteristics of the participating juveniles or the intervention programs, many important categories and combinations are addressed by few or no methodologically adequate studies. The more specific one attempts to be in regard to the nature of effective programs for particular sorts of juveniles, the fewer relevant studies there are to analyze.

The limitations of available research for supporting definitive conclusions about the effectiveness of the full range of rehabilitative intervention, nevertheless, do not diminish the fact that the general pattern of results is quite favorable. As shown in the meta-analysis reported here, the average effect on the recidivism of serious juvenile offenders of those interventions studied is positive, statistically significant, and, though modest, not trivial. This finding in itself demonstrates the error of the claim that nothing works made in the most pessimistic of the research reviews conducted in the era prior to the availability of systematic meta-analysis. If one asks categorically, then, whether rehabilitative intervention works with juvenile offenders, the answer is, essentially, yes. Not every intervention works in every application, but the research evidence, when carefully analyzed, unquestionably shows that, on average, those interventions subjected to study reduce recidivism. The premise that the

juvenile justice system can provide effective rehabilitative programs for the juvenile offenders that come under its authority is thus clearly justified by the available research.

The more significant question, however, does not have to do with the average effects of rehabilitation programs or categorical claims about whether such programs work. What is important for practice and policy is how much impact rehabilitative intervention might have if optimal programs were consistently applied. On this issue, this meta-analysis identifies some program approaches that produce quite sizable recidivism reductions for both institutionalized and noninstitutionalized offenders. This evidence shows that optimal combinations of program elements have the capability to reduce recidivism by 40-50 percent, that is, to cut recidivism rates to very nearly half of what they would be without such programming. Moreover, the program elements required for such impact do not entail exceptional efforts or costs. The high-impact programs identifiable in the research literature represent relatively straightforward application of selected types of intervention (interpersonal skill training, behavioral programs, multiple services) that are fully implemented by appropriate personnel over periods of six months or more.

A systematic and probing analysis of research on the effectiveness of intervention with juvenile offenders, therefore, does not lead to pessimism and uncertainty about whether the juvenile justice system can provide programs for youthful offenders that will significantly alter their reoffense rates, with corresponding benefits to the juveniles and the surrounding community. What it does show is that such beneficial effects do not come automatically as a result of the routine activities of the juvenile justice system. A focused effort must be made to establish effective types of programs and deliver the associated services at a consistently high level for a wide range of eligible offenders. The challenge presented by the research evidence is not to the premise that rehabilitative intervention can be effective, nor to the promise that its effects can be of meaningful magnitude, but to rehabilitative practice, which can be either very effective or very ineffective depending upon how it is carried out.

Note

1. The standard deviation is a statistical index of the range or dispersion of scores in a distribution. In a normal distribution, a range of ±1 standard deviation units around the mean takes in about two-thirds of all the scores.

References

Allen-Hagen, Betty. 1975. *Youth Crime Control Project: A Final Report on an Experimental Alternative to Incarceration of Young Adult Offenders*. Research Report 75-1. Washington, DC: D.C. Department of Corrections.

Auerbach, A. W. 1978. The Role of the Therapeutic Community "Street Prison" in the Rehabilitation of Youthful Offenders. Ph.D. diss., George Washington University.

Bean, J. S. 1988. The Effect of Individualized Reality Therapy on the Recidivism Rates and Locus of Control Orientation of Male Juvenile Offenders. Ph.D. diss., University of Mississippi.

Borduin, C. M., S. W. Henggeler, D. M. Blaske, and R. J. Stein. 1990. Multisystemic Treatment of Adolescent Sexual Offenders. *International Journal of Offender Therapy and Comparative Criminology: An Interdisciplinary Journal* 34(2):105-13.

Browne, S. F. 1975. *Denver High Impact Anti-Crime Program: Evaluation Report*. Denver, CO: Denver Manpower Administration.

Chandler, M. J. 1973. Egocentrism and Antisocial Behavior: The Assessment and Training of Social Perspective-Taking Skills. *Developmental Psychology* 9:326-33.

Cooper, Harris and Larry V. Hedges, eds. 1994. *The Handbook of Research Synthesis*. New York: Russell Sage Foundation.

Cullen, Francis T. and K. E. Gilbert. 1982. *Reaffirming Rehabilitation*. Cincinnati, OH: Anderson.

Delinquency Research Group. 1986. *An Evaluation of the Delinquency of Participants in the Youth at Risk Program*. Claremont, CA: Claremont Graduate School, Center for Applied Social Research.

Durlak, Joseph and Mark W. Lipsey. 1991. A Practitioner's Guide to Meta-Analysis. *American Journal of Community Psychology* 19(3):291-332.

Gendreau, Paul and B. Ross. 1979. Effective Correctional Treatment: Bibliotherapy for Cynics. *Crime & Delinquency* 25:463-89.

Glass, Gene, G. V. McGaw, and M. L. Smith. 1981. *Meta-Analysis in Social Research*. Beverly Hills, CA: Sage.

Glick, B. and A. P. Goldstein. 1987. Aggression Replacement Training. *Journal of Counseling and Development* 65:356-62.

Gordon, D. A., K. Graves, and J. Arbuthnot. 1987. Prevention of Adult Criminal Behavior Using Family Therapy for Disadvantaged Juvenile Delinquents. Ohio University. Manuscript.

Gottfredson, M. R. 1979. Treatment Destruction Techniques. *Journal of Research in Crime and Delinquency* 16:39-54.

Greenberg, D. F. 1977. The Correctional Effects of Corrections: A Survey of Evaluations. In *Corrections and Punishment*, ed. D. A. Greenberg. Beverly Hills, CA: Sage.

Guerra, N. G. and R. G. Slaby. 1990. Cognitive Mediators of Aggression in Adolescent Offenders: 2. Intervention. *Developmental Psychology* 26(2):269-77.

Hunter, J. E. and Frank L. Schmidt. 1990. *Methods of Meta-Analysis: Correcting Error and Bias in Research Findings*. Newbury Park, CA: Sage.

Jesness, C. F., F. S. Allison, P. M. McCormic, R. F. Wedge, and M. L. Young. 1975. *Evaluation of the Effectiveness of Contingency Contracting with Delinquents*. Sacramento: California Youth Authority.

Kawaguchi, R. M. 1975. *Camp Fenner Canyon Evaluation: Final Report*. NCJRS Document Reproduction Service no. NCJ036121. Los Angeles: Los Angeles County Probation Department.

Kirigin, K. A., C. J. Braukmann, J. D. Atwater, and M. M. Worl. 1982. An Evaluation of Teaching-Family (Achievement Place) Group Homes for Juvenile Offenders. *Journal of Applied Behavior Analysis* 15(1):1-16.

Lipsey, Mark W. 1992. Juvenile Delinquency Treatment: A Meta-Analytic Inquiry into the Variability of Effects. In *Meta-Analysis for Explanation: A Casebook*, ed. Thomas D. Cook, Harris Cooper, David S. Cordray, Heidi Hartmann, Larry V. Hedges, Richard J. Light, Thomas A. Louis, and Frederick Mosteller. New York: Russell Sage Foundation.

———. 1995. What Do We Learn from 400 Research Studies on the Effectiveness of Treatment with Juvenile Delinquents? In *What Works? Reducing Reoffending*, ed. J. McGuire. New York: John Wiley.

Lipsey, Mark W. and David B. Wilson. 1997. Effective Intervention for Serious Juvenile Offenders: A Synthesis of Research. In *Serious and Violent Juvenile Offenders: Risk Factors and Successful Interventions*, ed. Rolf Loeber and David P. Farrington. Thousand Oaks, CA: Sage.

Lipton, Douglas, R. Martinson, and J. Wilks. 1975. *The Effectiveness of Correctional Treatment: A Survey of Treatment Evaluation Studies*. New York: Praeger.

Lundman, R. J., P. T. McFarlane, and F. R. Scarpitti. 1976. Delinquency Prevention: A Description and Assessment of Projects Reported in the Professional Literature. *Crime & Delinquency* 22:297-308.

Martin, S. E., L. B. Sechrest, and R. Redner. 1981. *New Directions in the Rehabilitation of Criminal Offenders*. Washington, DC: National Academy Press.

Minnesota Governor's Commission on Crime Prevention and Control. 1973. *An Evaluation of the Group Residence Program for Juvenile Girls, June 1972 through April 1973*. St. Paul: Minnesota Department of Corrections.

Moore, R. H. 1987. Effectiveness of Citizen Volunteers Functioning as Counselors for High-Risk Young Male Offenders. *Psychological Reports* 61:823-30.

Morris, J. A. 1970. *First Offender: A Volunteer Program for Youth in Trouble with the Law*. New York: Funk & Wagnalls.

Palmer, Ted. 1975. Martinson Revisited. *Journal of Research in Crime and Delinquency* 12:133-52.

———. 1983. The Effectiveness Issue Today: An Overview. *Federal Probation* 47:3-10.

————. 1992. *The Re-emergence of Correctional Intervention*. Newbury Park, CA: Sage.

————. 1994. *A Profile of Correctional Effectiveness and New Directions for Research*. Newbury Park, CA: Sage.

Romig, D. 1978. *Justice for Our Children*. Lexington, MA: Lexington Books.

Rosenthal, Robert. 1991. *Meta-Analytic Procedures for Social Research*. Rev. ed. Newbury Park, CA: Sage.

Ross, R. R. and B. McKay. 1976. A Study of Institutional Treatment Programs. *International Journal of Offender Therapy and Comparative Criminology: An Interdisciplinary Journal* 20(2):167-73.

Schlicter, K. J. and J. J. Horan. 1981. Effects of Stress Inoculation on the Anger and Aggression Management Skills of Institutionalized Juvenile Delinquents. *Cognitive Therapy and Research* 5(4):359-65.

Sechrest, Lee, S. O. White, and E. D. Brown. 1979. *The Rehabilitation of Criminal Offenders: Problems and Prospects*. Washington, DC: National Academy of Sciences.

Seckel, J. P. and J. K. Turner. 1985. *Assessment of Planned Re-entry Programs (PREP)*. Sacramento: California Youth Authority.

Shivrattan, J. L. 1988. Social Interactional Training and Incarcerated Juvenile Delinquents. *Canadian Journal of Criminology* 30:145-63.

Spence, S. H. and J. S. Marzillier. 1981. Social Skills Training with Adolescent Male Offenders—II: Short-Term, Long-Term and Generalized Effects. *Behavior Research & Therapy* 19:349-68.

Thambidurai, G. A. 1980. A Comparative Outcome Study of a Contract Parole Program for Individuals Committed to the Youth Correctional Complex in the State of New Jersey. Ph.D. diss., Rutgers University.

Weisz, J. R., B. R. Walter, B. Weiss, G. A. Gernandez, and V. A. Mikow. 1990. Arrests Among Emotionally Disturbed Violent and Assaultive Individuals Following Minimal Versus Lengthy Intervention Through North Carolina's Willie M Program. *Journal of Consulting and Clinical Psychology* 58(6):720-28.

Wolf, M. M., E. L. Phillips, and D. L. Fixson. 1974. *Achievement Place: Phase II*. Vol. 1. Rockville, MD: Center for Studies of Crime and Delinquency, National Institute of Mental Health.

Wright, W. E. and M. C. Dixon. 1977. Community Prevention and Treatment of Juvenile Delinquency: A Review of Evaluation Studies. *Journal of Research in Crime and Delinquency* 14:35-67.

ANNALS, *AAPSS*, **564**, July 1999

Get-Tough Juvenile Justice Reforms: The Florida Experience

By CHARLES E. FRAZIER, DONNA M. BISHOP, and LONN LANZA-KADUCE

ABSTRACT: Get-tough reforms aimed at juvenile offenders have become commonplace in the United States. In the last decade, almost every state has modified laws relating to juvenile crime in some way, and the direction of the reforms has been very clear. States are getting tougher on juvenile offenders either by shifting away from traditional rehabilitation models to punishment-oriented juvenile justice or by legislating new or expanded legal means by which greater numbers of juvenile offenders may be moved to criminal court for adult processing and punishment. The present study focuses on a major set of juvenile justice reforms in Florida and the impact on actual practice. Florida is unique in a historical sense because it has transferred large numbers of juveniles to criminal court for two decades, and, currently, because it has more juveniles in its prisons than any other state. Despite incremental get-tough reforms, the new transfer provisions have had a negligible impact. The effects of Florida's get-tough laws and practices should be instructive for those other states that have begun such reforms more recently.

Charles E. Frazier is professor of sociology and affiliate professor of criminology in the Center for Studies in Criminology and Law at the University of Florida.

Donna M. Bishop is associate professor of criminal justice and legal studies at the University of Central Florida.

Lonn Lanza-Kaduce is professor of sociology and criminology in the Center for Studies in Criminology and Law at the University of Florida.

NOTE: Some of the research for this article was part of a project funded under grant no. 95-JN-FX-0030 from the Office of Juvenile Justice and Delinquency Prevention, Office of Justice Programs, U.S. Department of Justice. Points of view or opinions in this article are those of the authors and do not necessarily represent the official position or policies of the U.S. Department of Justice.

D URING the last decade, legislatures throughout the country have modified juvenile codes to "get tough" on juvenile crime (Torbet et al. 1996; Bishop, Lanza-Kaduce, and Frazier 1998). The culmination of much of this legislature activity may be illustrated in the debate over two bills in the 105th United States Congress, H.R. 3 and S. 10. Both bills offered federal support for additional legislation to get tough on juvenile offenders. The present study focuses on the impact of most recent get-tough juvenile justice reforms in Florida, especially the effects of transfer provisions on transfer rates. It also examines the extent to which these provisions and the philosophical momentum that generated them affected the way transfer cases were handled in the criminal justice system.

Since 1978, Florida has transferred more juveniles to criminal court than most other states together. During the past 10 years, 6000 to 7000 cases have been transferred annually (Bishop et al. 1998; Frazier et al. 1995; Bishop, Frazier, and Henretta 1989). As a consequence, Florida has more juveniles in adult prison, including those under 16 years of age, than any other state (Schwartz, Hsieh, and Kenagy 1996). Because Florida initiated extensive use of transfer prior to other states, provided more methods of transfer, transferred more juveniles, and allowed a wider variety of sentencing options, we may consider it something of a policy laboratory for the rest of the country.

In 1978, Florida introduced prosecutorial waiver (or direct file) to supplement traditional, and rather cumbersome and time-consuming, judicial waiver procedures (Florida Statutes, section 39.04(2)(e)4. [Supp. 1978]). The 1978 legislation, which was slightly modified in 1981 (Florida Statutes, section 39.04(2)(e)4. [Supp. 1981]), gave prosecutors the authority to charge directly in criminal court any 16- or 17-year-old juvenile accused of any felony; any 16- or 17-year-old accused of any misdemeanor who previously had been found to have committed at least two delinquent offenses, one of which involved a felony; and any child 14 years of age or older who had been previously adjudicated delinquent for one of several violent felonies and who was accused a subsequent time of one of those offenses. In addition to these prosecutorial waiver provisions, Florida law already provided for traditional *Kent*-style judicial waiver proceedings (*Kent* v. *United States*, 383 U.S. 541, 86 S.Ct. 1045, 16 L.Ed. 2d 84 [1966]) for youths over age 13 (see Florida Statutes, section 39.09(2) and (d) [1975]), and for grand jury indictment of youths of any age who were accused of capital or life felonies (see Florida Statutes, section 39.02(6)(c) [1969]). Similarly, the Florida Constitution (1968, articles 1 and 15) had long provided for a voluntary or demand waiver of the case against any juvenile who demanded to be tried as an adult if the juvenile was joined by a parent, guardian, or a guardian *ad litem* and the waiver request was presented in writing and prior to the juvenile court adjudicatory hearing (Florida Statutes, section 985.226(1) [1997]).

The broad statutory authority granted with respect to prosecutorial waiver provided the framework within which transfers to criminal court increased dramatically over the next 15 years. The introduction of prosecutorial direct file also marked the beginning of the end of judicial waiver as a method of moving juveniles to criminal court jurisdiction. In 1979, for example, 48 percent of transfers were direct-filed (Bishop, Frazier, and Henretta 1989). By 1993, 93 percent were direct-filed (Florida Juvenile Justice Advisory Board 1994). Beginning in 1990, a series of events occurred that culminated, in 1994, in the passage of very punishment-oriented reforms.

First, in 1990, the Florida legislature passed the Juvenile Justice Reform Act (Florida Statutes, chapter 39 [Supp. 1990]). The reforms were prompted in large measure by settlement of the *Bobby M.* case (*Bobby M.* v. *Martinez*, Civ. case no. TCA 83-7003 MMP, consent decree entered 8 May 1987), a federal class action lawsuit filed in 1983 on behalf of residents of the state's training schools. The lawsuit alleged overcrowding, inadequate medical care, abuse, and lack of treatment. The litigation ended in a 1987 consent decree that mandated, among other things, reductions in youth populations within institutional facilities and the development of a continuum of placement options for juvenile offenders. The 1990 Juvenile Justice Reform Act included provisions for additional programs and services consistent with the consent decree (Florida Juvenile Justice Advisory Board 1994).

Second, although the legislature initially provided significant funding for the reforms, subsequent budget cuts reduced the funds to a fraction of what was necessary to provide the additional placements called for in the legislation (Florida Juvenile Justice Advisory Board 1994). Waiting lists for placement of committed youths grew, waiting periods lengthened to months, and the Department of Health and Rehabilitative Services—the social welfare agency charged with administering juvenile delinquency programs at that time—was forced to reduce lengths of stay in placement facilities to accommodate the backlog of incoming offenders. Although the department was essentially hamstrung due to fiscal limitations, it was nonetheless the target of strong and sharp criticism for what was characterized as a "soft" and "ineffectual" approach to juvenile crime (Martinez 1997).[1]

Third, during the early 1990s, juvenile arrest rates rose in Florida—especially for felony offenses—and commitment rates increased correspondingly (Florida Juvenile Justice Advisory Board 1994). Many committed youths awaited actual juvenile correctional placement in their homes because they were ineligible for detention for more than 15 days under then-existing law. In a widely distributed report issued in 1992, it was suggested that these youths were largely responsible for increases in juvenile crime (Krzycki and Cass 1992). This report further contributed to the erosion of support for the Department of Health and Rehabilitative Services.

Fourth and finally, a series of killings of tourists in 1993 constituted another impetus for get-tough reforms.

The response to the killings rocked Florida's economy and threatened its annual $30 billion tourism industry. Because several of the perpetrators were juveniles, even stronger calls to get tough on violent young offenders were heard. Then Secretary of State Jim Smith went so far as to state, "We should shoot them down like the mad dogs that they are" (*Orlando Sentinel* 1993). A special legislative session on crime was held in November 1993, resulting in authorization for 1000 new prison beds in the adult system that were to be used for serious juvenile offenders.[2]

On the juvenile side, the legislature in 1994 also passed a new Juvenile Justice Reform Act (hereinafter called the 1994 reforms), which presaged an era in which punishment and accountability were to become watchwords of the juvenile justice system (Florida Statutes, chapter 39 [Supp. 1994]). Several provisions of the 1994 reforms illustrate this point. Prohibitions against the use of detention for punishment purposes were removed. New deep-end Level 10 placements were authorized for serious offenders who were retained in the juvenile system (Florida Juvenile Justice Advisory Board 1996). Restrictions on the use of post-dispositional detention were relaxed. Post-dispositional detention of unlimited duration was mandated for youths committed to deep-end (Level 8 and 10) programs. Most important, the Department of Health and Rehabilitative Services was divested of its authority over juvenile justice programs and all operations were transferred to a newly created Department of Juvenile Justice (DJJ). The first head of the new agency was a former police chief.

The 1994 reforms made several modifications in the state's transfer provisions consistent with the get-tough orientation. Three major revisions were made, two of which involved mandatory transfer. The first applied to juveniles 14 years of age or older who had three prior adjudications (or adjudications withheld) for felonies, one or more of which involved violence against a person or the use or possession of firearms (Florida Statutes, section 985.236(2)(b) [1997]). A second provision mandated direct file for youths of any age who were charged with any offense and who had a history of three separate felony residential commitments (Florida Statutes, section 985.227(2)(b) [1997]). A third provision authorized discretionary direct file for 14- and 15-year-old youths charged with any of 15 enumerated person and property felony offenses (Florida Statutes, section 985.227(1)(a) [1997]).

The implications of the 1994 changes in transfer law for juvenile and criminal justice in Florida were serious. Extrapolating from cases and practices in 1993, we projected that roughly 13,000 additional juvenile cases might be formally charged in the criminal courts (Lanza-Kaduce et al. 1996). Pursuing the same line of reasoning, we also estimated that two-thirds of those 13,000 prosecuted cases could result in sentences carrying adult sanctions. Of those that received adult sanctions, our projection was that 7300 new cases annually could flow

TABLE 1
JUVENILE CASES REFERRED, FILED,
AND TRANSFERRED, FISCAL YEARS 1992-93 THROUGH 1996-97

	(1) Cases Referred to Intake	(2) Cases Referred to Court	(3) Cases Transferred to Criminal Court	(4) Percentage of Court Cases Transferred
1992-93	141,084	75,669	7,229	9.6
1993-94	156,780	82,645	6,729	8.1
1994-95	169,500	92,352	7,019	7.6
1995-96	172,276	92,633	7,315	7.9
1996-97	173,753	95,993	6,570	6.8

into the adult correctional institutions (approximately 5500 in prison and 1800 in jail), with the remaining cases sentenced to community-based sanctions. We now have new data to assess what in fact happened after the 1994 reforms, and these data are the focus of the remainder of this article.

TRANSFER IN FLORIDA BEFORE
AND AFTER THE 1994 REFORMS

In this section, we draw from two automated statewide data sets with an eye toward assessing the impact of changes in transfer provisions produced by the 1994 Juvenile Justice Reform Act. These are the Client Information System (CIS), currently maintained by the Florida DJJ, and the Offender Based Transaction System (OBTS) maintained by the Office of the State Courts Administrator. The first of these data systems tracks all delinquency referrals in Florida from the point of initial intake to case disposition. For cases[3] transferred to criminal court, the end point of the CIS database is the point at which the transfer is made. Once a case is transferred, information on criminal

case processing can be obtained from the OBTS. The OBTS tracks charging, adjudicatory, and sentencing outcomes with the state's criminal courts.[4]

CIS DATA

Information from the CIS on juvenile cases referred, filed, committed, and transferred to criminal court for fiscal years 1992-93 through 1996-97 is presented in Table 1. The data are compiled from public access information provided by the Florida Department of Juvenile Justice (1998).

The table shows that the number of cases referred to DJJ intake and then to juvenile court increased throughout this five-year period. However, the rate of increase in the number of cases referred to intake and to court was lower after the 1994 reforms.

Table 1 also presents both the new numbers of cases transferred and those numbers calculated as a percentage of all court cases. While the number of transfer cases fluctuated throughout the period covered in the table, the percentage of all court cases that were transferred clearly declined. The 1994 reforms did not increase transfers (Lanza-Kaduce, Bishop, and Winner 1996). Some would suggest that this is because effects of policy tend not to appear immediately after a change. The lack of impact of the changes in law shown here cannot be explained in terms of a delayed effect. In fact, our data show that the transfer rate continued to decline three years after the reforms.

Changes in juvenile justice commitment practices may have blunted the impact of the 1994 transfer reforms. This explanation is supported by noting that the number of cases that resulted in juvenile justice commitments increased steadily from 6160 in 1992-93 to 10,748 in 1996-97. This constitutes a 74.48 percent increase in juvenile commitments (Florida Department of Juvenile Justice 1998). Further, the rate of commitment to juvenile justice programs also increased steadily across all offense categories. During the same time period, the rate of transfer to adult court declined across all offense categories (data not shown). In other words, the juvenile justice system was being used increasingly after the 1994 reforms even for serious and violent offenders— indeed, for offenders who were clearly eligible for transfer.

The major transfer reform in 1994 authorized direct file of 14- and 15-year-old juveniles. The number of youths in these age categories who were transferred increased between 1992-93 and 1995-96 (from a low of 731 to a high of 921). The rates of transfer, however, showed a downward trend. The transfer rates started at 2.6 percent of court referrals in the fiscal year 1992-93 and ended at 2.2 percent in fiscal year 1996-97 (see Table 2).

In sum, the CIS data show four significant patterns across the period preceding and following the 1994 reforms. First, the number of transfer cases stabilized. Second, the rate of transfer declined. Third, the fact that transfers did not increase cannot be explained by a delayed effect. Fourth, commitments to juvenile justice facilities and programs increased dramatically.

OBTS DATA

The issue of whether the 1994 reforms had an impact on transfer can also be addressed with the OBTS data. We use OBTS data to examine what happens at each of several stages of processing for cases transferred to the criminal court.[5] If the get-tough mood that influenced the 1994 reforms was more generally present in Florida, we would expect an effect on the way criminal courts handled juvenile transfers. We would also expect to see more cases involving serious crimes or offenders going to the criminal court and receiving harsher penalties in 1995 than was true in 1993.

The OBTS data are dynamic. Florida's Office of the State Courts Administrator constantly receives input from court clerks on criminal court cases. The clerks update the OBTS records as court actions are taken. For the period under observation here, eight counties were dropped from both 1993 and 1995 because they failed to update records

TABLE 2
REFERRALS, COMMITMENTS, AND TRANSFERS BY AGE, FISCAL YEARS 1992-97

	Age	(1) Intake Referrals	(2) Court Referrals	(3) Commitments	(4) Percentage of Court Referrals Committed	(5) Transfers	(6) Percentage of Court Referrals Transferred
1992-93	16-17	59,915	33,036	2,563	7.8	6,144	18.6
	14-15	50,170	28,010	2,858	10.2	731	2.6
	<14	28,241	12,935	739	5.7	27	0.2
1993-94	16-17	66,642	35,648	3,232	9.1	5,720	16.0
	14-15	56,199	30,849	3,714	12.0	607	2.0
	<14	30,967	14,230	989	7.0	31	0.2
1994-95	16-17	72,425	40,400	3,809	9.4	5,850	14.5
	14-15	60,346	34,587	4,164	12.0	793	2.3
	<14	33,392	15,266	1,053	6.9	47	0.3
1995-96	16-17	74,158	40,928	4,413	10.8	6,012	14.7
	14-15	60,365	33,716	4,223	12.5	921	2.7
	<14	34,010	15,541	1,152	7.4	41	0.3
1996-97	16-17	75,111	45,572	4,969	11.7	5,441	12.8
	14-15	60,397	34,318	4,536	13.2	762	2.2
	<14	34,513	16,565	1,243	7.5	29	0.2

each year. When records are updated, some of them may be expunged from the system altogether and, in other instances, a number of charges may be absorbed into other cases. This continual refinement of the data amounts to what we have come to call a maturation effect, in that the OBTS data become more complete over time and a better reflection of actual processing and final case outcomes.

Sizable decreases in the number of cases occur over time as a result of this maturation effect. For this reason, the OBTS data cannot be used to compare numbers of cases across years. These data do, however, provide a very useful basis for determining the percentages of cases that are processed in various ways from one year to another. As the data for a year mature, the percentages remain relatively stable.[6] Thus the OBTS data can be used to gain insight into

whether the 1994 reforms have had an impact by examining percentage differences in cases at four stages of processing in 1993 and in 1995. They are (1) initiation of counts and cases, (2) cases proceeding to court adjudication, (3) cases disposed in court, and (4) cases sentenced.

COUNTS AND CASES INITIATED

Table 3 presents percentages in 1993 and 1995 for both the counts initiated and the cases that grow from them (by level and degree of offense) at the initial phase of criminal court processing.

The first two columns of percentages show that the overall distribution of counts in any given offense category remained remarkably stable from 1993 to 1995. The last two columns indicate that the percentages of cases across these same

TABLE 3

**PERCENTAGE OF TOTAL COUNTS AND CASES INITIATED
BY LEVEL AND DEGREE OF OFFENSE, 1993 AND 1995**

	Counts		Cases	
	1993	1995	1993	1995
All serious felonies	15.9	15.8	22.3	22.6
Capital	0.8	1.1	1.6	1.6
Life	3.2	2.7	4.0	3.5
First-degree	11.9	12.0	16.7	17.6
Second-degree felonies	18.5	17.8	21.2	23.4
Third-degree felonies	41.3	42.8	28.3	28.8
All misdemeanors	24.3	22.4	28.2	25.1
First-degree	12.9	12.0	14.9	12.0
Second-degree	10.6	10.5	11.3	10.9
Other infractions	0.9	1.1	2.0	2.0
Total number	10,092	11,088	3,778	4,175

offense categories also did not change much between 1993 and 1995 either. The biggest difference by offense category between 1993 and 1995 occurred for transfer cases initiated on misdemeanors. Given the maturation of the OBTS data, however, we are reluctant to make much of a 3 percentage point difference. These data suggest the get-tough 1994 reforms had minimal impact on the kinds of cases initiated in adult court.[7]

CASES PROCEEDING TO
COURT FOR ADJUDICATION

Nearly all (99 percent) of the cases in which criminal prosecutions were initiated moved on to court for adjudication according to the OBTS data for both 1993 and 1995. The percentages of cases moving to the adjudication stage varied little from 1993 to 1995. In 1993, over 22 percent of the cases proceeding to court for adjudication involved capital, life, or first-

degree felonies, compared with 23 percent in 1995. In 1993, about 21 percent of the cases proceeding to adjudication were for second-degree felonies, as compared with 23 percent in 1995. Twenty-eight percent of the cases in 1993 and 29 percent of them in 1995 were for third-degree felonies. The largest difference for this stage of processing is in the category of misdemeanor or other infraction: 28 percent in 1993 and 25 percent in 1995.

CASES DISPOSED IN COURT

We can also examine whether the disposition of cases that were adjudicated reflects a get-tough approach. For a quarter of the cases in both 1993 and 1995 (25 percent in 1993 and 26 percent in 1995), no court action was recorded as of the time the OBTS data were obtained. Of these cases reaching a court disposition, 91 percent in 1993 and 93 percent in 1995 had a conviction recorded. The percentages indicate that between 1993 and 1995 much stayed the same in the rate of convictions for juvenile cases transferred into adult court.

Not all convictions in Florida are the same, however. Transferred offenders can be convicted by being adjudicated delinquent (and sentenced back to juvenile sanctions), by having adjudication formally withheld (although they are sanctioned as adults), or by being formally convicted (and sanctioned as adults). About 81 percent of the 1993 transfer cases are recorded as adult convictions, but only 74 percent of the 1995 transfer cases had such an entry recorded.[8] This difference, while not large, indicated a disposition trend away from get-tough sanctions.

The increase in the percentage of cases adjudicated as delinquent in adult court (from 6.2 percent in 1993 to 8.9 percent in 1995) is interesting and potentially a significant indication of counterforces at work. Now that more cases are eligible for transfer, judges may be exerting some additional checks. This may be part of the reason why the new transfer provisions have not been utilized more often.

A difference is also seen for cases having adjudication withheld. Adjudication was withheld in nearly 13 percent of the 1993 cases but in about 18 percent of the 1995 cases.

CASES SENTENCED

We turn now to information on sentences that have been imposed by the criminal court. Cases that have resulted in an adjudication of delinquency would have received juvenile

sanctions and are omitted from this discussion. At the time these data were obtained, 56 percent of the 1993 cases had proceeded to the sentencing phase and 51 percent of the 1995 cases had gone to sentencing. The higher percentage of cases going to sentencing in 1993 probably reflects the maturation effect characteristic of these data.

For the 1993 cases, over three-quarters (77 percent) of those who had pled or been found guilty as adults were sentenced to some form of incarceration (43 percent in prison and 34 percent in jail). A fairly similar pattern was found for the 1995 cases. In 1995, 74 percent of those who had pled or been found guilty as adults were sentenced to incarceration (39 percent in prison and 35 percent in jail).[9]

When we examined more detailed sentencing information, differences between 1993 and 1995 emerged. The 1995 cases received less severe sanctions. Fifty-three percent of those convicted of a felony offense in 1995 were sentenced to prison terms, down 8 percentage points from 1993. About 31 percent of those convicted of felony offenses in 1995 were sentenced to jail, about 6 percentage points higher than was the case in 1993.[10] Forty-six percent of the cases prosecuted for misdemeanors or other minor violations of law in 1995 were sentenced to jail, a rate that is 10 percentage points less than was found in 1993.

The OBTS data for 1993 and 1995 also show differences in the length of prison sentences. There was an increase in the number of sentences in the 1- to 5-year range (from 36 percent in 1993 to 46 percent in 1995), but a substantial decrease in other categories of sentence length. Special note should be taken of the reduction of nearly 9 percentage points in the 5- to 10-year sentencing range between 1993 and 1995. We doubt that the shift from 5- to 10-year prison sentences to 1- to 5-year prison sentences is due to ongoing maturation of the 1993 OBTS data, especially since the distribution of offenses for which persons were convicted was stable between 1993 and 1995. Instead, these data probably indicate that the criminal court is scaling back the most severe sentences for juvenile offenders, most likely because of expansion and greater use of adult-system provisions for youthful offenders (these provisions often entail shorter prison sentences followed by probation).[11]

This scaling back in sentences is also seen when we examine incarceration by the level and degree of the offense for which youths were convicted. For the 1993 cases, 65 percent of those incarcerated for felonies of the first degree or higher received sentences of five years or more. By contrast, in 1995, about 45 percent of those incarcerated for felonies of the first degree or higher received prison sentences of five years or more. It is likely that some part of this difference reflects a shift toward scaling back the severity of court sentences for juvenile offenders in criminal court. Some part of the difference may also reflect system adaptations to legislation in 1994 that eliminated automatic gain time. Those sentenced in 1995 may actually have served about the same amount of

time as those sentenced in 1993, given that those sentenced in 1995 were forced to serve a longer portion of their sentences. The criminal justice system has an uncanny ability to resist changes in the going rate.[12]

For cases from both 1993 and 1995, over 70 percent of those juveniles sentenced to incarceration had terms greater than six months. The average stay in a residential facility for juvenile offenders prior to 1994 (the year of the juvenile justice reforms) was generally less than six months. As late as 1995-96, lengths of stay at even the deep-end juvenile programs still averaged only six to nine months, though the range varied widely (Florida Juvenile Justice Advisory Board 1998). Clearly, offenders sentenced to incarceration as adults in 1993 received longer sentences than those who were retained in the juvenile system. The difference is so large that it would exist even after making adjustments for gain time and other early-release credit in the adult correctional system. With the 1994 reforms (and the new Level 10 juvenile justice programs), the average length of incarceration in deep-end juvenile facilities has increased. The authorized length of stay for Level 8 juvenile justice programs now ranges from 6 to 12 months and that for Level 10 facilities ranges from 18 to 36 months (Florida Juvenile Justice Advisory Board 1998). For those who want to get tough with young offenders, the terms for juvenile sentences after 1994 may be as long as those for many juveniles sentenced as adults. At least in 1995, a large plurality of the sentences to adult incarceration fell in the 1- to 5-year range. Now that the juvenile justice system can institutionalize its wards for similar periods of time, one critical difference between the adult and juvenile systems has been diminished. Subsequent to the 1994 reforms, the availability of stiffer juvenile justice sanctions combined with treatment may offer an attractive alternative to transfer.

PERCEPTIONS OF JUSTICE
OFFICIALS: RESULTS FROM
A TELEPHONE SURVEY

According to the CIS and OBTS data, Florida's 1994 juvenile reforms have had little appreciable effect on transfer practices. To explore why reforms that expanded transfer eligibility to thousands of additional cases had such little impact, we turn to the results of a telephone survey conducted as part of our current research project. The survey was administered to both prosecutors and judges familiar with transfer practices in Florida.

Although the survey was conducted in 1997, its central purposes were to determine what prosecutors and judges thought about the 1994 reforms (Bishop et al. 1998) and how they perceived the reforms had affected local practice.[13] Here we draw on several items from the survey that take us another step toward understanding why the 1994 reforms had a negligible impact on actual practice. Before discussing the particular findings, we note that Florida prosecutors (representing juvenile divisions of circuit state attorneys' offices and a major statewide

professional organization) have been a considerable force in juvenile justice legislation for at least 20 years. During that same time frame, the juvenile bench has been much less influential in juvenile justice reform (Bishop, Lanza-Kaduce, and Frazier 1998). This context will help us understand the respective perspectives about juvenile justice and transfer that emerged in our survey.

Judges tended to be more satisfied than prosecutors with the sweeping reforms of 1994—reforms that were in large measure a response to political pressure brought by the prosecutors. While 80 percent of the judges thought that the direct file provisions were now adequate, only 29 percent of the prosecutors thought they were. The large majority of judges (80 percent) thought the judicial waiver and indictment procedures for juveniles were also adequate. A majority of the prosecutors (75 and 71 percent, respectively, on waiver and indictment) also were accepting of these two methods of transfer. In short, judges were very satisfied with all current transfer provisions and had little or no interest in proposing more change.

Direct file was the preferred method of transfer for 79 percent of the prosecutors (but only 36 percent of the judges), and prosecutors wanted to expand its availability even more. Over 60 percent of them favored further lowering of the age of eligibility for direct file (Florida Department of Juvenile Justice 1998). Direct file is, after all, far quicker and easier for the prosecutors than is either judicial waiver or indictment, and direct file gives prosecutors sole responsibility to make the transfer decision.[14] No wonder it is so frequently used in Florida (currently 99 percent of transfers result from direct files) (Florida Department of Juvenile Justice 1998).

Although direct file was not the preferred method of transfer among judges, they were not concerned that their authority under judicial waiver provisions had been circumvented. The pattern of responses across several survey items (including both fixed and open-ended response formats) suggests that most judges in our survey were relatively satisfied with the amount of transfer authority being placed with prosecutors. Judges, for example, did not think that direct file was overused. Only about a quarter of the judge respondents reported that juveniles were wrongly transferred often or occasionally—a percentage that was similar to that for prosecutors.

Prosecutors and judges hold somewhat different perceptions about how often transfer should be used. Over 60 percent of the prosecutors thought that, on occasion, juveniles who should be transferred are not. By stark contrast, only 4 percent of the judges thought there were such cases. After Florida's two-decade experiment with expanding transfer authority, judges seem well satisfied with the status quo and lack strong opinions on many of the transfer issues covered in the survey. Paradoxically, prosecutors, who are utilizing little of their expanded power to transfer (according to CIS and OBTS data), still believe that law and practice need to go further to reach all the offenders who deserve transfer to adult court.

The judges in our sample showed strong opinions about the future of the juvenile court. The vast majority (84 percent) did not favor abolishing the juvenile court.[15] This was true of a smaller majority of the interviewed prosecutors (64 percent). While prosecutors clearly would like to see more change in the direct file provisions of Florida law, indications are that most of them currently accept the existence of a separate juvenile court.

Despite their desire for authority to direct file even younger juveniles and their concern that some juveniles slip through the new transfer provisions, the prosecutors we interviewed were relatively content with the relationship between the goals and practice of transfer. When asked if they thought there was a significant gap between the goals of transfer and how transfer is practiced, 79 percent of the prosecutors said there was not. Prosecutors apparently believe the goals they have for transfer are generally achievable under existing law and that they are being realized in practice.

Prosecutors' satisfaction with practice is, at first glance, hard to reconcile with their interest in greater direct file authority, particularly in the area of lowering the age of direct file eligibility. Their survey responses suggest that they want essentially total authority to direct file juvenile offenders at any age if, in their view, it will be in the best interest of public safety. Prosecutors already have the authority to seek indictments through the grand jury for juveniles of any age who are charged with capital or life felonies and must direct file for those who have been adjudicated and committed for felonies on three separate occasions.

Discretionary direct file would be faster and more convenient for prosecutors. Given current mandatory direct file and indictment alternatives for very young serious offenders, however, the prospect remains low that more expansive direct file provisions would capture a new group of transfers who are under 14 years of age. Our present analyses show little evidence of the existence of a sizable group of serious and violent offenders in this younger age range (Bishop et al. 1998). The comparison of actual transfer practices (using both the CIS and OBTS findings presented earlier) with the projections of the number of youths eligible for transfer under the 1994 reforms (Lanza-Kaduce et al. 1996) shows that expanding authority does not necessarily translate into more transfers.

What we know from these survey results is that prosecutors, who have been the primary players in the transformation of Florida's juvenile justice system, are basically satisfied with a separate juvenile justice system and its current transfer provisions. If the prosecutors surveyed in this study are representative, the only change they would make is to further reduce the age of eligibility for direct file. Little else in the survey would lead to a conclusion that there is more that is wanted by either group of juvenile justice officials. Indeed, little more could be added

that would enable juvenile prosecutors to use their transfer powers in a substantially larger number of cases.

DISCUSSION

Prosecutors have infrequently used their new authority under the 1994 reforms to transfer 14- and 15-year-old offenders. If they had, we would have seen a greater impact of the 1994 reforms according to the official state data. The paradox of expanded prosecutorial powers and an indiscernible impact raises questions about how to understand the 1994 get-tough reforms.

Broad system and societal forces probably need to be taken into account to fully appreciate and explain the Florida situation. Toward that end, we will consider two system explanations, "saturation" and "adaptation," and one larger societal explanation regarding the "expressive functions of legal change" (Mays and Gregware 1996) for a system response discussion and explanation of recent reforms in New Mexico.

From a system point of view, Florida prosecutors may have reached a saturation point in their transfer practices. The data on transfer rates in Florida over a very long period suggest that transfer provisions and practice have come together so that prosecutors can now transfer almost any juvenile whom they deem a threat to public safety. The relatively stable number of transfers and the declining rate of transfer indicate that (at the local level, at least) prosecutors are transferring with ease every case they believe deserves it.[16] Philosophically, they may want still more discretion with regard to age limitations, but judging from the data we have presented previously, having it is unlikely to change their practices in any major way.

Other literature also compels us to consider the possibility of saturation. Walker (1998), for example, has long argued that the criminal justice system establishes a going rate and that punitive policies are unlikely to have major impacts on serious cases. For example, he cites the negligible impact that preventive detention provisions had on bail practices in Washington, D.C. (Thomas 1976; *Preventive Detention* 1972). Judges were already detaining serious offenders under previous bail provisions. Walker's argument may apply to Florida's recent situation. Given that extensive transfer provisions were established as early as 1978 in Florida, the 1994 reforms may well have been an unnecessary addition— the going rate for transfer had already been established.

Florida's experience may go beyond system saturation. Some evidence also points to a major adaptation, by the juvenile justice system, to years of get-tough rhetoric and reform. The removal of juvenile justice administration in 1994 from the unwieldy and widely discredited Department of Health and Rehabilitative Services and its placement in the newly created DJJ allowed the system to adapt. The new DJJ was able to shed the image of being soft on crime and coddling delinquents. The new department essentially leveraged this image change into bigger budgets with additional funds to expand the capacity for juvenile commit-

ments. As a result, the DJJ was first granted credibility, and then it worked effectively to enhance its status in the politics of crime— credibility that its predecessor Department of Health and Rehabilitative Services had lost.

The DJJ also distanced itself from the rehabilitative ideal. For example, it effectively showcased its new long-term deep-end residential facilities. It stressed a new get-tough approach to detention, which, after 1994, was authorized for longer periods both for those awaiting adjudication and for those awaiting deep-end placements in correctional facilities after being adjudicated.

The expanded capacity for juvenile commitments to deep-end facilities and the DJJ's public relations program seem to have reduced the pressure to transfer juveniles into adult court in Florida. Interestingly, most of that deep-end commitment capacity is now privatized, albeit with not-for-profit corporations under contract with the state (Florida Juvenile Justice Advisory Board 1998).[17] As a consequence of such contracts, the DJJ is less directly involved, and rehabilitation and treatment programs are associated with the service providers with whom the department contracts. Contracts with nongovernmental providers, therefore, serve to distance the DJJ from the sorts of rehabilitative efforts that have, in the past, fallen from political favor.[18]

The 1994 reforms' lack of impact may also reflect larger societal forces. Law may be more a result of general political and social factors than it is a specific instrument of social change. Our initial projections of the potential impact of Florida's 1994 transfer reforms (Lanza-Kaduce et al. 1996) tacitly assumed an instrumental effect of law. In retrospect, we are reminded of Gusfield's distinction (1963) between instrumental law formation (where reform goals reflect efforts to alter society) and expressive law formation (where law is enacted solely for the sake of expression). Florida's 1994 reforms could be merely expressive of general public frustration (including frustration over youth crime) that prevailed just a few short years ago—before the economy improved and crime rates declined.

Current beliefs and practices reflected in the Florida data presented earlier belie the get-tough language of the 1994 provisions. Indeed, in Florida, there may be a new openness to juvenile sanctions and programs instead of an increased reliance on transfer to criminal court and adult corrections. Interview data show continued acceptance of a separate juvenile system among prosecutors and judges. Official data on juvenile cases processed indicate stable numbers of transfer cases and lower rates of transfer. These were accompanied by increases in commitments to juvenile justice programs (which have been expanded in both number and variety) as well as a moderation of lengthy adult prison sentences for transferred youths. The overall pattern may indicate that the pendulum in Florida has begun to swing back to a less punitive and more treatment-oriented approach to juvenile offenders. It will take time and focused

research to determine whether juvenile justice will evolve or dissolve in other jurisdictions. While Florida's experiences are instructive in a broad sense, the next several years in those many states that have just begun to expand their transfer provisions and practices (Torbet et al. 1996) are critically important pieces to a yet unfinished justice puzzle.

Notes

1. Elvin Martinez was a long-time member of the Florida legislature, and, for several years, he was chairman of the powerful criminal justice committee. The interviews cited in this article were held shortly after Mr. Martinez had retired from the legislature and become a circuit judge.

2. Reflecting a pervasive get-tough mentality, the state legislature in 1994 initiated an ambitious prison-expansion program, funding 20,000 additional beds. The early-release discretion of the Control Release Authority (the state's reformulated parole commission) was curbed, and offenders sentenced to prison were required to serve 85 percent of their sentences prior to release.

3. Cases are comprised of all referral charges for an individual that are recorded on the same day. Each case is characterized by the most serious of those referral charges.

4. It should be noted that both of these databases have weaknesses. CIS misidentifies some cases as being transferred and some as not being transferred. The data are, nevertheless, widely used by the state both to make decisions on individual cases (for example, to establish a juvenile's prior record) and to estimate rates and trends of transfer. The OBTS is incomplete because 14 of the state's 67 counties do not participate in the system. Again, while these data would be of little use were we trying to determine how many cases are transferred statewide, they are quite helpful when our interest is in assessing whether there have been changes over time in the ways in which the state's criminal courts respond to juvenile offenders.

5. The OBTS tracks criminal court charges or counts (rather than persons or

cases) based on information obtained from county criminal court clerks' offices. It does not include cases retained in the juvenile court system. Each of the counts is tracked in OBTS as it moves through the system. Our analysis of OBTS data focuses on cases that have been constructed by combining counts or charges for an individual that were recorded on the same date. The cases are then followed from initial prosecutorial consideration, to taking the prosecution to court, to adjudication, and to sentencing. We have OBTS data for the year before the juvenile justice reforms (1993) and the year after the reforms (1995). Cases for both years have been selected to include only those defendants who were under age 18 at the time of their offense.

6. OBTS data for 1993 obtained in 1994 were compared with OBTS data for 1993 obtained in 1998. Over 40 percent of the 1993 cases studied using the 1994 entries were no longer in the OBTS data by 1998. This is partly because several counties that had begun reporting to OBTS did not continue updating case records. Thus, eight additional counties were dropped from the data set. Even with this adjustment, however, the percentages processed for various levels and degrees of offenses were comparable. For example, for the 1998 edition of the 1993 cases, 22 percent of the cases involved serious felonies, 21 percent involved second-degree felonies, 28 percent involved third-degree felonies, and 28 percent involved misdemeanors or other infractions. For the 1994 edition of the 1993 OBTS cases, 21 percent of the cases involved serious felonies, 24 percent involved second-degree felonies, 29 percent involved third-degree felonies, and 26 percent involved misdemeanors or other infractions.

7. The 1993 and 1995 cases were also examined for differences by race, gender, and age. Few differences were found. The largest one was in the percentage of 14- and 15-year-old offenders who were transferred to adult court. The percentage rose from 8.3 in 1993 to 11.4 in 1995. Although this is consistent with the enabling transfer provisions passed in 1994, the increase is still quite small—much smaller than projected. (See Lanza-Kaduce et al. 1996.)

8. In the aggregate, there are some noteworthy differences in conviction by age, race, and gender. For example, older juveniles are more likely than younger ones to be convicted as adults, females are more likely than males to have adjudication withheld, and whites are more likely than blacks to be adjudicated delinquent. These differences, however, might be reduced or even disappear if controls for offender history variables were introduced into the analysis. Unfortunately, we could not pursue this issue because OBTS data do not include information on important potential control variables such as prior record.

9. The number of prison cases in 1995 can be expected to increase as the data set matures over the next couple of years. When probation is violated, for example, the case comes back to court and is often changed after revocation of probation to a prison sentence.

10. Generally in Florida, jail sentences can be for terms up to 12 months and prison sentences are for terms greater than 12 months.

11. Changes may also have resulted from the 1994 legislation that stemmed early release and required inmates to serve 85 percent of their sentences. Prosecutors and judges may have adjusted their decision making because offenders will now serve 85 percent of a four-year sentence, which is longer than the previous 50 percent of a six-year sentence.

12. For an excellent discussion of this point, see Walker 1998.

13. A full report of the item-by-item results can be found in Bishop et al. 1998. The instrument was nearly 40 pages long, and each interview lasted an hour or more. In the present article, we report only selected results that may shed some light on what prosecutors and judges thought about transfer in 1997. We targeted each of Florida's 20 judicial circuits and tried to obtain an interview with one judge with experience in the juvenile court and one with experience in the criminal court (or a single person who had experience in both courts). The same strategy was used to obtain the sample of prosecutors. Twenty-eight prosecutors and 25 judges responded to the survey. At least one prosecutor responded from each circuit, and all circuits but two were represented by at least one judge respondent.

14. Unlike the *Kent*-style criteria generally in place for judicial waiver hearings, prosecutors are guided by "their judgement of the best interest of public safety" and any statutory considerations tied to direct file of 14- and 15-year-olds. Critics describe waiver as "cumber-

some, time-consuming, and function[ing] as a 'mini-trial' considering factors which have often been previously determined at a detention hearing" (Florida Legislature 1978, 59).

15. This is especially noteworthy considering that most judge respondents had been on the bench less than two years and on the juvenile bench less than one year. In Florida, the tendency is for judges at the circuit level to rotate through the juvenile bench rather than to hold the position as a career post.

16. One telephone survey item showed that 57 percent of the prosecutors believed there was considerable variation in transfer practices across jurisdictions, but a follow-up item showed that 86 percent of the prosecutors were not in favor of measures that would promote greater consistency across circuits. Understandably, prosecutors preferred local control of policy relating to transfer practice.

17. The Florida Juvenile Justice Advisory Board (1998) lists over 130 specific commitment programs for classification Levels 4-10 (and various unspecified local programs). Of the named programs, only 8 are state operated and only 10 are operated by county sheriffs' offices.

18. Privatization may serve other functions as well. A recent analysis of recidivism rates for adult inmates released from the first privately operated prisons in Florida compared with those for inmates released from Florida's publicly operated prisons found lower recidivism among the releasees from the private prisons (Lanza-Kaduce, Parker, and Thomas 1999).

References

Bishop, Donna M., Charles E. Frazier, and John C. Henretta. 1989. Prosecutorial Waiver: A Case Study of a Questionable Reform. *Crime & Delinquency* 35(2):179-201.

Bishop, Donna M., Charles E. Frazier, Lonn Lanza-Kaduce, and Henry G. White. 1998. *Juvenile Transfers to Criminal Court Study: Phase I.* Tallahassee, FL: Juvenile Justice Accountability Board.

Bishop, Donna M., Lonn Lanza-Kaduce, and Charles E. Frazier. 1998. Juvenile Justice Under Attack: An Analysis of the Causes and Impact of Recent Reforms. *University of Florida Journal of Law and Public Policy* 10(1):129-56.

Florida Department of Juvenile Justice. 1998. www.djj.state.fl.us.

Florida Juvenile Justice Advisory Board. 1994. *Annual Report and Juvenile Justice Fact Book.* Tallahassee: Florida Juvenile Justice Advisory Board.

———. 1996. *Annual Report and Juvenile Justice Fact Book.* Tallahassee: Florida Juvenile Justice Advisory Board.

———. 1998. *1998 Outcome Evaluation Report.* Vol. 1. Doc. no. 98-001-OE. Tallahassee: Florida Legislature.

Florida Legislature. House. Committee on Health and Rehabilitative Services. Ad Hoc Committee on Children and Youth. 1978. *Report of the Ad Hoc Committee on Children and Youth.* Florida State Archives, Department of State. Series 19, Carton 370.

Frazier, Charles E., Donna M. Bishop, Lonn Lanza-Kaduce, and Lawrence Winner. 1995. *Juvenile Justice Transfer Legislation in Florida: Assessing the Impact on the Criminal Justice and Correctional Systems.* Tallahassee, FL: Task Force for the Review of Criminal Justice and Correctional Systems and the Collins Center for Public Policy.

Gusfield, Joseph R. 1963. *Symbolic Crusade.* Urbana: University of Illinois Press.

Krzycki, Leonard A. and Elizabeth Cass. 1992. Issues Relating to the Implementation of the Juvenile Justice Reform Act. Florida Commission on Juvenile Justice. Report.

Lanza-Kaduce, Lonn, Donna M. Bishop, Charles E. Frazier, and Lawrence Winner. 1996. Changes in Juvenile Waiver and Transfer Provisions: Projecting the Impact in Florida. *Law & Policy* 18(1-2):137-50.

Lanza-Kaduce, Lonn, Donna M. Bishop, and Lawrence Winner. 1996. *Juvenile Case Processing in Florida: A Comparison of Cross-Jurisdictional Variations in Timing Sequences and Outcomes 1993-1995*. Tallahassee, FL: Juvenile Justice Advisory Board.

Lanza-Kaduce, Lonn, Karen Parker, and Charles Thomas. 1999. Measuring the Effectiveness of Private and Public Prisons: A Comparative Recidivism Analysis. *Crime & Delinquency* 45(1):28-47.

Martinez, Elvin. 1997. Interviews by Donna M. Bishop. 1-15 Sept.

Mays, G. L. and Peter R. Gregware. 1996. The Children's Code Reform Movement in New Mexico: The Politics of Expediency. *Law & Policy* 18(1-2): 179-93.

Orlando Sentinel. 1993, 12 Oct.

Preventive Detention in the District of Columbia: The First Ten Months. 1972. Washington, DC: Georgetown Institute for Law and Procedure.

Schwartz, Ira M., Chang-ming Hsieh, and Gretchen P. Kenagy. 1996. *Juveniles in Adult Prisons*. Philadelphia: University of Pennsylvania, School of Social Work, Center for the Study of Youth Policy.

Thomas, Wayne. 1976. *Bail Reform in America*. Berkeley: University of California Press.

Torbet, Patricia, Richard Gable, Hunter Hurst IV, Imogene Montgomery, Linda Szymanski, and Douglas Thomas. 1996. *Responses to Serious and Violent Juvenile Crime*. Washington, DC: Department of Justice, Office of the Juvenile Justice and Delinquency Prevention.

Walker, Samuel. 1998. *Sense and Nonsense About Crime and Drugs*. 4th ed. Belmont, CA: Wadsworth.

ANNALS, *AAPSS*, **564**, July 1999

Challenging Girls'
Invisibility in Juvenile Court

By MEDA CHESNEY-LIND

ABSTRACT: Despite the fact that girls account for one of four arrests of juveniles, discussions of delinquency and juvenile justice generally ignore young women and their problems. A review of the nature of female delinquency as well as the juvenile justice system's long-documented bias against girls suggests that careful consideration of girls' issues would shed considerable light on the shortcomings of the juvenile justice system as a whole. Specifically, the unique problems of girls, like sexual abuse, were long ignored by a system that purported to seek "the best interests of the child." Instead, girls' survival strategies, like running away from home, were criminalized. Contemporary congressional efforts to reform juvenile justice, focused almost exclusively on boys' violence, are likely to produce changes that will result in the compounding of girls' problems due to contact with a system that ignores their unique situations.

Meda Chesney-Lind is professor of women's studies at the University of Hawaii at Manoa. Her books include Girls, Delinquency and Juvenile Justice, *which was awarded the American Society of Criminology's Michael J. Hindelang Award for the "outstanding contribution to criminology, 1992" and* The Female Offender: Girls, Women and Crime *(1998). She is currently at work on an edited collection entitled* Female Gangs in America.

E VERY year, girls account for one of four arrests of young people in America (U.S. Department of Justice 1997, 219). Despite this, young women are almost always forgotten when juvenile justice issues are discussed.

There are many ways in which girls' invisibility can be measured. For example, in the most significant congressional overhaul of the juvenile justice system in the last three decades, no one is talking about girls. A quick review of the initiatives being considered by Congress finds an almost exclusive focus on "violent" juvenile offenders (meaning boys) and the need to "get tough" on youth violence (Schiraldi and Soler 1998). A closer reading though, suggests a less public congressional agenda— one that would again permit the juvenile justice system to discriminate against girls and jail them for running away from home—no matter how abusive. It turns out that the invisibility of girls in the juvenile justice system has also often facilitated practices that could in no way be justified as in the best interest of girls.

This article will briefly address some of the critical issues confronted by those attempting to understand both female delinquency and creative, girl-centered responses to the problems of young women. It will also suggest that no discussion of the future of juvenile justice is complete without consideration of girls and their unique problems.

GIRLS' TROUBLES AND GIRLS' CRIME: ARE GIRLS GETTING MEANER?

Shortly after a study by the American Association for University Women (1992) documented the dramatic and widespread drop in the self-esteem of girls during early adolescence, a curious thing happened in the media. There was a dramatic surge of journalistic interest in girls, often girls of color, engaged in nontraditional, masculine behavior— notably, joining gangs, carrying guns, and fighting with other girls.

This fascination with a presumably new, violent female offender is itself not really new, however. In the 1970s, a notion emerged that the women's movement had caused a surge in women's serious crimes, but this discussion focused largely on an imagined increase in crimes of adult women, usually white women (Chesney-Lind 1997). The current discussion has settled on girls' commission of violent crimes, often in youth gangs. Indeed, there has been a veritable siege of these news stories with essentially the same theme—today girls are more violent, they are in gangs, and their behavior does not fit the traditional stereotype of girls' delinquency.

On 2 August 1993, for example, in a feature spread on teen violence, *Newsweek* had a box entitled "Girls Will Be Girls" that noted that "some girls now carry guns. Others hide razor blades in their mouths" (Leslie et al. 1993, 44). Explaining this trend, the article notes, "The plague of teen violence is an equal-opportunity scourge. Crime by girls is on the rise, or so various jurisdictions report" (Leslie et al. 1993, 44).

A review of girls' arrests for violent crime for the last decade (1987-96) initially seems to provide support for the notion that girls have become more violent. Arrests of girls for all Crime Index[1] violent offenses were up 118.1 percent (U.S. Department of Justice 1997, 219), and arrests of girls for "other assaults" were up 142.6 percent. But a closer look at these and other data on girls' violent behavior presents a more complex picture.

First, and most important, boys' arrests for these offenses have been climbing sharply as well; as a result, girls' share of serious crimes of violence has changed only slightly during the time period. In 1987, arrests of girls accounted for 11 percent of all arrests of youths for serious crimes of violence; in 1996, the comparable figure was 15 percent (U.S. Department of Justice 1997, 219). Second, serious crimes of violence still constitute only a small proportion of all girls' delinquency, and that figure has remained essentially unchanged. Only 2.0 percent of girls' arrests in 1987 were for serious crimes of violence. By 1996, this figure had climbed to 2.9 percent (13,995 arrests out of a total of 481,164 arrests) (compared to 5.6 percent of boys' arrests).

But what about those increases, particularly in "other assaults"? Relabeling as violent offenses behaviors that were once categorized as status offenses (noncriminal offenses like running away from home and "person in need of supervision") cannot be ruled out in explanations of arrest rate shifts, nor can changes in police practices with reference to domestic violence. A review of the more than 2000 cases of girls referred to Maryland's juvenile justice system for "person-to-person" offenses revealed that virtually all of these offenses (97.9 percent) involved "assault." A further examination of these records revealed that about half were "family centered" and involved such activities as "a girl hitting her mother and her mother subsequently pressing charges" (Mayer 1994).

Other mechanisms for relabeling status offenses as criminal offenses include police officers' advising parents to block the doorways when their children threaten to run away and then charging the youths with assault when they shove their way past their parents (Shelden 1995). Such relabeling, which is also called bootstrapping, has been particularly pronounced in the official delinquency of African American girls (Robinson 1990; Bartollas 1993), and this practice also facilitates the incarceration of girls in detention facilities and training schools— something that would not be possible if the girls were arrested for noncriminal status offenses.

When exploring the dramatic increases in the arrests of girls for "other assaults" (which increased by 142.6 percent in the last decade), it is also likely that enforcement practices have dramatically narrowed the gender gap. Minor or "other" assaults can range from schoolyard tussles to relatively serious but not life-threatening assaults (Steffensmeier and Steffensmeier 1980). Steffensmeier and Steffensmeier first noted an increasing tendency to arrest girls for these offenses in the 1970s and commented that "evidence suggests that female arrests for 'other assaults' are relatively non-serious in nature and tend to consist of being bystanders or companions to males involved in skirmishes, fights, and so on" (70). Currie adds to this the fact that these "simple assaults without injury" are often "attempted" or "threatened" or "not completed" (Currie 1998, 40). At a time when official concern about youth violence is almost unparalleled and school principals are increasingly likely to call police onto their campuses, it should come as no surprise that youthful arrests in this area are up.

Detailed comparisons drawn from supplemental homicide reports based on unpublished data from the Federal Bureau of Investigation also hint at the central, rather than peripheral, way in which gender colored and differentiated girls' and boys' violence. Loper and Cornell's study (1996) of these FBI data on the characteristics of girls' and boys' homicides between 1984 and 1993 found that girls accounted for "proportionately fewer homicides in 1993 (6%) than in 1984 (14%)" (324). Their work shows that girls' choice of weapons differed from that of boys; in comparison to boys' homicides, girls who killed were more likely to use a knife than a gun and to murder someone as a result of conflict (rather than in the commission of a crime). Girls were also more likely than boys to murder family members (32 percent) and very young victims (24 percent of their victims were under the age of 3, compared to 1 percent of the boys' victims) (328). When involved in a peer homicide, girls were more likely

than boys to have killed "as a result of an interpersonal conflict"; in addition, girls were more likely to kill alone, while boys were more likely to kill with an accomplice (328). Loper and Cornell concluded that "the stereotype of girls becoming gun-toting robbers was not supported. The dramatic increase in gun-related homicides . . . applies to boys but not girls" (332).

Finally, a note about self-report data. These have always shown that girls committed more assaults than official statistics reflected (Chesney-Lind and Shelden 1997). A summary of recent studies of self-reported aggression also reflects that while about a third of girls reported having been in a physical fight in the last year, this was true of over half of the boys (Girls Incorporated 1996, 13). Girls are far more likely than boys to fight with a parent or sibling (34 percent compared to 9 percent), whereas boys are more likely to fight with friends or strangers. Finally, boys are twice to three times more likely to report carrying a weapon in the past month (13).

Trends in self-report data of youthful involvement in violent offenses also fail to show the dramatic changes found in official statistics. Specifically, a matched sample of "high-risk" youths (aged 13-17) surveyed in the 1977 National Youth Study and the more recent 1989 Denver Youth Survey revealed significant decreases in girls' involvement in felony assaults, minor assaults, and hard drugs, and no change in a wide range of other delinquent behaviors, including felony theft, minor theft, and index delinquency (Huizinga 1997).

Finally, girls' behavior, including violence, needs to be put in its patriarchal context. In her analysis of self-reported violence by girls in Canada, Artz (1998) did precisely that, and the results were striking. First, she noted that violent girls reported significantly greater rates of victimization and abuse than their nonviolent counterparts, and that girls who were violent reported great fear of sexual assault, especially from their boyfriends. Specifically, 1 in 5 violent girls felt they were physically abused at home compared to 1 in 10 violent males and only 6.3 percent of nonviolent girls. Patterns for sexual abuse were even starker; roughly 1 in 4 violent girls had been sexually abused compared to 1 in 10 nonviolent girls (47). Follow-up interviews with a small group of violent girls found that the girls had learned at home that "might makes right" and engaged in "horizontal violence" directed at other powerless girls (often with boys as the audience). Certainly, these findings provide little ammunition for those who would contend that the "new," violent girl is a product of any form of emancipation.

While the media has focused attention on girls' violent, nontraditional delinquency, most delinquency by girls is not of that sort at all. Examining the types of offenses for which girls are actually arrested, it is clear that most are arrested for the less serious criminal acts and status offenses (noncriminal offenses for which only youths can be taken into custody, like running away from home). In 1995, well over half of girls' arrests were for either larceny theft (25.8 percent), much of which, particularly for girls, is shoplifting (Shelden and Horvath 1986), or status offenses (23.4 percent). Boys' arrests were far more dispersed.

Running away from home and prostitution remain the only two arrest categories where more girls than boys are arrested. Despite the intention of the Juvenile Justice and Delinquency Prevention (JJDP) Act of 1974, which, among other things, encouraged jurisdictions to divert and deinstitutionalize youths charged with status offenses, arrests for these have been climbing in recent years. Between 1987 and 1996, for example, girls' runaway arrests increased by 20.7 percent, and arrests of girls for curfew violations increased by 155.2 percent (U.S. Department of Justice 1997, 219).

Status offenses have always played a significant role among the offenses that bring girls into the juvenile justice system. They accounted for about a quarter of all girls' arrests in 1996, but less than 10 percent of boys' arrests—figures that remained relatively stable during the last decade. In 1996, over half (57.5 percent) of those arrested for one status offense—running away from home—were girls (U.S. Department of Justice 1997, 219).

Why are girls more likely to be arrested than boys for running away from home? There are no simple answers to this question. Studies of actual delinquency (not simply arrests) show that girls and boys run away from home in about equal numbers. As an example, Canter (1982) found in a National Youth Survey that there was no evidence of greater female involvement, compared to that of males, in any category of delinquent behavior. Indeed, in this sample, males were significantly more likely than females to report status offenses.

There is some evidence to suggest that parents and police may be responding differently to the same behavior. Parents may be calling the police when their daughters do not come home, and police may be more likely to arrest a female than a male runaway youth.

Another reason for different responses to running away from home speaks to differences in the reasons that boys and girls have for running away. Girls are, for example, much more likely than boys to be the victims of child sexual abuse, with some experts estimating that roughly 70 percent of the victims of child sexual abuse are girls (Finkelhor and Baron 1986). Not surprisingly, the evidence is also suggesting a link between this problem and girls' delinquency, particularly running away from home.

Studies of girls on the streets or in court populations show high rates of both sexual and physical abuse. A study of a runaway shelter in Toronto found, for example, that 73 percent of the female runaways and 38 percent of the males had been sexually abused. This same study found that sexually abused female runaways were more likely than their nonabused counterparts to engage in delinquent or criminal activities such as substance abuse, petty theft, and prostitution. No such pattern was found among the male runaways (McCormack, Janus, and Burgess 1986).

Detailed studies of youths entering the juvenile justice system in Florida have compared the "constellations of problems" presented by girls and boys entering detention (Dembo, Williams, and Schmeidler 1993, 1995). In these studies, it was found that female youths were more likely than male youths to have abuse histories and contact with the juvenile justice system for status offenses, while male youths had higher rates of involvement with various delinquent offenses. Further research on a larger cohort of youths (N = 2104) admitted to an assessment center in Tampa concluded that "girls' problem behavior commonly relates to an abusive and traumatizing home life, whereas boys' law violating behavior reflects their involvement in a delinquent life style" (Dembo, Williams, and Schmeidler 1995, 21).

Girls on the run from these sorts of homes clearly need help. For many years, however, their accounts of abuse were ignored, and they were inappropriately institutionalized in detention centers and training schools as delinquents if they refused to stay at home.

THE FAMILY COURT AND
THE FEMALE DELINQUENT

While girls have long been invisible to those who crafted theories of delinquency, concerns about girls' immoral conduct were at the center, rather than at the periphery, of the movement that established the juvenile court (Platt 1969; Odem 1995; Kunzel 1993). As a result, in the earliest years of the court, girls were frequently institutionalized for such offenses as "sexual immorality" or "waywardness," and well into the 1970s, contemporary status offenses such as running away from home often functioned as "buffer charges" for the court's concern about the sexual behavior of girls (see Chesney-Lind and Shelden 1997 for a discussion of these issues).

Correctional reformers, concerned about abuse of the status offense category by juvenile courts (though not necessarily concerned about girls), were instrumental in urging the U.S. Congress to pass the JJDP Act of 1974. This legislation required that states receiving federal delinquency prevention moneys begin to divert and deinstitutionalize their status offenders. Despite erratic enforcement of this provision and considerable resistance from juvenile court judges, girls were the clear beneficiaries of the reform. Incarceration of young women in training schools and detention centers across the country have fallen dramatically in the decades since its passage, in distinct contrast to patterns found early in the century.

National statistics on girls' incarceration reflect both the official enthusiasm for the incarceration of girls during the early part of this century and the impact of the JJDP Act of 1974. Girls' share of the population of juvenile correctional facilities increased from 1880 (when girls were 19 percent of the population) to 1923 (when girls were 28 percent). By 1950, the proportion of girls had climbed to 34 percent of the total, and in 1960 they were still 27 percent of those in correctional facilities. By 1980, this pattern appeared to have reversed, and girls were again 19 percent of those in correctional facilities (Cahalan 1986, 130). In 1993, girls composed 10 percent of those held in public detention centers and training schools (Hsieh 1998).

Despite its success in reducing the number of status offenders, and hence girls, in facilities, the reform effort faced broad resistance from the outset. In 1980, the National Council of Juvenile and Family Court Judges was able to narrow the definition of a status offender in the amended act so that any child who had violated a "valid court order" would no longer be covered under the deinstitutionalization provisions (Pub. L. 96-509). This change effectively gutted the 1974 JJDP Act by permitting judges to reclassify a status offender who violated a court order as a delinquent. This meant that a young woman who ran away from a court-ordered placement (a halfway house or foster home, for example) could be relabeled a delinquent and locked up.

Judges have long used techniques like charging youths with "violation of a valid court order" or issuing contempt citations as ways to "bootstrap" status offenders into categories that permit their detention. They thereby circumvent the deinstitutionalization component of the JJDP Act (Costello and Worthington 1981, 42).

These judicial maneuvers clearly disadvantage girls. For example, a Florida study (Bishop and Frazier

1992) reviewed 162,012 cases referred to juvenile justice intake units during 1985-87. The researchers found only a weak pattern of discrimination against female status offenders compared to the treatment of male status offenders. However, when they examined the impact of contempt citations, the pattern changed markedly. They found that female offenders referred for contempt were more likely than females referred for other criminal-type offenses to be petitioned to court, and substantially more likely to be petitioned to court than males referred for contempt. Moreover, the girls were far more likely than boys to be sentenced to detention. Specifically, the typical female offender in their study had a probability of incarceration of 4.3 percent, which increased to 29.9 percent if she was held in contempt. Such a pattern was not observed among the males in the study. The researchers concluded that "the traditional double standard is still operative. Clearly, neither the cultural changes associated with the feminist movement nor the legal changes illustrated in the JJDP Act's mandate to deinstitutionalize status offenders have brought about equality under the law for young men and women" (1186).

During the early part of this decade, things seemed to be turning around for girls. Hearings held in 1992 in conjunction with the reauthorization of the JJDP Act addressed for the first time the "provision of services to girls within the juvenile justice system" (U.S. House 1992). At this hearing, the double standard of juvenile justice was discussed, as was the paucity of services for girls. The chair of the hearing, Representative Matthew Martinez, noted the high number of girls arrested for status offenses, the high percentage of girls in detention as a result of violation of court orders, and the failure of the system to address girls' needs. He ended with the question, "I wonder why, why are there no other alternatives than youth jail for her?" (U.S. House 1992, 2).

As a result of this landmark hearing, the 1992 reauthorization of the act included specific provisions requiring plans from each state receiving federal funds to include "an analysis of gender-specific services for the prevention and treatment of juvenile delinquency, including the types of such services available and the need for such services for females and a plan for providing needed gender-specific services for the prevention and treatment of juvenile delinquency" (Pub. L. 102-586). Additional moneys were set aside as part of the JJDP Act's challenge grant program for states wishing to develop policies to prohibit gender bias in placement and treatment and to develop programs that ensure girls equal access to services. As a result, 23 states embarked on such programs—by far the most popular of the 10 possible challenge grant activity areas (Girls Incorporated 1996, 26). Finally, the legislation moved to make the bootstrapping of status offenders more difficult (U.S. House 1992, 4983).

Sadly, these changes, while extremely hopeful, were short-lived. Currently, Congress is undertaking a major overhaul of the JJDP Act, and virtually all of the initiatives being considered are ominous for girls. The bills introduced to date intend to refocus national attention on the "violent and repeat juvenile offender" (read "boys") while also granting states "flexibility" in implementing the four core mandates of the JJDP Act. Key among these mandates, of course, is the deinstitutionalization of status offenders, though conservative lawmakers are also taking aim at efforts to separate youths from adults in correctional facilities, efforts to reduce minority overrepresentation in juvenile detention and training schools, and efforts to remove juveniles from adult jails (National Criminal Justice Association 1997, 2-3).

Most ominous for girls are efforts to loosen restrictions on the detention of status offenders. An example is Senate Bill 10, the Violent and Repeat Juvenile Offender Act of 1997: it allows for the incarceration of runaways if a hearing determines that "the behavior of the juvenile constitutes a clear and present danger to the juvenile's physical or emotional well being" or when "secure detention is necessary for guarding the safety of the juvenile" or, finally, when "the detention is necessary to obtain a suitable placement" (Coalition for Juvenile Justice 1997). Both House and Senate bills currently under consideration weaken the 1992 initiatives in the area of the detention of youths for violation of a valid court order. Even more worrisome, all the bills make it easier to hold youths in adult jails. The latter provision is most disturbing, since girls were not infrequently held in

such situations in the past (such as de facto detention centers in rural America). Sadly, abuse is not uncommon in such settings. In Ohio, for example, a 15-year-old girl was sexually assaulted by a deputy jailer after having been placed in an adult jail for a minor infraction (Ziedenberg and Schiraldi 1997, 2). Due to the isolation and abuse in these settings, girls are also at great risk for suicide (Chesney-Lind 1988).[2]

These initiatives should not surprise any student of the court's history, since they represent a return to the court's backstopping the sexual double standard (and parental authority) at the expense of girls' freedom. Indeed, a careful review of the data on incarceration patterns (during deinstitutionalization) signaled the resilience of the court's bias against girls as well as the special meaning of this for girls of color. Specifically, recent research suggests that the impact of deinstitutionalization has produced a racialized, two-track system of juvenile justice, one in which white girls are placed in mental hospitals and private facilities, while girls of color are detained and institutionalized.

DEINSTITUTIONALIZATION
UNDER SIEGE

While the JJDP Act stressed the need to deinstitutionalize status offenders, we have seen that the numbers of girls and boys arrested for these noncriminal offenses continued to increase. What has emerged from this pressure is a complex and not necessarily equitable system. Notably, over the last two decades, there has been a distinct rise in the number of youths confined in private facilities, and this trend has special meaning for girls.

In 1991, girls were 11 percent of those in public institutions but over a quarter (29 percent) of those held in private institutions (Moone 1993a, 1993b). Another way to look at this is to say that, of girls held in facilities of any sort, over half (62 percent) are held in private facilities. The vast majority of girls (85 percent) held in private facilities are being held for "nondelinquent" offenses including status offenses, dependency, and neglect, and due to "voluntary" admissions; for boys, only slightly over half (58 percent) are held for these reasons, with the rest being held for criminal offenses (Jamieson and Flanagan 1989, 596).

Ethnic differences are also apparent in the populations of these institutions; whites constituted about 40 percent of those held in public institutions in 1989 but 60 percent of those held in private facilities (Krisberg et al. 1991, 57-59). A more recent census (1995) of private facilities showed that well over half (53 percent) were white and, more important, that most youths in these facilities were "detained" or "committed" rather than admitted voluntarily (Moone 1997, 2).

Finally, the numbers indicate that, after a dramatic decline in the early 1970s, the number of girls held in public training schools and detention centers has not declined much, and meanwhile the number of girls in private facilities has soared. As an example, on one day in 1979, there were 6067 girls in public facilities

(mainly detention centers and training schools); in 1991 the figure was 6328. Meanwhile, the number of girls held in private facilities increased 27 percent, from 8176 in 1979 to 10,389 in 1991 (Krisberg et al. 1991, 43; Moone 1993a, 1993b). Between 1991 and 1995, the number of girls held in private facilities increased by 7.62 percent (Moone 1997, 1).

Some research indicates a reason for this pattern. Deinstitutionalization may have actually signaled the development of a two-track juvenile justice system—one track for girls of color and another for white girls. In a study of investigation reports from one area office in Los Angeles, Jody Miller (1994) examined the impact of race and ethnicity on the processing of girls' cases during 1992-93.

Reviewing the characteristics of the girls in Miller's group reveals the role played by color in the current juvenile justice system; Latinas composed the largest proportion of the population (43 percent), followed by white girls (34 percent), and African American girls (23 percent) (Miller 1994, 11). Predictably, girls of color were more likely to be from low-income homes, but this was especially true of African American girls (53 percent were from families participating in Aid to Families with Dependent Children, compared to 23 percent of white girls and 21 percent of Hispanic girls). Most important, Miller found that white girls were significantly more likely to be recommended for a treatment-oriented placement, as opposed to a "detention oriented" one, than either African American or Latina girls. In fact, 75 percent of the white girls were recommended for a treatment-oriented facility, compared to 34 percent of the Latinas and only 20 percent of the African American girls (Miller 1994, 18).

Examining a portion of the probation officers' reports in detail, Miller found key differences in the ways that girls' behaviors were described, reflecting what she called "racialized gender expectations." In particular, African American girls' behavior was often framed as products of "inappropriate 'lifestyle' choices," while white girls' behavior was described as resulting from low self-esteem, being easily influenced, and the result of "abandonment" (Miller 1994, 20). Latina girls, Miller found, received "dichotomized" treatment, with some receiving the more paternalistic care that white girls received, while others received the more punitive treatment (particularly if they had committed "masculine" offenses like car theft).

Robinson's in-depth study of girls in the social welfare (CHINS) and juvenile justice system (DYS) in Massachusetts documents the racialized pattern of juvenile justice quite clearly (1990). Her social welfare sample (N = 15) was 74 percent white/non-Hispanic and her juvenile justice system sample (N = 15) was 53 percent black or Hispanic.

Her interviews, though, document the remarkable similarities of the girls' backgrounds and problems. As an example, 80 percent of the girls committed to DYS reported being sexually abused, compared to 73 percent of the girls "receiving services as a child in need of supervision" (Robinson 1990, 311). The difference

between these girls was in the offenses for which they were charged; all the girls receiving services were charged with traditional status offenses (chiefly running away from home and truancy), while the girls committed to DYS were charged with criminal offenses. Here, though, her interviews reveal clear evidence of bootstrapping. Consider, for example, the 16-year-old girl, Beverly, who was committed to DYS for "unauthorized use of a motor vehicle." In this instance, Beverly, who is black, had presumably stolen her mother's car for three hours to go shopping with a friend. Previous to this conviction, according to Robinson's interview, she had been committed to CHINS for "running away from home repeatedly." Beverly told Robinson that her mother had been "advised by the DYS social worker to press charges for unauthorized use of a motor vehicle so that Beverly could be sent to secure detention whenever she was caught on the run" (202).

Other evidence of this pattern is reported by Bartollas (1993) in his study of youths confined in juvenile "institutional" placements in a midwestern state. His research sampled female adolescents in both public and private facilities. The state sample (representing the girls in public facilities) was 61 percent black, while the private sample was 100 percent white. Little difference, however, was found in the offense patterns of the two groups of girls. Seventy percent of the girls in the state sample were "placed in a training school as a result of a status offense" (473). This state, like most states, does not permit youths to be institutionalized for these offenses; however, Bartollas noted that "they can be placed on probation, which makes it possible for the juvenile judge to adjudicate them to a training school" (473). In the private sample, only 50 percent were confined for status offenses; the remainder were there for "minor stealing and shoplifting-related offenses" (473). Bartollas also noted that both of these samples of girls had far less extensive juvenile histories than did their boy counterparts.

Programming for girls

National data indicate that, between 1989 and 1993, detentions involving girls increased by 23 percent, compared to an 18 percent increase in boys' detentions (Poe-Yamagata and Butts 1995, 12). Shorter et al. (1996), examining the situation of girls in San Francisco's juvenile justice system, concluded that girls would languish in detention centers waiting for placement, while the boys were released or put in placement. As a result, 60 percent of the girls were detained for more than seven days, compared to only 6 percent of the boys (12).

Despite figures like these, a recent study by the U.S. General Accounting Office of services to status offenders that had, as a major goal, the exploration of the "availability of facilities and services for female and male status offenders" reported that "most of the juvenile justice officials and service providers interviewed told us that status offenders did not need gender-specific treatment or services, except for gynecological services and prenatal care for females" (U.S. General Accounting Office

1995, 5.3). These comments reflect a system that has failed to develop programs shaped by girls' unique situations and failed to address the special problems girls have in a gendered society.

Clearly, after decades of "deinstitutionalization efforts," girls continue to be "all but invisible in programs for youth and in the literature available to those who work with youth" (Davidson 1983, viii; Bergsmann 1989). As an example, the 1993 study by the San Francisco Chapter of the National Organization for Women found that only 8.7 percent of the programs funded by the major organization in San Francisco that funded children and youth programs "specifically addressed the needs of girls" (Siegal 1995). Not surprisingly, then, a 1995 study of youth participation in San Francisco after-school or summer sports programs found that only 26 percent of the participants were girls (Siegal 1995).

In addition, people who work in the juvenile justice system typically prefer working with boys and routinely stress the difficulty of working with girls. Belnap and her colleagues in Ohio reported, in their study of youth workers, that "most of the professionals, unless they worked exclusively with girls, had a difficult time not talking solely about the male delinquents" (Belnap, Dunn, and Holsinger 1997, 28). Likewise, Alder (1997) has noted that "willful" girls produce problems for a system initially devised to handle boys: girls in these systems get constructed as "hysterical," "manipulative," "verbally aggressive," and "untrusting," while boys are "honest," "open," and "less complex." Clearly, the juvenile justice system has its work cut out for it if it hopes to deal fairly with girls, to say nothing of creating programs and services tailored to girls' problems and needs.

What are the specific needs of young women in general and, in particular, those who come into contact with the juvenile justice system, either as victims or offenders? Davidson (1983) argues that "the most desperate need of many young women is to find the economic means of survival" (ix). Other research has stressed homeless girls' urgent needs for housing, jobs, and medical services (Iwamoto, Kameoka, and Brasseur 1990).

The Minnesota Women's Fund noted that the most frequent risk factors for girls and boys differ and that for girls the list includes emotional stress, physical and sexual abuse, negative body image, disordered eating, suicide, and pregnancy. For boys the list included alcohol use, polydrug use, accidental injury, and delinquency (Advisory Task Force 1994). While, clearly, not all girls at risk will end up in the juvenile justice system, this gendered examination of youth problems sets a standard for the examination of delinquency prevention and intervention programs.

Among other needs that girls' programs should address are the following: dealing with the physical and sexual violence in their lives (from parents, boyfriends, pimps, and others), confronting the risk of AIDS, dealing with pregnancy and motherhood, drug and alcohol dependency, facing family problems, vocational and career counseling, managing stress, and developing a sense of efficacy and empowerment. Many of these needs are universal and should be part of programs for all youths (Schwartz and Orlando 1991). Most of these, however, are particularly important for young women.

Alder (1986, 1995) points out that serving girls effectively will require different and innovative strategies since "young men tend to be more noticeable and noticed than young women" (1995, 3). When girls go out, they tend to move in smaller groups, there are greater proscriptions against girls "hanging out," and they may be justly fearful of being on the streets at night. Finally, girls have many more domestic expectations than their boy counterparts, and these may keep them confined to their homes. Alder notes that this may be a particular issue for immigrant girls.

Programs must also be scrutinized to ensure that they are culturally specific as well as gender specific. As increasing numbers of girls of color are drawn into the juvenile justice system (and bootstrapped into correctional settings), while their white counterparts are deinstitutionalized, there is a need for programs to be rooted in specific cultures. Since it is clear that girls of color have different experiences of their gender, as well as different experiences with the dominant institutions in the society (Amaro and Aguiar 1994; Amaro 1995; Orenstein 1994; LaFromboise and Howard-Pitney 1995), programs to divert and deinstitutionalize must be shaped by the unique developmental issues confronting minority girls. In addition, such programs must incorporate the specific cultural resources available in ethnic communities.

The content of gender-specific programs formed within the juvenile justice system requires special vigilance, since the family court has a long history of sexism, particularly in the area of policing girls' sexuality. In fact, the one area where the General Accounting Office found evidence of gender difference was the focus on girls' sexuality. In addition to a fairly routine focus on girls' ability to become pregnant or be pregnant, the researchers reported that institutions that served girls exclusively included testing for sexually transmitted diseases while "at similar male-only facilities operated by the same organizations, such testing was not done unless requested by the males" (U.S. General Accounting Office 1995, 5.2.3). As Kimberly Kempf-Leonard (1998) has recently cautioned, the juvenile justice system's long history of paternalism and sexism makes it a problematic site for gender-specific services. Certainly, the existence of such services should not be used as justification for incarcerating girls, and girl-specific programming should never be an excuse to return to the good old days of girls' institutions where working-class girls were trained in the womanly arts.

Some might even extend Kempf-Leonard's argument to a more general call for an end to the juvenile justice system, given evidence that the system has had a notable lack of success in controlling its own excesses when it comes to policing the non-criminal activities of girls. Certainly,

many of the worst excesses of "state maternalism" (Odem 1995) would be avoided if girls were tried in adult courts.

As is often the case, however, the crafting of solutions to complex problems may produce unanticipated consequences. A quick look at the recent trends in the adult criminal justice system reveals, for example, a disturbing tendency to subject women offenders to a form of justice that might be called vengeful equity. Here, in the name of equal treatment, women are tried, sentenced, and incarcerated as if they were men (Chesney-Lind 1997). The most tangible consequence of this pattern of equality has been the soaring number of women in U.S. prisons. In 1980, there were just over 12,000 women in U.S. state and federal prisons. By 1997, there were 79,624. In about a decade and a half, the number of women being held in the nation's prisons had increased sixfold (Cahalan 1986; U.S. Department of Justice 1998).

In essence, if the juvenile justice system represents the worst excesses of a system that policed and reinforced gender difference, the contemporary adult system epitomizes a system that embraces, often with a troubling zest, a form of equality that penalizes women by failing to recognize real differences (both biological and social) between men and women. This, coupled with the fact that the adult system, and most particularly the adult correctional system, is being overwhelmed by admissions of women inmates, argues for seeking solutions to the problems of girls in a system that, at least currently, is able to entertain the notion of innovation and reform.

The major challenge to those seeking to address the needs of girls within the juvenile justice system remains the invisibility of these young women. The short-lived congressional focus on girls has, unfortunately, been followed by a major retreat from such initiatives. Not only that, but Congress is apparently encouraging the recriminalization of status offenses, which suggests that without powerful, local advocacy, the nation could again see large numbers of young girls incarcerated "for their own protection." A girl-centered response to this backlash, as well as continued pressure on the juvenile justice system to do more to help girls, is essential. Much more, not less, work needs to be done to support the fundamental needs of girls on the margin.

Notes

1. Defined by the Federal Bureau of Investigation as murder, forcible rape, robbery, burglary, aggravated assault, larceny theft, automobile theft, and arson.

2. Both of these bills died at the end of the session of Congress that concluded in December 1998. However, at least one bill with many of the same features was introduced shortly thereafter. On 20 January 1999, Senators Orrin Hatch and Jeff Sessions introduced S. 254, the Violent and Repeat Offender Accountability and Rehabilitation Act of 1999. There are indications that the bill may not have hearings and will be placed on the Senate calendar for a vote.

References

Advisory Task Force on the Female Offender in Corrections. Adolescent Female Subcommittee. 1994. *Needs Assessment and Recommendations for Adolescent Females in Minnesota*. St. Paul: Minnesota Department of Corrections.

Alder, Christine. 1986. "Unemployed Women Have Got It Heaps Worse": Exploring the Implications of Female Youth Unemployment. *Australian and New Zealand Society of Criminology* 19:210-24.

———. 1995. Delinquency Prevention with Young Women. Paper presented at the Delinquency Prevention Conference, Terrigal, New South Wales, Australia.

———. 1997. "Passionate and Willful" Girls: Confronting Practices. Paper presented at the annual meeting of the Academy of Criminal Justice Sciences, Louisville, KY.

Amaro, Hortensia. 1995. Love, Sex, and Power: Considering Women's Realities in HIV Prevention. *American Psychologist* 50(6):437-47.

Amaro, Hortensia and Maria Aguiar. 1994. *Programa Mama: Mom's Project. A Hispanic/Latino Family Approach to Substance Abuse Prevention*. Washington, DC: Department of Health and Human Services, Mental Health Services Administration, Center for Substance Abuse Prevention.

American Association for University Women. 1992. *How Schools Shortchange Girls*. Washington, DC: AAUW Educational Foundation.

Artz, Sibylle. 1998. *Sex, Power and the Violent School Girl*. Toronto: Trifolium Books.

Bartollas, Clemens. 1993. Little Girls Grown Up: The Perils of Institutionalization. In *Female Criminality: The State of the Art*, ed. Concetta Culliver. New York: Garland Press.

Belnap, Joanne, Melissa Dunn, and Kristi Holsinger. 1997. *Gender Specific Services Work Group: Report to the Governor*. Columbus, OH: Office of Criminal Justice Services.

Bergsmann, Ilene R. 1989. The Forgotten Few: Juvenile Female Offenders. *Federal Probation* 53(1):73-78.

Bishop, Donna and Charles Frazier. 1992. Gender Bias in the Juvenile Justice System: Implications of the JJDP Act. *Journal of Criminal Law & Criminology* 82(4):1162-86.

Cahalan, Margaret. 1986. *Historical Corrections Statistics in the United States, 1850-1984.* Washington, DC: Department of Justice, Bureau of Justice Statistics.

Canter, Rachelle J. 1982. Sex Differences in Self-Report Delinquency. *Criminology* 20:373-93.

Chesney-Lind, Meda. 1988. Girls in Jail. *Crime & Delinquency* 34(2):150-68.

———. 1997. *The Female Offender: Girls, Women and Crime.* Thousand Oaks, CA: Sage.

Chesney-Lind, Meda and Randall G. Shelden. 1997. *Girls, Delinquency, and the Juvenile Justice System.* 2d ed. Belmont, CA: Wadsworth.

Coalition for Juvenile Justice. 1997. Legislative Summary. Internal memo, 8 Aug.

Costello, Jan C. and Nancy L. Worthington. 1981. Incarcerating Status Offenders: Attempts to Circumvent the Juvenile Justice and Delinquency Prevention Act. *Harvard Civil Rights–Civil Liberties Law Review* 16:41-81.

Currie, Elliot. 1998. *Crime and Punishment in America.* New York: Metropolitan Books.

Davidson, Sue. 1983. *The Second Mile: Contemporary Approaches in Counseling Young Women.* Tucson, AZ: New Directions for Young Women.

Dembo, Richard, Linda Williams, and James Schmeidler. 1993. Gender Differences in Mental Health Service Needs Among Youths Entering a Juvenile Detention Center. *Journal of Prison and Jail Health* 12:73-101.

———. 1995. Gender Differences in Service Needs Among Youths Entering a Juvenile Assessment Center: A Replication Study. Paper presented at the annual meeting of the Society of Social Problems, Washington, DC.

Finkelhor, David and Larry Baron. 1986. Risk Factors for Child Sexual Abuse. *Journal of Interpersonal Violence* 1:43-71.

Girls Incorporated. 1996. *Prevention and Parity: Girls in Juvenile Justice.* Indianapolis, IN: Girls Incorporated National Resource Center.

Hsieh, Chang-ming. 1998. Personal communication with the author.

Huizinga, David. 1997. *Over-Time Changes in Delinquency and Drug-Use: The 1970's to the 1990's.* Boulder: University of Colorado, Institute of Behavioral Science.

Iwamoto, Juanita J., Keith Kameoka, and Yvette C. Brasseur. 1990. *Waikiki Homeless Youth Project: A Report.* Honolulu, HI: Catholic Services to Families.

Jamieson, Katherine M. and Timothy Flanagan, eds. 1989. *Sourcebook of Criminal Justice Statistics—1988.* Washington, DC: Department of Justice, Bureau of Justice Statistics.

Kempf-Leonard, Kimberly. 1998. Disparity Based on Sex: Is Gender Specific Treatment Warranted? University of Missouri, St. Louis. Paper.

Krisberg, Barry, Robert DeComo, Norma C. Herrera, Martha Steketee, and Sharon Roberts. 1991. *Juveniles Taken into Custody: Fiscal Year 1990 Report.* San Francisco: National Council on Crime and Delinquency.

Kunzel, Regina. 1993. *Fallen Women and Problem Girls: Unmarried Mothers and the Professionalization of Social Work, 1890-1945.* New Haven, CT: Yale University Press.

LaFromboise, Teresa D. and Beth Howard-Pitney. 1995. Suicidal Behavior in American Indian Female

Adolescents. In *Women and Suicidal Behavior*, ed. S. Canetto and D. Lester. New York: Springer Publishing.

Leslie, Connie, Nina Biddle, Debra Rosenberg, and Joe Wayne. 1993. Girls Will Be Girls. *Newsweek*, 2 Aug., 44.

Loper, Ann B. and Dewey G. Cornell. 1996. Homicide by Girls. *Journal of Child and Family Studies* 5:321-33.

Mayer, Judith. 1994. Girls in the Maryland Juvenile Justice System: Findings of the Female Population Taskforce. Presentation at Gender Specific Services Training, Minneapolis, MN.

McCormack, A., M. D. Janus, and A. W. Burgess. 1986. Runaway Youths and Sexual Victimization: Gender Differences in an Adolescent Runaway Population. *Child Abuse & Neglect* 10:387-95.

Miller, Jody. 1994. Race, Gender and Juvenile Justice: An Examination of Disposition Decision-Making for Delinquent Girls. In *The Intersection of Race, Gender and Class in Criminology*, ed. Martin D. Schwartz and Dragan Milovanovic. New York: Garland Press.

Moone, Joseph. 1993a. *Children in Custody: Private Facilities*. Washington, DC: Department of Justice, Office of Juvenile Justice and Delinquency Prevention.

———. 1993b. *Children in Custody: Public Facilities*. Washington, DC: Department of Justice, Office of Juvenile Justice and Delinquency Prevention.

———. 1997. *Juveniles in Private Facilities, 1991-1995*. Washington, DC: Department of Justice.

National Criminal Justice Association. 1997. Congressional Roundup. *Justice Bulletin* 17(4):1-3.

Odem, Mary E. 1995. *Delinquent Daughters*. Chapel Hill: University of North Carolina Press.

Orenstein, Peggy. 1994. *School Girls*. New York: Doubleday.

Platt, Anthony M. 1969. *The Child Savers*. Chicago: University of Chicago Press.

Poe-Yamagata, Eileen and Jeffrey A. Butts. 1995. *Female Offenders in the Juvenile Justice System*. Pittsburgh, PA: National Center for Juvenile Justice.

Pub. L. 96-509. 94 Stat. 2697, 1981.

Pub. L. 102-586. 106 Stat. 498, 1992.

Robinson, Robin. 1990. Violations of Girlhood: A Qualitative Study of Female Delinquents and Children in Need of Services in Massachusetts. Ph.D. diss., Brandeis University.

Schiraldi, Vincent and Mark Soler. 1998. *The Will of the People? The Public's Opinion of the Violent and Repeat Juvenile Offender Act of 1997*. Washington, DC: Justice Policy Institute and Youth Law Center.

Schwartz, Ira M. and Frank Orlando. 1991. *Programming for Young Women in the Juvenile Justice System*. Ann Arbor: University of Michigan, School of Social Work, Center for the Study of Youth Policy.

Shelden, Randall. 1995. Personal communication with the author.

Shelden, Randy and John Horvath. 1986. Processing Offenders in a Juvenile Court: A Comparison of Male and Female Offenders. Paper presented at the annual meeting of the Western Society of Criminology, Newport Beach, CA.

Shorter, Andrea D., Laurie Schaffner, Shelley Shick, and Nancy Stein Frappier. 1996. *Out of Sight, Out of Mind: The Plight of Girls in the San Francisco Juvenile Justice System*. San Francisco: Center for Juvenile and Criminal Justice.

Siegal, Nina. 1995. Where the Girls Are. *San Francisco Bay Guardian*, 4 Oct.

Steffensmeier, Darrell J. and Renee Hoffman Steffensmeier. 1980. Trends in Female Delinquency: An Examination of Arrest, Juvenile Court, Self-

Report, and Field Data. *Criminology* 18:62-85.

U.S. Department of Justice. Bureau of Justice Statistics. 1998. *Prisoners in 1997*. Washington, DC: Department of Justice.

U.S. Department of Justice. Federal Bureau of Investigation. 1997. *Crime in the United States 1996*. Washington, DC: Government Printing Office.

U.S. General Accounting Office. 1995. *Juvenile Justice: Minimal Gender Bias Occurring in Processing Non-Criminal Juveniles*. Washington, DC: General Accounting Office.

U.S. House. Committee on Education and Labor. Subcommittee on Human Resources. 1992. *Hearings on the Juvenile Justice and Delinquency in Prevention Act of 1974*. 102d Cong., 2d sess.

Ziedenberg, Jason and Vincent Schiraldi. 1997. *The Risks Juveniles Face When They Are Incarcerated with Adults*. Washington, DC: Justice Policy Institute.

ANNALS, *AAPSS*, **564**, July 1999

The Attack on Juvenile Justice

By RUSSELL K. VAN VLEET

ABSTRACT: As juvenile crime increased during the last two decades, the juvenile justice system came under unprecedented scrutiny and criticism for its perceived inability to respond to this increase and to provide interventions that might thwart juvenile crime. As this offending became more lethal, with juvenile homicide rates increasing by more than 200 percent in some jurisdictions, the abolishment of the juvenile court was called for. Get-tough reforms, mostly in the form of boot camps, were established in the hope that physical exercise and discipline would provide a welcome relief to the perceived softness of the juvenile system. These camps also embodied the popular notion that punishment had disappeared and that its reintroduction would somehow lead to a general deterrence causing crime rates to plummet. Violent crime rose, but general crime rates dropped. Research efforts could not connect these declines to the boot camp phenomenon, however. In addition, violent juvenile crime led to an increase in the waiver of many young offenders to the adult criminal justice system, bringing into question the notion of diminished capacity and its relationship to crime and punishment.

Russell K. Van Vleet is an adjunct assistant professor and director of the Center for the Study of Youth Policy, University of Utah. He was formerly the director of the Utah State Division of Youth Corrections and was a prominent figure when Utah transformed its youth corrections system into a national model. He has served as a consultant to organizations in 49 states, has conducted workshops and training, and has authored several booklets and articles pertaining to juvenile justice reform.

THE juvenile court, anticipating its hundredth anniversary in 1999, finds itself the subject of an unwonted attack suggesting that it has failed in its mission of rehabilitation. Its perceived failure and the rise in juvenile offending, specifically in violent crime, have raised the question of the efficacy of the juvenile court and clouded its future. This breach of confidence and the concomitant failure of the juvenile court, while caught in this maelstrom, to exert its purpose in a powerful and united manner have led to a partial abandonment of that system and lent credence to the assertion of Professor Barry Feld that the juvenile court should be abolished (Feld 1990).

Get-tough measures, mostly in the form of boot camps and waiver to the adult system, have gained favor in most state legislatures, have returned much of the youth correction system to the training school mentality that was largely abandoned during the decades of deinstitutionalization (the 1970s and 1980s), and have left the court in the philosophical and political quagmire of an institution without a purpose or a defined constituency. That an increase in juvenile offending should give rise to a question of the efficacy of a juvenile justice system is without precedent, somewhat defiant of explanation, and suggestive of a society pushed to its limit with adolescents packing guns and menacing entire neighborhoods.

Juvenile offending began to rise in the 1970s and continued its growth into the 1990s. This alone would not have been so remarkable or elicited a national reaction except for one major characteristic of these offending patterns: their lethality. Kids began killing other kids in record numbers, and, even more frightening, they began to threaten to kill the rest of us. Gang members' killing gang members was not necessarily news, especially if the killing was confined to the proper barrio. When the killing fields expanded into mainstream society and middle-class neighborhoods, with drive-by shootings and killings of tourists, and, incredibly, into the schools in Kentucky, Oregon, and Arkansas, a national panic commenced that initiated a search for an explanation.

The juvenile justice system became the scapegoat. It became symbolic of a generation of youths perceived as being without discipline or respect. The juvenile court was viewed as being part of this modern adolescent social anomie. Judges were too sympathetic and were not sufficiently punitive to restore the lost social order. They were seemingly lost in a sea of juvenile crime and became the target for those wishing to affix blame for the rise in violent juvenile offending. A society impatient for a juvenile justice response adequately punitive to warrant its retention began to expose what many viewed as the rehabilitative failure of the juvenile court.

Last year, Arizona passed Proposition 102, giving local prosecutors much more discretion to waive large numbers of youths from the juvenile court to the adult courts. This was done, in effect, to express a vote of no confidence for the juvenile justice system in that state and is, to date, the most literal expression of this public loss of conviction in the juvenile justice system.

WAIVER

Waiver to the adult court has been a tool that prosecutors have utilized for those youths who, theoretically, would benefit from the sanctions available in the adult corrections system, mainly incarceration in adult prisons. Frazier, Bishop, and Lanza-Kaduce (1996) confirmed what many practitioners had experienced with waiver. Many youths waived to the adult court were not always the most chronic or severe offenders, nor did they receive the harsher sanctions available in the adult system. Often these youths would be remanded to the adult court only to be out on bail, placed on probation, and infrequently receiving incarceration in an adult corrections facility. Notwithstanding this research, legislators rushed to enact legislation empowering local prosecutors to greatly expand their options for waiver because the expectation of harsh punishment, embodied within the get-tough philosophy, was seen as a solution to youth crime (Schwartz et al. 1995).

In virtually all states, in response to public pressure, legislatures are lowering the minimum age at which waiver could be considered, lowering the maximum age of juvenile court jurisdiction, shifting the burden to the defendant to prove that he or she should remain in the juvenile system, and increasing legislative waiver that mandates to the courts the ages and offending histories of those youths who will be waived

(Schwartz et al. 1995). Most important, Frazier, Bishop, and Lanza-Kaduce (1996) found that "the best available evidence indicates that the rush to impose adult status on juveniles is neither reducing juvenile crime nor enhancing public safety" (40). In other words, as waivers to the criminal justice system increased, it became clear that waiver was not having the desired effect. Adult jurisdictions were still reluctant, regardless of juvenile histories, to impose prison sentences on many chronic and serious juvenile offenders. Moreover, in some jurisdictions, youths in state youth correctional facilities were committing assaults on staff in order to be waived since that option carried with it the opportunity of bail and probation. Indeed, some youths actually received, through the waiver process, a lesser sanction than they would have received had they been retained within the juvenile system. Not only was waiver not consistently getting tough, but in some instances it was getting softer.

The get-tough movement has also affected the behaviors of the juvenile system. The juvenile court, for example, wanting to be perceived as responsive to the offending patterns of juveniles of the 1990s and to the demands for harsher treatment by the public, is placing more emphasis on incarceration. We are also witnessing a growing tendency to send to the juvenile court youths for whom the juvenile justice system has spent the previous 20 years developing community-based sanctions through various deinstitutionalization initiatives. This includes petty juvenile offenders and, most recently, status offenders, with a reintroduction of female and minority offenders to detention centers that had been deinstitutionalized through the Office of Juvenile Justice and Delinquency Prevention mandates enacted by Congress in 1974. Detention centers in particular are feeling the impact. In just a few short years, these centers have become akin to the "hidden closets" (Schwartz et al. 1987) that existed prior to the Juvenile Justice and Delinquency Prevention Act of 1974, which mandated, for those choosing to participate under the act, that status offenders be removed from detention.

FEDERAL ROLE

The federal government has also begun to weigh in on the juvenile justice issue. Years ago, the federal government operated youth correctional facilities for those youths in need of incarceration after committing federal offenses. The utility of those facilities came under question, and they were closed. Currently, there are efforts to enact legislation in Congress designed to federalize juvenile crime by giving U.S. Attorneys options to prosecute youths as adults "if there is a prevailing Federal interest" (Violent and Repeat Offender Act of 1997, 8). This legislation would eliminate most of the mandates that were part of the original Juvenile Justice and Delinquency Prevention Act of 1974, including the incarceration of juveniles in adult jails for up to 72 hours, elimination of the interest in responding to issues of disproportionate minority confinement,

and encouragement of states to reduce the waiver age to 14.

JUVENILE OFFENDING

An interesting thing has happened, however, on the way to blaming and perhaps dismantling the juvenile justice system. Juvenile offending has declined. Juvenile crime has been decreasing since 1993 according to the official reports of the Federal Bureau of Investigation and annual reporting from the Office of Juvenile Justice and Delinquency Prevention. More important, violent offending also has decreased (Snyder 1998). There may be many reasons for this downward trend. For example, improved police activity, including a renewed emphasis on community policing and targeting large urban areas where the majority of killings by juveniles occurred, and an increased emphasis on incarceration of young offenders are possible reasons. Regardless of the reasons that offending is down, however, it is important to ask the question, Why is there a continued effort to discredit the juvenile court and to replace it with adult sanctions, including a federal component?

PURPOSE OF THE JUVENILE JUSTICE SYSTEM

Even the most ardent critic of the juvenile court would be unlikely to claim that its continued existence depends on the elimination of delinquency. But the very least it should do is punish the perpetrators. Punishment should lead to a suppression of future delinquency through generalized fear. Therein lies the controversy. The historical mission of the juvenile system has primarily been to rehabilitate offenders, not to punish them. *Parens patriae* ("in the interest of") continues to be a key organizing factor of the court. We put the young people in secure care, not in jail or prison. Punishment was part of the system during its formative stages (in the form of sheltered workshops or youth indenturing) (Boss 1967), but a hundred years later, its proper place is unclear, leading to confusion and disagreement about the system's real purpose.

In the past decade about one quarter of the states have redefined the purposes of their courts (Feld 1988, 842, n. 84). These amendments de-emphasize the role of rehabilitation and the child's "best interest," and elevate the importance of public safety, punishment, and individual and juvenile justice system accountability (Walkover 1984). (Feld 1992, 72)

CURRENT STATUS

The problem with determining the propriety of punishing or not punishing is that punishment in the adult criminal justice system oftentimes closely resembles treatment in the juvenile justice system (Feld 1990). Regardless of carefully worded mission statements that purport to offer rehabilitation, juvenile systems in the United States have been providing punishment, although calling it something else, for most of its existence (U.S. Department of Justice 1994). For example, the 1967 report of the President's Commission on Law Enforcement and the Administration of Justice declared that training schools (secure care facilities for youths) in the United States were a failure. They did not protect the public because rates of unallowed absences were high, and youths who graduated from such facilities were more likely than not to continue committing crimes. Moreover, in the name of treatment, youths, regardless of the crimes they committed, were often housed in large open campuses that were severely overcrowded, that had virtually no individualized programming, and that were staffed by individuals who were ill equipped to work with troubled and troubling youths. Because all youths who committed crimes in a particular state were housed together in these facilities regardless of the nature and severity of their offenses, smaller, less sophisticated, and weaker residents were often housed alongside hardened and tougher youthful offenders and subjected by the latter to sexual assaults, intimidation, harassment, and physical confrontations commonly associated with prisons.

Could we not call placement in many, if not most, of those facilities punishment? If one questions this assumption, it is only necessary to examine the number of public juvenile facilities under court order due to conditions of confinement that could not meet the minimum professional standards established by the American Corrections Association or the American Bar Association. My own experience, from visiting training schools in the majority of these United States, is that most are overcrowded, understaffed, abusive, and therefore punitive.

From the start of the training school system, which began about the same time as the juvenile court, it has been a fundamental component of the juvenile justice system. Any objective observer would have to conclude that it was punishment and not rehabilitation that defined that system. Since punishment has been an integral part of the juvenile justice system since its inception, the get-tough-through-waiver movement is ill advised. An objective look at the juvenile system, especially the legacy of the nation's training schools, cannot suggest that a lack of punishment within that system has somehow led to an increase in youth crime; the remedy is more punishment within the adult criminal justice system. Since punishment has always been inherent within the juvenile system, the debate should be about treatment, not punishment. Treatment is ill defined, devoid of outcome measures, and confused with punishment for at least two reasons: diminished capacity, and deterrence.

DIMINISHED CAPACITY

Diminished capacity (Morse 1984) is the concept that youths, simply by virtue of their age, are less culpable for their acts than are adults. The entire premise for the development of a separate juvenile court was a general acceptance that youths are not simply little adults. Due to their brief life span, they have not had the opportunity to achieve adult capacities physically, intellectually, or emotionally. This lack of maturation requires a separate and presumably less punitive response to their actions. This has, for the past 100 years, been reinforced through the adoption by the juvenile court of legal processes that differed substantially from those of the criminal court.

The criminal court has generally been reserved for those whose chronological age assumed a maturation level consistent with adult sanctions. The juvenile court began to change with the *In re Gault* decision (*In re Gault*, 387 U.S. 1 [1967]), and states have modified legal processes allowing youths, usually due to certain kinds of offending and with a minimum age requirement, most commonly 14, to be waived to the adult court to stand trial as an adult. This was necessary because some acts, most notably homicide, are so reprehensible that maturation levels are less important with respect to culpability than is the need to punish in order to provide a portion of retribution to the community, especially surviving family members of the victims.

The juvenile systems in most states would allow incarceration only to age 18. The simple matter of time served for a specific act mandated adult court prosecution. As juvenile offending has become more violent, the issue of diminished capacity has become lost in the rush to assess punishment that presumably is available in the adult criminal justice system. What is missing in much of the discussion regarding the transfer of youths to the adult courts is that the expectation of reducing juvenile crime or enhancing public safety is secondary, in the mind of the public, to retribution for the act committed by the delinquent.

How much do we care, as a society, about diminished capacity? We retain this concept for almost every other rite of passage for our children: voting, marriage, driving, drinking, and so on. A person is presumed to attain certain capacities with the passing of years that enable him or her emotionally to assume responsibility for the privileges accorded only to those with adult status.

We are quite reluctant, given the current collective public attitude toward juvenile crime, to allow a lack of responsibility to mitigate punishment for youthful offenders. What this may suggest, of course, is not so much a lack of confidence in the juvenile court as a lack of jurisdiction. Adults can be held for life. Youths cannot. It seems quite clear that youths responsible for multiple homicides (as evidenced by the recent shootings in the public schools of Arkansas, Oregon, and Kentucky) are not going to be sufficiently punished within the limitations of time imposed by the jurisdictional requirements of the juvenile systems within those states. Is anyone within the juvenile system willing to defend time and its relationship to developmental stages, thus suggesting that time served is quite different for youths and for adults? Does six years of punishment of a 12-year-old equal 12 years of punishment for an adult? If the average adult receiving a life sentence is paroled in 10 years, then why would 6 years within a juvenile system not equal approximately the same sentence? Even if the

developmental theorists could provide a convincing argument for parity of time served due to maturation differences, would that be sufficient to convince the courts and, more important, the public that such a sentence was justice? Probably not, and for at least one related reason: deterrence.

DETERRENCE

Treatment and rehabilitation are, in the minds of most people, antithetical to punishment and deterrence. The juvenile system, with its emphasis on rehabilitation, is viewed as soft and incapable of exerting the necessary punishment to deter youths from future offending. Only incarceration in a relatively harsh environment would be sufficiently punitive to shock young offenders into a realization that crime does not pay. So say many politicians in what they claim is a response to the general attitude of their constituents. The problem is that empirical evidence supporting incarceration as a general deterrence to future offending, at least among chronically delinquent youths, is mostly lacking. "Few if any practitioners believe that strict discipline and harsh living conditions on their own will lead to behavioral changes" (Greenwood 1995, 110). The evidence supporting the crime-reduction effect of punishment-oriented policies is lacking or negative (Krisberg 1987, cited in Schwartz 1992, 14).

Juvenile justice often views the deprivation of freedom, whether through incarceration or other staff-secure alternatives, as punishment with treatment components added on. Treatment, as viewed by those offering it, is not soft nor is it always welcomed by the offenders. It is not uncommon for youthful offenders to opt for incarceration in lieu of treatment alternatives since many of them would simply rather do time than be required to engage in a treatment regime that is less certain, often is more labor intensive, and requires some emotional and intellectual commitments.

A commonsense approach to juvenile justice continues to be the kick in the pants. While that is a metaphor for punishment, meaning incarceration, it includes an expectation that once the kick is administered, it will result in an awakening within the offender. It will be a lesson well learned, and the recalcitrant youth, having learned the error of his ways, will now emerge repentant and prepared to lead a productive, law-abiding life. The most recent example of the translation of this attitude into action is the proliferation of boot camps in the last several years. Fueled by a belief that juvenile justice is soft and that a little toughening up would be in everyone's best interest, boot camps were developed in jurisdictions from coast to coast. Unhappily, the research on boot camps is similar to that on deterrence. Parent (1993) conducted an extensive literature review of boot camps and found "no evidence of significant impact on recidivism rates" (146). "There are numerous studies and evaluations of the boot camp correctional model, virtually all of them finding that the evidence of their efficacy is either negative or inconclusive" (Nabors 1997, 2).

UNINTENDED CONSEQUENCE

While we continue to be enamored of deterrence and remain hopeful that somehow a national get-tough response will affect offending, the more likely result will be a reexamination of the proper role of the juvenile court and a possible renewed emphasis on prevention. The reason that prevention may finally be given serious consideration is the realization that the cost of incarceration, regardless of its real or perceived general deterrent benefit, is simply too high. Costs of prison construction and operation are beginning to outstrip dollars spent on education in some states, leaving the politician to ponder his commitment to incarceration against the reality of the dollars available for total government spending.

Prevention may finally be given consideration because juvenile justice agencies are recognizing that early intervention, as defined by the courts, is traditional probation services. Traditional probation services are not instituted until the youth has become a delinquent, usually as a result of school failure and minor delinquency such as truancy, smoking, or shoplifting. These services are still too little (caseloads are large) too late (the youth already has adopted a delinquent pattern). Various programs may show success, but intervening with a 12- or 13-year-old who already has a seven- or eight-year history of offending is less likely to be successful than a similar intervention with a 5- to 6-year-old who has been identified by the school system as delinquency prone. Factors such as poor school performance, apathy, behavioral problems, low self-esteem, and feelings of inferiority, often the result of broken homes and cultural, social, or economic deprivation, may also contribute.

Catalano and Hawkins (1996) have developed a theory of antisocial behavior, the social development model, which looks at risk and protective factors for delinquency, crime, and substance abuse. The risk factors include the following:

community norms favorable to [delinquency, crime, and substance abuse], neighborhood disorganization, extreme economic deprivation, family history of drug abuse or crime, poor family management practices, family conflict, low family bonding, parental permissiveness, early and persistent problem behaviors, academic failure, peer rejection in elementary grades, association with drug-using or delinquent peers or adults, alienation and rebelliousness, attitudes favorable to drug use and crime, and early onset of drug use or criminal behavior. (152-53)

As we have become more aware of the relationship between these factors and delinquency, the role of the juvenile court as a change agent has been brought into question since these youths often become known to the court at an early age.

NEW ROLE FOR THE COURT

Over the last several decades, the jurisdiction of the juvenile court has eroded considerably. The deinstitutionalization movement of the 1970s suggested diversion from the court for status offenders (offenses that are offenses only for minors). Thus the role of the court as an intervening agent with these offenders through court programs for truant, ungovernable, and runaway youths became confused. During the 1980s and into the 1990s, the national get-tough response said that since the juvenile court did not punish youths, it could not be trusted with the more serious and violent offenders. The passing of youthful offender legislation (to enhance prosecutorial discretion in the use of the adult system with certain classes of youthful offenders) began removing this population from the juvenile court. What was left was a so-called burglary court, that is, a court reserved for a class of offenders, mostly property offenders, who were too old for early intervention, too young for punishment, and the least likely, due to chronicity of offending, to respond to treatment opportunities available to them within the juvenile court system.

There are many signs that the juvenile court of the pre-1970s is coming back. As the court's jurisdiction over serious offenders is eroded by legislation, survival seems to dictate the renewed inclusion of status offenders, along with "burglars" (a generic term for minor property offenders), as the proper clientele for the juvenile court of the next decade. The court needs to advocate clearly and strongly for the remanding of a certain percentage of youths to the adult courts. Dr. Marvin Wolfgang, in his famous Philadelphia cohort study, told us that a very small percentage, 6 percent, of offenders commit the majority of crimes. By the time youths are 15 to 18 years old, if they have been part of a progressive juvenile justice system, they would have been exposed to many opportunities for rehabilitation. After that exposure and if offending continues, the youths should be waived to the adult court. This should be done because these youths can be presumed to have been self-identified as part of the criminal cohort described by Dr. Wolfgang or, failing that assumption, because they simply do not warrant additional expenditure of very scarce resources.

The adult system is not confused about its role. Incarceration is for the protection of the public. The juvenile system needs to become just as clear. There are youths who require transfer to the adult system, thus liberating additional resources for those youths more susceptible to rehabilitative efforts. The court should place renewed emphasis on younger offenders, recognize the connection between school failure and delinquency, and arm probation departments with resources for earlier intervention. Success in school may well be the best delinquency-prevention tool available to any of us.

In Farmington, New Mexico, youths known to the court who are also failing in school are referred to a grade court. School attendance and school assignments become part of the probation experience. An evaluation of this court is currently being conducted by the Social Research Institute of the University of Utah. The goal of the court is to help youths

succeed in school. Truancy and school failure are again, after many years of absence, an integral concern of the court, at least in this jurisdiction. It is appropriate to question the propriety of this intervention not because of its intent but because of the possible or probable unintended consequences. Some fear that the intervention is not warranted and that introducing these youths into the system simply greases the banister for their deposit into the black hole of criminal justice. They are penetrating a system, and the further the penetration, the worse they will become. Why are we not, as a society, asking why the schools do not assume this responsibility? School failure as a precursor of delinquency is documented in detail throughout the literature, yet it becomes a function of the court only through the failure of other social institutions to more appropriately intervene.

In most states, the family services division of the social services agency would be the most appropriate agency for youngsters in danger of failing out of school, but just try to find one out there that is taking this responsibility. Education departments are responding to these youths with expulsion, claiming that their mandate is to educate those who are willing and eager to learn effectively and to eliminate those at-risk youths who we all know are our next juvenile delinquents. The expulsion becomes a self-fulfilling prophecy for these kids. Youthful-offender categories should be established in each state. Waiving youths to the adult system is not the answer;

incarceration within a juvenile system for the most chronic and serious offenders is. Rather than reducing the role of juvenile justice on the punishment end of juvenile offending, that role should be acknowledged, welcomed, and expanded. Age limitations should be extended to 21. Questions regarding diminished capacity would mostly be addressed with this change.

Concurrent jurisdiction should be established for those youths who are both very young and in need of long-term incarceration. Currently, the juvenile system, with only a few exceptions, requires placement in either the adult or juvenile system. This is appropriate for most offenders. The nature of the offending and the history of the offender can be examined, and the judicial process can allow for a decision to be made regarding proper prosecution, either juvenile or adult. A few select cases—almost exclusively concerning young males under 14 years of age who commit multiple homicides—create legal dilemmas for us. States can develop guidelines for concurrent jurisdiction so that these offenders, meeting strict criteria, could be placed in a juvenile system pending their maturation. Hearings held annually could determine continued length of stay and appropriate system, either adult or juvenile, for their continued incarceration.

THE FUTURE OF
THE JUVENILE COURT

Lisbeth Schorr (1988) talks about the high cost of "rotten outcomes" (3-7). One of the "rotten outcomes," delinquency, can be reduced because we have the benefit of the past 100 years of experience to help us link our knowledge of factors that lead to delinquency to interventions that will help ameliorate the delinquency-promoting conditions that currently plague our neighborhoods. The frustration in our current society is that, although the knowledge is available, its application defies us. Agencies grapple with responsibility, courts struggle with jurisdiction, and both try to determine the best application of scarce resources. The end result seems to be a perpetuation of the norm.

References

Boss, Peter. 1967. *Social Policy and the Young Delinquent*. London: Routledge & Kegan Paul.

Catalano, Richard F. and J. David Hawkins. 1996. The Social Development Model: A Theory of Antisocial Behavior. In *Delinquency and Crime: Current Theories*, ed. J. David Hawkins. New York: Cambridge University Press.

Feld, Barry C. 1988. Juvenile Court Meets the Principle of Offense: Punishment, Treatment, and the Difference It Makes. *Boston University Law Review* 68:821-915.

———. 1990. Transformed but Unreformed: Juvenile Court and the Criminal Court Alternative. Paper presented at the meeting of the American Society of Criminology, Baltimore, MD.

———. 1992. Criminalizing the Juvenile Court: A Research Agenda for the 1990s. In *Juvenile Justice and Public Policy: Toward a National Agenda*, ed. Ira M. Schwartz. Lexington, MA: Lexington Books.

Frazier, Charles E., Donna M. Bishop, and Lonn Lanza-Kaduce. 1996. "Get Tough" Juvenile Reforms: Does "Adultification" Make Matters Worse? Paper presented at a symposium at the University of Pennsylvania School of Law, Philadelphia.

Greenwood, Peter W. 1995. Juvenile Crime and Juvenile Justice. In *Crime*, ed. James Q. Wilson and Joan Petersilia. San Francisco: Institute for Contemporary Studies.

Krisberg, Barry. 1987. Preventing and Controlling Violent Youth Crime. In *Violent Youth Crime: What Do We Know About It and What Can We Do About It?* ed. Ira M. Schwartz. Minneapolis: University of Minnesota, Hubert H. Humphrey Institute of Public Affairs.

Morse, Stephen J. 1984. Undiminished Confusion in Diminished Capacity. *Journal of Criminal Law & Criminology* 75:20-21.

Nabors, Finis. 1997. Boot Camps and Therapeutic Interventions: Correctional Treatment Options for Juvenile Offenders. Paper presented at Laurel Ridge Hospital.

Parent, D. C. 1993. Boot Camps Failing to Achieve Goals. *Overcrowded Times* 4(1):12-15.

President's Commission on Law Enforcement and the Administration of Justice. 1967. *Juvenile Delinquency and Youth Crime*. Washington, DC: Department of Justice.

Schorr, Lisbeth. 1988. *Within Our Reach*. New York: Doubleday.

Schwartz, Ira M., ed. 1992. *Juvenile Justice and Public Policy: Toward a National Agenda*. Lexington, MA: Lexington Books.

Schwartz, Ira M., Gideon Fishman, Radene Rawson Hatfield, Barry A. Krisberg, and Zvi Eisikovits. 1987. Juvenile Detention: The Hidden Closets Revisited. *Justice Quarterly* 4(2): 220-34.

Schwartz, Ira M., Russell Van Vleet, Frank Orlando, and Suzanne McMurphy. 1995. A Study of New Mexico's Youthful Offenders. Center for the Study of Youth Policy, University of Pennsylvania. Study.

Snyder, Howard. 1998. Decline in Juvenile Violent Crime. *NCJJ in Brief* Apr.

U.S. Department of Justice. Office of Juvenile Justice and Delinquency Prevention. 1994. *Conditions of Confinement: Juvenile Detention and Corrections Facilities*. NCJ 141873.

Walkover, A. 1984. The Infancy Defense in the New Juvenile Court. *University of California at Los Angeles Law Review* 31:503-62.

Book Department

INTERNATIONAL RELATIONS AND POLITICS

COHEN, RAYMOND. 1997. *Negotiating Across Cultures: International Communication in an Interdependent World.* 2d ed. Pp. xvi, 268. Washington, DC: U.S. Institute of Peace Press. Paperbound, $19.95.

In 1995, the United States and India negotiated rights for their airlines. Air India sought the right to take on passengers in London and fly them to Chicago, while United Airlines wanted to land in New Delhi as part of its new round-the-world service. United advertised the inauguration date of this service even before the negotiations concluded. An example of the American "habit of urgency," as Cohen puts it, this—coupled with an obligation to succeed—left U.S. negotiators "without a leg to stand on."

This is just one of the 35 bilateral negotiations between the United States and five other countries (China, Egypt, India, Japan, and Mexico) that Cohen taps in his attempt to demonstrate the effects of cultural dissonance on negotiation outcomes and parties' broader relationships. Each main chapter of his book focuses on a stage of negotiation (pre-negotiation, opening moves, middle game, end game) and contrasts American actions and interpretations with those of the other countries. Ultimately, Cohen argues that these countries generally do not follow the result-oriented, individualistic, American approach; their "high context" alternative centers on parties' relationships, concern about status and face, and use of language to maintain harmony rather than to transmit information or to persuade.

What Cohen does best is show us how and why "cultural gaps" occur. He also effectively synthesizes streams of work in anthropology, linguistics, and negotiation. There are gems of insight throughout his book, as seen in the chapter "What Is Negotiable" and in the concluding chapter, which lists action recommendations for American negotiators.

On the other hand, the book does not make a convincing causal link between cultural dissonance and inferior negotiation outcomes. Cohen's stated purpose is cultural analysis that targets meaning, not causation, but his position on the significance of culture rests on its consequences. The negotiation vignettes highlight culture, outside the context of other influencing factors such as interests and power, so the reader cannot assess culture's relative impact. Further, the organization of the book produces only a fragmentary picture of the alternative, "high context" negotiation paradigm. Finally, the book's title suggests a more inclusive treatment of culture than dissonance alone—treatment that would address also the up side of cross-cultural interaction.

This is an enjoyable compilation that complements the literature on interna-

215

tional negotiation that has ignored cultural factors. For scholars and practitioners anchored in an American perspective on the subject, it is a must read.

STEPHEN E. WEISS
York University
Toronto
Ontario
Canada

HAMMOND, SUSAN WEBB. 1998. *Congressional Caucuses in National Policy Making*. Pp. xiv, 257. Baltimore, MD: Johns Hopkins University Press. No price.

For approximately two decades, Susan Webb Hammond has chronicled the formation, activities, and influence of congressional caucuses. Her early work brought the existence of these actors on the congressional stage to the attention of the community of congressional scholars. Her more recent work has focused on the influence of these caucuses at various points in time. In the present book, she has drawn a complete picture, showing the variety of congressional caucuses and how different types of caucuses have affected the Congress in different ways.

In part, the difficulty of Hammond's task results from the variety of organizations that have been collectively referred to as congressional caucuses. While her database includes information on more than 150 different caucuses that have been in existence for all or part of the three decades since the formation of the first such group, the Democratic Study Group, she manages those data by creating a typology of caucus types: party caucuses (such as the Democratic Study Group or the Conservative Opportunity Society); personal-interest caucuses (such as the Arms Control and Foreign Policy Caucus); national-constituency caucuses (such as the Congressional Black Caucus); regional caucuses (such as the Northeast-Midwest Congressional Coalition); state or district caucuses (such as the Rural Caucus); and industry caucuses (such as the Coal Caucus).

Hammond proceeds to look at the formation, life cycle, membership, and influence of caucuses, examining each type of caucus separately for each topic. She also analyzes how each type of caucus interacts with party leaders, with the executive branch, with congressional committees, and with members (distinguishing caucus members from nonmembers) as they cast votes on the floor. While Hammond demonstrates a familiarity with a wide array of theoretical literature on the Congress, her guiding principle is organization theory. Her focus is on how caucuses develop and adapt as organizations and on how they interact with the Congress as an organization.

While the book is not without fault—at times stating the obvious and often repeating similar examples in different sections—it makes an important contribution by gathering an incredible wealth of information in one place and putting it in an appropriate context. Particularly cogent is Hammond's discussion of the persistence of the caucuses after the Republicans gained control of the Congress in 1994 and the House passed a resolution eliminating so-called legislative service organizations, the institutional umbrella under which the most prominent caucuses existed. The adaptation of the caucuses demonstrates the point she makes throughout, that they represent an institutional response to needs of the members reacting to a changing environment and that the wide variety seen in the experiences of these caucuses speaks to the principal reason for their adaptability and success, which is that they are more flexible than the formal subunits of the Congress and thus remain capable of meeting members' changing needs for information, for ways to represent their constituents, and for means to coordinate efforts on emerging issues.

L. SANDY MAISEL

Colby College
Waterville
Maine

KEENAN, THOMAS. 1997. *Fables of Responsibility, Aberrations and Predicaments in Ethics and Politics.* Pp. x, 251. Stanford, CA: Stanford University Press. $45.00. Paperbound, $16.95.

Fables concerns important issues surrounding the problem of thinking through political and ethical stances without recourse to universals. It is situated within the lineage of deconstruction, and one must be conversant, even fluent, with those discussions to appreciate the subtlety of the contributions Keenan is making. This carefully written book is cast at such a level of exhilarating abstraction that when, from time to time, it does touch on a recognizable political action, the disproportion between the discursive apparatus and what it is applied to is dizzying.

Fables covers a range of topics, among them fables and paradoxes. The longest essay in the book is on Michel Foucault. It treats the attacks leveled against Foucault for not having a clearly stated and grounded position from which his politics could proceed "responsibly." Keenan undertakes a patient, detailed, and respectful tour through the objections (especially Habermas) and then presents a carefully constructed case for what Foucault's response is or was or should have been. Keenan convincingly shows through multiple citations that most of the negative readings of Foucault's use of such paired terms as "power-knowledge" are misreadings conflating power with

knowledge or knowledge with power. He quotes Foucault's denial of such readings and his frustration at their persistence. Showing what Foucault really meant is harder and always contestable. Keenan's reading is plausible; he emphasizes the "hyphen" in "power-knowledge" as showing the space, discursive in Keenan's reading, opened by that disjunction. For example, Keenan shows Foucault's consistent unwillingness to simply abandon the usage of human rights while he (like Derrida and many others) was devoting so much effort to show their lack of originary foundations and the weaknesses of traditional humanist positions based on them. This paradoxical space, so infuriating to the critics when they even notice it, is carefully presented and defended by Keenan. From this a primordially discursive type of politics is said to flow or be made possible or to be appropriate to contemporary challenges.

Fables comes adorned with the highest praise ("brilliant") from the leading figures in theory, Judith Butler, Guyatri Chakravorty Spivak, and Slavoj Zizak (others are thanked in the acknowledgments). Its cover contains a photo of what appears to be an airline highjacking with the worried face of pilot and gun-toting bearded, dark-complexioned highjacker staring out at the reader. Is this an image from a newspaper or a film? Fact or fiction? Regardless, we are being interpellated.

PAUL RABINOW

University of California
Berkeley

PAGE, BENJAMIN I. 1996. *Who Deliberates? Mass Media in Modern Democracy.* Pp. xii, 167. Chicago: University of Chicago Press. $29.00. Paperbound, $10.95.

The conditions under which public deliberation takes place in our democratic system and the role of the media in this process come under scrutiny in this volume, the first in the series American Politics and Political Economy by the University of Chicago Press.

This book is organized into five chapters: an introduction, three case studies, and a conclusion. The cases are drawn from episodes in the early 1990s, each illustrating some very useful, interesting, and provocative points.

Chapter 2 deals with *New York Times* editorial and op-ed pages leading up to the Persian Gulf war. Page argues provocatively that the *Times*'s editorial opinions were embedded in op-ed page discourse that was carefully crafted to make them appear more balanced and reasonable than they really were.

Chapter 3 examines the controversy touched off by President Bush's spokesman Marlin Fitzwater in 1992 when he said that an important cause of urban problems in the United States, such as the Los Angeles riots in the spring of 1992, was liberal social programs enacted at the federal level during the 1960s and 1970s. Page uses the flurry of media stories about this episode to articulate five characteristics of mediated deliberation in the United States today. These characteristics include the great speed of communication and intertextuality of discourse in which a kind of debate occurs between various media; the central role of officials and other professional communicators; distinctive editorial positions staked out by various media outlets; the tendency of editorial stands to affect news judgments; and the active role of elite media in framing issues and shaping the nature of the debate.

The final case, in chapter 4, examines the role of talk radio in overcoming indifference among both elites and elite journalists to the charges that Clinton attorney general nominee Zoe Baird had hired illegal aliens as domestic workers and had not paid the required Social Security tax on their salaries. A key lesson here, according to Page, is that the media and elite decision makers were out of touch with popular sentiment on this matter in their initial sympathetic portrayals of Baird. The fact that these forces were brought into line through the lead of populist talk-show discourse highly critical of Baird represents a victory for populistic deliberation, Page argues.

Page, who is Gordon Scott Fulcher Professor of Decision Making in the Department of Political Science at Northwestern University, is well known for his work in American politics and public opinion, but, with this book, he emerges as a major original voice in political communication.

GERALD M. KOSICKI

Ohio State University
Columbus

THOMAS, IAN Q. R. 1997. *The Promise of Alliance: NATO and the Political Imagination.* Pp. xii, 304. Lanham, MD: Rowman & Littlefield. $67.50. Paperbound, $24.95.

Since the end of the Cold War, we have had a barrage of rhetoric from the North Atlantic Treaty Organization (NATO) and its supporters, aimed at convincing us that the alliance still has important work to do, even without a great-power enemy. This verbal blitzkrieg led Ian Q. R. Thomas to wonder what role official language might have played in the long-term evolution of the alliance. In his timely book, *The Promise of Alliance*, Thomas surveys the major public statements about the alliance by leaders of the United States, the United Kingdom, France, and Germany and the official declarations of NATO itself, from its beginnings in the late 1940s to the recent debate about enlargement. He traces the rise and decline of such large ideas as "North Atlantic community," "self-help and mutual aid," "interdependence," "partnership," and "stability," as well as (more briefly) military doctrines like "the long haul," "flexible response," and "balanced and collective forces." He demonstrates that the alliance has always been conceived as an expression of community values going well beyond military security. Official declarations often drew upon such basic values to foster alliance cohesion. Rhetorical change sometimes was driven by external stimuli and sometimes by factors internal to the alliance or its members. The collapse of Soviet power and the consequent threat to the alliance's survival generated a rhetoric of transformation centered on peacekeeping in eastern Europe and partnership with the former adversary.

Yet the book is analytically disappointing. It never makes clear why political rhetoric is important and worth studying in its own right. One looks in vain for any sustained general discussion of the purposes and functions of NATO's rhetoric, or of its impact on policies and policymaking. All we are given are occasional hints: the function of rhetoric is to persuade and to "propagate conceptions" of the alliance; rhetoric provides "clues" to explain the alliance's cohesion and longevity; one of its effects is to "constrain policy options." But these assertions go largely unsupported. No distinction is made between rhetoric intended for public consumption and arguments employed in intra-alliance bargaining and decision making. It is left unclear to what extent rhetoric has diverged from reality. Thomas apparently makes no use of theoretical literature from the academic discipline of rhetoric. He seems innocent of recent writings in political science about the independent impact of ideas on foreign policy.

In extenuation, Thomas might very well argue that all one can do analytically with political rhetoric is to trace its variation over time and correlate it with changing events. The book does accomplish this limited task. Moreover, it will stand as a good short history of the alliance itself, rhetoric aside.

GLENN H. SNYDER

University of North Carolina
Chapel Hill

VERTZBERGER, YAACOV Y. I. 1998. *Risk Taking and Decisionmaking: Foreign Military Intervention Decisions.* Pp. xi, 519. Stanford, CA: Stanford University Press. $69.50. Paperbound, $24.95.

What makes a Saddam Hussein, a Mao Zedong, or a Harry Truman "ignore the odds" and risk taking on military opponents who are either larger or more powerful than their own forces, as Hussein did in Iran and Mao and Truman both did in Korea? This question, which involves the notions of deterrence and risk acceptance, has fascinated policy and decision analysts.

Vertzberger, an international relations professor at Israel's Hebrew University, carefully dissects the concept of risk—perceived, actual, and acceptable— in international conflict situations, particularly those involving decisions to intervene militarily in foreign conflicts. He develops theories of both risk "acceptance and aversion" and of intervention decision making, and he "tests" them through five historical cases of "high and low risk" U.S., Soviet, or Israeli decision making. In a sense, his conclusions are that leaders, both groups and individuals, do not ignore odds but define and calculate risks for themselves—risks involving such factors as loss of life, government survival, or control over prized foreign countries or regions—according to alternate projected consequences of action or inaction.

Economists, as well as political scientists such as Bruce Bueno de Mesquita, have closely modeled risk taking according to supposed costs and benefits. Vertzberger, however, seeks to take us inside the decision makers' frames of reference by applying "sociocognitive" reasoning and by testing, albeit subjectively, the importance of culture, personality, and organizational setting. Indeed, he treats risky situations as those in which outcomes are to some degree ambiguous and potentially dangerous or adverse (short of desired goals).

Although it is not entirely clear why Vertzberger seized upon military interventions for analysis, they appear to be nonroutine situations of inherent outcome ambiguity. Leaders are never sure beforehand of what might result if they act or not, but come to estimate outcome probabilities (for example, third-party reactions) based on available information—tainted, of course, by pride (ambition) and prejudice (fear).

The integration of cognitive and decision-making approaches is enlightening, and intervention caveats are useful, but by focusing on the risk concept, overstressing military considerations, obscuring motivation versus rationalization, and studying only cases of intervention (rather than nonintervention or nonmilitary intervention), Vertzberger limits his contributions to intervention theory. Risk assessment is only one component of intervention calculus. Although factors of perceived capability and power balances are important, answers to "Why use force as opposed to other available means?" or "When to negotiate or extricate?" (for example, a Khrushchev versus a Gorbachev) can hinge on definitions of what "the game" itself is all about.

FREDERIC S. PEARSON

Wayne State University
Detroit
Michigan

AFRICA, ASIA, AND LATIN AMERICA

MENDELSON, SARAH E. 1998. *Changing Course: Ideas, Politics, and the Soviet Withdrawal from Afghanistan.* Pp. xiii, 140. Princeton, NJ: Princeton University Press. $35.00.

The war in Afghanistan was a watershed event in recent world history. The Soviet invasion in December 1979 signaled the death of East-West détente and contributed to a sharp rise in international tension. The Soviet withdrawal, completed in February 1989, demonstrated how dramatically Soviet foreign policy had changed under the leadership of Mikhail Gorbachev. His "new thinking," backed by major initiatives, heralded the end of the Cold War.

In this small but important book, Sarah Mendelson explains how the old generation of Soviet leaders, represented by Leonid Brezhnev, made the decision to invade Afghanistan and how Gorbachev and his allies succeeded in getting Soviet troops out. Mendelson was one of the first students of Soviet foreign policy to interview prominent Soviet officials during the Gorbachev period (including the Soviet leader's top foreign policy aides and the former chief of the general staff, Marshal Sergei Akhromeev), and she has combined those interviews with archival documents to put together a persuasive account of Soviet decision making.

Mendelson's book goes beyond a simple description of Soviet policymaking in three respects. First, she addresses an important theoretical debate in the field of international relations over the relative influence of ideas and domestic politics versus international systemic constraints in accounting for changes in countries' foreign policies. She highlights the role of expert communities in promoting new ideas and policies and undermining the resistance from "old thinkers." Second, she engages the related public debate about whether the policies of "peace through strength" pursued by the administrations of Ronald Reagan and George Bush deserve credit for the Soviet withdrawal from Afghanistan. She casts doubt on that claim and is particularly effective in demonstrating that the deployment of the much-vaunted Stinger missiles to the Afghan mujahideen had little impact on Soviet policy (not least because the decision in principle to withdraw had already been taken by the time the weapons appeared and also because their overall impact on Soviet military operations was limited). Third, she puts the changes in Soviet foreign policy in the broader context of the major domestic political and economic transformation whose origins predate Gorbachev's formal assumption of power in 1985. Thus her book serves as a useful introduction to the Gorbachev era as well as a concise account of major Soviet decisions on Afghanistan.

MATTHEW EVANGELISTA

Cornell University
Ithaca
New York

EUROPE

MAGNUS, SHULAMIT S. 1997. *Jewish Emancipation in a German City: Cologne, 1798-1871.* Pp. xiv, 336. Stanford, CA: Stanford University Press. $49.50.

In her masterful treatment of Jewish emancipation in Cologne, Shulamit Magnus has not simply fleshed out the struggle for Jewish civic and political equality on the local level; she has provided a compelling analysis of the forces that first impeded Jewish rights and then ultimately led to Jewish emancipation in nineteenth-century Germany. Based on a close reading of municipal records, and extensive knowledge of local, national, and Jewish issues, Magnus's book convincingly demonstrates the centrality of the Jewish experience to the history of liberalism, municipal politics, and Germany itself. An example of local history at its best, *Jewish Emancipation in a German City* is a revisionist work that all students of Jewish and German history will have to read.

Cologne provides an excellent case study in Jewish emancipation. In the early nineteenth century, city leaders sought to restrict Jewish rights, but by the 1840s, liberals in Cologne were at the forefront of the struggle for Jewish equality in Prussia. Magnus provides an economic explanation for Cologne's early opposition and later support for Jewish rights. After Prussia took over the Rhine province, the economy of Cologne stagnated and its old elite feared an influx of Jewish competitors. By the mid-1830s, capitalist expansion had created a new worldview that welcomed those who contributed to Cologne's economic growth, including the previously detested Jews. Moreover, as the Jews themselves became embedded in new capitalist enterprises, they became more acceptable to the urban elite, who shared with them in building the railroads and insurance companies that led to Cologne's prosperity.

Even if economic considerations remained paramount, Magnus does not reduce history to economics alone. She makes a compelling case that the struggle over Jewish status in Cologne can be understood only within the context of the tension between a city eager to preserve its former autonomy and the expectation of the Prussian state to impose its authority. Moreover, religious demographics played a role as well. The Protestant minority, mindful of past discrimination, supported tolerance; the Catholic majority lived in a Protestant state and preferred the government not to interfere in religious matters.

Magnus has revised many conventional assumptions about Jewish emancipation and integration in Germany. She has convincingly demonstrated that the 1850s and 1860s were not a period of Jewish communal passivity. On the contrary, the Jewish community of Cologne, which did not receive full emancipation until 1871, nevertheless convinced the municipal authorities to accord Judaism parity with other religious denominations by subsidizing the Jewish elementary school. Similarly, the new Moorish-style synagogue, erected in 1861, reflected the Jews' confidence in their distinctiveness even as they announced their firm integration in the urban landscape.

This book is not without some minor faults. Occasionally, Magnus claims to be more revisionist than she actually is, especially on the role of liberalism. She might have provided a bit more background on the course of Jewish emancipation in Prussia for those not well versed in its intricacies. She does not fully explain the absence of religious reform in Cologne. Nevertheless, *Jewish Emancipation in a German City* is an important book, filled with significant insight into the complicated relationship of Germans and Jews in modernity.

MARSHA L. ROZENBLIT

University of Maryland
College Park

UNITED STATES

ANCHETA, ANGELO N. 1998. *Race, Rights, and the Asian American Experience.* Pp. xv, 209. New Brunswick, NJ: Rutgers University Press. $47.00. Paperbound, $18.00.

In America, race is a black-and-white issue, literally and figuratively. However, as Ancheta notes from the very beginning of his book, Asian Americans are neither black nor white, though at various times in our nation's history they have been treated as one or the other. Usually considered blacks, Asian Americans have suffered the same social and legal problems as blacks have: violence, segregation, and discrimination. Being looked upon as whites in more recent years has presented Asian Americans with a set of unique problems, particularly being singled out as a "model minority" with admirable cultural values and enviable educational achievements. As Ancheta shows, the model-minority stereotype has been used to make invidious comparisons with other people of color.

On the occasions when they have been dealt with as Asian Americans, the emphasis has been on the Asian rather than the American part of their identity, a perception that has resulted in such tragedies as the internment of Japanese Americans during World War II. Bearing the burden of being regarded as foreigners in their own country is part and parcel of the Asian American experience.

Using his considerable experience as a community-based lawyer, Ancheta focuses on civil rights laws and their application to Asian Americans to broaden the discussion of race relations in America. At the center of his analysis is the argument that discrimination against Asian Americans is qualitatively different from discrimination against blacks because it is based on citizenship rather than color. By stigmatizing Asian Americans as foreigners, racists have alienated them from the rest of society.

As to be expected in works of this sort, Ancheta begins with a historical overview of discrimination against Asian Americans, reminding us that many of the legal doctrines used against them in the past continue as legal precedents in the present system of jurisprudence. The bulk of the book is devoted to an analysis of the various psychological and social theories that underlay anti-Asian discrimination as well as the legal doctrines and policies that realized it in practice. In the course of his discussion, he evaluates existing civil rights laws as applied to Asian Americans, pointing out their deficiencies. One of the conclusions that Ancheta draws is that, before significant headway can be made against anti-Asian discrimination, people must appreciate the differences between various Asian American ethnic groups as well as the differences between Asian Americans and other people of color.

Ever since the 1960s, activists concerned about race relations have known that the black-white model is simplistic and limited, for it fails to convey the complexity of race relations in America. What makes Ancheta's work important is that it captures that complexity, using the Asian American experience as the main means of doing so. In illuminating the complex nature of anti-Asian discrimination, he has deepened our understanding of race and the unfortunate role it plays in American society. It is only with a deeper understanding of race that the problem of racism in America will ever be solved.

WILLIAM WEI

University of Colorado
Boulder

DeSIPIO, LOUIS and RODOLFO O. DE LA GARZA. 1998. *Making Americans,* *Remaking America: Immigration and Immigrant Policy.* Pp. xii, 156. Boulder, CO: Westview Press. $45.00. Paperbound, $15.95.

This volume, by two well-known and highly respected political scientists, is the latest entry in the Westview Press series Dilemmas in American Politics. Its contents are somewhat narrower than the title suggests (for example, the consequences of immigration and important aspects of immigrant adaptation are neglected), but what this compact volume does it does superbly.

The book's objective is to examine U.S. immigration, naturalization, and settlement policy and to identify the dilemmas the United States has faced as a nation of immigrants that sets as a national ideal the political incorporation of new immigrants. Four such dilemmas are identified. First, how many immigrants should the United States admit and what characteristics should they have? Second, to which immigrants should citizenship be extended and on what terms? Third, how should the state structure the relationship between immigrants and natives in areas such as the rights and privileges to extend to noncitizens or the resources the state should expend to smooth the transition of immigrants into American society? Fourth, which levels of government should be empowered to formulate and supervise immigration, naturalization, and settlement policy?

Each of these dilemmas is addressed in a separate chapter. Along the way, DeSipio and de la Garza make several interesting points. The federal government has generally pursued a more liberal immigration policy than the American public says it wants. With some exceptions, the state has historically taken a relatively neutral stance toward immigrants' political incorporation, leaving to private institutions policies to accelerate the process of immigrant adaptation. Frustrated with the federal government's seeming inability to reduce undocumented immigration, individual states are now attempting to take more control over their immigration destinies. Finally, although the United States has no explicit immigrant or settlement policy, it does have a de facto policy that often consists of extending to immigrants policies and programs designed to help disadvantaged members of America's domestic minority population.

DeSipio and de la Garza rightly point out that more attention has been paid to immigration policy than to policies surrounding naturalization or settlement. In addition, they seem to favor a set of settlement policies designed specifically for immigrants that would speed the transition of immigrants into equal citizens. Because they conclude that the success or failure of the political incorporation of today's immigrants will depend in part on "what the country offers these immigrants once they are here," this reader wishes the authors had seized the opportunity to outline the shape they believe U.S. immigrant policies should take.

THOMAS J. ESPENSHADE

Princeton University
New Jersey

FAUST, DREW GILPIN. 1996. *Mothers of Invention: Women of the Slaveholding South in the American Civil War.* Pp. xvi, 326. Chapel Hill: University of North Carolina Press. $29.95.

This is the first book to broadly consider Confederate women's wartime lives since Mary Massey published *Bonnet Brigades* in 1966. Beautifully written and lavishly illustrated (one photo shows socks knitted by Winchester's Mary Lee out of unraveled tent canvas), it describes the dismantling of familiar race and gender relations in Southern communities between 1861 and 1865. Domestic upheaval obliged planter women to construct new selves, but they did so "to resist change," Faust writes, and "to fashion the new out of as much of the old as could survive in the altered postwar world of defeated Confederates, regional poverty, and black freedom."

Faust attends to the material and spiritual conditions of elite lives in chapters on women's war work, the changed configuration of Confederate households, refugee life, the collision between Confederate women and Yankee men, and narrative representations of the war. With the loss of male protection, Southern women became not only physically but also psychologically vulnerable—a state that encouraged class conflict and undermined sectional solidarity. Like George Rable in *Civil Wars* (1989), Faust observes that Southern institutions attempted to squelch female identity but argues that the literary output of Confederate women evidenced a "bolder claim to a public voice and political identity" than others have credited them with.

Although Faust's subjects are the women of the slaveholding South who were white, we see much of mistress-slave relations and the racism that "white southern women readily embraced." Considering slaves as "enemies" in their households, white women uneasily assumed the management of their human property. The frustrations of this obligation reduced some to brutality; most, however, considered violence a male prerogative and shrank from administering punishment, like Lizzie Neblett of Texas, who called in a neighbor to whip recalcitrants. More intimate contact between slaves and mistresses served only to weaken white women's enthusiasm for the peculiar institution.

Faust maintains that despite the deprivations of wartime, elite women were loath to labor, leaving teaching, government clerkships, and factory work to their social inferiors. Well-to-do widows, who were "outside the structures of direct patriarchal control," seem to have been among the few elite women to engage in hospital and relief work, although the war's presence on Southern turf would suggest their wider participation in relieving human suffering.

Faust's extensive reading in southern archives will help us better understand the paradoxical construction of Southern womanhood in the postwar era. The human face of her achievement will make *Mothers of Invention* a pleasure to academic and nonacademic audiences alike.

JANE E. SCHULTZ

Indiana University-
Purdue University
Indianapolis

KLEHR, HARVEY, JOHN EARL HAYNES, and KYRILL M. ANDERSON. 1998. *The Soviet World of American Communism*. Pp. vii, 378. New Haven, CT: Yale University Press. $35.00.

This book is the sixth volume published in Yale's important Annals of Communism series and the second written by Klehr, Haynes, and a Russian coauthor. Their previous work, *The Secret World of American Communism* (1995), documented the ties between the Communist Party of the USA (CPUSA) and Soviet intelligence and espionage agencies. Here they concentrate on the political relationship between the CPUSA and its parent bodies in Moscow. "Parent" is the operative word, for from its beginnings in 1919 until the fall of the Soviet Union in 1991, the CPUSA was a creature of the Soviets, who provided some of its funds and all of its direction. Moscow chose the American party's leaders and dictated policy to them. When they objected, it was for practical reasons or be-

cause an order could not be carried out. Klehr, Haynes, and Anderson found not a single document in Soviet archives "that show American Communist leaders refusing to carry out Comintern orders as a matter of principle."

Historians have long believed this, but it is the authors' great achievement to have found the smoking guns. Their book contains 95 documents, some excerpted and 11 reproduced in facsimile, that leave no room for doubt as to the slavishness of the CPUSA and its complicity in Stalin's crimes. The most notable of these was its support of the arrest and conviction of several hundred Finnish American Communists who had gone to Soviet Karelia to revitalize its timber industry. Most died in the gulag, as did hundreds of other American Communists who were caught up in Stalin's mad purges.

In addition to proving what had been thought to be true, Klehr, Haynes, and Anderson have come up with some new information. As an instance, they discovered that John L. Lewis, the imperious head of the Congress of Industrial Organizations, had negotiated directly with the CPUSA over the terms of its support in the 1930s. That such an arrangement existed was widely believed at the time, but it was always assumed that Lewis had kept his distance from the Party. Amusingly, American Communists had a debate with Moscow over the question of who had the upper hand in this relationship, the Soviets suspecting correctly that the CPUSA was not the user but the used.

In recent years, a small group of historians has been attempting, at least in part, to rehabilitate the CPUSA. *The Soviet World of American Communism* establishes beyond a doubt the pointlessness of such efforts.

WILLIAM L. O'NEILL

Rutgers University
New Brunswick
New Jersey

SOCIOLOGY

MARSHALL, GORDON. 1997. *Repositioning Class: Social Inequality in Industrialized Society.* Pp. xiii, 236. Thousand Oaks, CA: Sage. $85.00. Paperbound, $26.50.

Gordon Marshall is a leading member of a group of sociologists at Nuffield College, Oxford, with a distinct and important approach to empirical sociological research, especially sociological class analysis. The approach is identified by its methodological sophistication, suspicion of grand theory, and the use of a particular class scheme developed by the senior member of the Nuffield group, John Goldthorpe.

Repositioning Class is a collection of 11 essays, all previously published except for part of the introduction. The volume provides an exceptionally useful presentation of the contributions of the Nuffield approach to macrosociological research and Gordon Marshall's particular contributions. The essays are very well written, the methodology superb, and the arguments cogent and well justified in theory and evidence. They cover a wide range of topics. Specific issues include a treatment of the debate about the unit of class analysis, an issue that has important implications for the treatment of gender in class analysis. It covers cross-national similarities in mobility regimes, comparing Britain to the United States, Scandinavia, and the former Communist countries of Eastern Europe, including the Soviet Union. There are analyses of the impact of class voting and on the development of the particular attitudes that have been identified with the underclass. Finally, Marshall provides a lucid discussion of meritocracy and social justice.

The main conclusion is that class is very important for almost everything and everywhere. Marshall's essays are meant to demonstrate that the Nuffield brand of class analysis is in a very healthy state. Whether this will satisfy those who claim class is dead and replaced by cultural, ethnic, and gender divisions will obviously depend on what is meant by social class. The Nuffield branch of class analysis is clear about this. Class is what is captured by the 11 categories of the Goldthorpe class scheme reflecting divisions by employment relations, market situation, and working conditions. It captures homogeneous categories according to living conditions. It does not, and is not meant to, capture positions in social structure that might generate antagonistic interests, conflict, and social change in the tradition of Marx. Why the Goldthorpe scheme works so well is perhaps not so clear, but Marshall's essays provide abundant evidence for the scheme's empirical usefulness and the important insights class analysis provides into the social structures of industrialized societies.

AAGE B. SØRENSEN

Harvard University
Cambridge
Massachusetts

O'KEEFE, GARRETT J., DENNIS P. ROSENBAUM, PAUL J. LAVRAKAS, KATHALEEN REID, and RENEE A. BOTTA. 1997. *Taking a Bite out of Crime: The Impact of the National Citizens' Crime Prevention Media Campaign.* Pp. vii, 158. Thousand Oaks, CA: Sage. $52.00. Paperbound, $23.95.

Taking a Bite out of Crime presents an evaluation of a nationwide media campaign designed to increase citizen awareness of and responsibility for crime prevention activities. The campaign, whose central figure is a trench-coated dog named McGruff, is called Take a Bite out of Crime. The first chapter of this book describes crime prevention programs in the United States and explores their impact. Chapter 1 also discusses public service advertisements (PSAs) and the factors that make them effective.

Chapter 2 traces the evolution of McGruff, distinguishes between different types of McGruff PSAs, and summarizes previous research on crime prevention programs in general and on McGruff in particular. In addition, the chapter contains examples of McGruff PSAs and an overview of the methodology employed to evaluate the McGruff campaign.

To place the McGruff evaluation in a larger context, chapter 3 examines citizens' general views of crime and crime prevention behaviors. Most people interviewed in the opinion survey by O'Keefe and his colleagues believed that crime prevention was the joint responsibility of citizens and the police. Those interviewed also wanted more information about crime prevention strategies.

Chapters 4 through 6 discuss the specific findings of the national evaluation of McGruff. O'Keefe and his colleagues report that media managers overall rated the campaign's PSAs favorably, particularly for their capacity to increase public awareness of drug and crime prevention issues. Furthermore, the authors report that McGruff was a cost-effective mechanism for increasing citizens' "knowledge [and] perceived responsibility, [evoked] feeling[s] of efficacy, and [encouraged] personal actions with regard to crime prevention."

Chapter 7 provides recommendations for improving anticrime PSAs. The authors emphasize the importance of high production quality and flexibility (for example, campaigns should be responsive to changing trends in crime and crime control policies) and the need to avoid fear-inducing messages. The researchers also stress the benefit of including in PSAs concrete examples and demonstrations of actual crime prevention activities.

Taking a Bite out of Crime is comprehensive and well written. It covers a topic of genuine interest to crime prevention scholars, law enforcement practitioners, and media experts, especially those investigating the media's power to influence people's attitudes and to change their behaviors. The book is sweeping in its appeal and highly informative, yet it is basic enough in its content to engage readers of varying backgrounds and levels of knowledge about media and crime prevention research.

ARTHUR J. LURIGIO

Loyola University
Chicago
Illinois

ROSENZWEIG, ROBERT M. 1998. *The Political University: Policy, Politics, and Presidential Leadership in the American Research University.* Pp. xvii, 201. Baltimore, MD: Johns Hopkins University Press. $31.95.

The Political University falls into two parts. The first half is essentially a personal memoir—although highly analytical—of author Robert Rosenzweig's tenure from 1983 to 1993 as president of the Association of American Universities (AAU). The second half ponders the internal governance of universities largely from a presidential perspective. The distinctive treatment of both topics arises from the engagement and insight of the author. Rosenzweig combines unabashed admiration for American research universities, honesty about their real-world shortcomings, keen appreciation for academic quality, and apprehension bordering on congenital pessimism about looming threats to their continued effectiveness.

As the chief national voice for research universities, the AAU had to deal with a steady erosion of the stature of these institutions in Washington. Universities came to be regarded as just another interest group—fair game for one-sided attacks by self-promoting politicians. With characteristic irony, Rosenzweig recognizes how his role as a lobbyist drew universities more deeply into these political waters. He is especially adept at portraying the clash of cultures as, for example, when the AAU vainly championed academic peer review against the congressional prerogative of earmarking porkbarrel appropriations for home districts.

In the chapters treating internal governance, Rosenzweig's own analysis has been enriched with the views of 16 current and former university presidents, whom he convened for a daylong symposium. Although these chapters are punctuated by lengthy quotations from the meeting, the reader is left with the impression that the collective knowledge of the university presidency must have greatly exceeded the scope allotted to it in this book. The general view conveyed is of the precarious nature of presidential leadership. Faculty constitute much of the problem, being crucial to the success of any institutional initiative yet largely preoccupied with their own intellectual and professional interests.

The critical lens with which Rosenzweig examines the university is the source of the originality and occasionally the weakness of this volume. At times, it leads the author to depict situations in far more dire terms than are ultimately warranted, but it also precludes any simple admonitions or formulas. He perceives the political process within and around universities as messy, complex,

and often contradictory—much like reality itself. Perhaps that is reason enough for anyone concerned with the leadership and fate of these institutions to read *The Political University*.

ROGER GEIGER

Pennsylvania State University
University Park

YOON, IN-JIN. 1997. *On My Own: Korean Businesses and Race Relations in America*. Pp. 256. Chicago: University of Chicago Press. $45.00. Paperbound, $17.95.

In-Jin Yoon's *On My Own* makes an important contribution to the growing literature on Korean American entrepreneurs. While Yoon takes the familiar template of transpacific immigration, immigrant settlement, ethnic solidarity, and interracial conflict to examine Korean American small businesses, his work advances the discussion on two important fronts. First, the narrative of Yoon's book is driven by the theoretical debates within the existing literature on Korean American entrepreneurs. He effectively marshals his rigorous use of aggregate and survey data to engage the previous research on the topic. In particular, he uses his own revealing and fascinating survey data from Chicago and Los Angeles to advance the theoretical discussion on several fronts, including a longitudinal examination of Korean immigrant economic adaptation. His analysis powerfully demonstrates why ethnic entrepreneurship has become such a compelling choice for middle-class Korean Americans who seek to reproduce their class position in the limited opportunity structure of the U.S. labor market.

Second, Yoon's book expands the narrow "black-Korean conflict" framework in understanding the social impact of Korean American entrepreneurs. Yoon includes in his analysis the role of Latinos in the Korean American entrepreneurial experience as employees, neighborhood residents, and potential economic competitors. His analysis of why the Korean American relationship with African Americans has been marked by overt conflict while the relationship with Latinos has not provides an interesting and insightful discussion on the role of nativity and uneven levels of political mobilization in shaping race relations. While his engagement with the existing theoretical debates and an expansive approach to the social impact of Korean American entrepreneurs represent the strength of the book, Yoon's insistence that all of the major features of Korean American social life can be examined through the lens of entrepreneurship represents its weakness. While Korean American entrepreneurs represent a sizable portion of the community (24.3 percent in 1990), the community itself is tremendously diverse and many facets of it cannot be understood exclusively through the activities of entrepreneurs alone. The fixation on entrepreneurs leaves other areas of Korean American community life—such as the demand for more equitable distribution of social services and political representation—largely untouched. This is especially unfortunate since in these other areas of urban life, Korean Americans have much in common with African Americans and Latinos, providing grounds for interracial cooperation and coalition building. Nonetheless, Yoon has made an invaluable contribution to a more critical understanding of Korean American entrepreneurs.

EDWARD J. W. PARK

University of Southern California
Los Angeles

ECONOMICS

LANDES, DAVID S. 1998. *The Wealth and Poverty of Nations: Why Some Are So Rich and Some So Poor.* Pp. xxi, 650. New York: Norton. $30.00.

Here at last is an excellent presentation of world history on a grand scale, free of the Marxist and anti-Western frameworks that have distorted our understanding in the past three decades. Here, also, is an economic history of the modern world that manages to retain the anecdotal, little details that make the reading of good history so enjoyable for both specialists and a wider intellectual public. Very few historians or economists, if any, can match David Landes's deep learning, balanced judgment, wit, and clarity.

The central thesis, backed by mountains of convincing evidence, is clear. Western Europe, eventually led by the Netherlands and Britain, created the modern world of rapid economic growth and perpetual technological advance. This was because of markets that were somewhat freer and political systems that were more tolerant, more concerned with individual freedom, and less stifling than in most of the rest of the civilized world. This combination resulted in a greater respect for property rights, a more open mind toward innovation and scientific advances, and a greater willingness to accept commercial success as a measure of social worth.

This is not a new thesis, but the popularity of "world system" or "dependency" theories of economic development, combined with the constant denigration of anything Western, has obscured the essential aspects of the economic rise of the West. So, aside from economists, most of whom have never been fooled by either Marxism or political correctness, few scholars in either the social sciences or the humanities now understand why and how our contemporary world has been shaped. The economists, for all their theoretical sophistication, rarely know as much history as they should, particularly detailed cultural history. Nor can many communicate, as can Landes, with a broader public. With this magnificent book at hand, perhaps this ignorance will begin to be rolled back.

Let us not forget that such issues are not merely matters of scholarship. Important public policies have been made on the basis of theories of economic development, and to have picked the wrong ones, as did the Communists and many anti-Western nationalists, has led to many disasters. Landes shows that today, as in the past, those societies that are relatively more tolerant, more democratic, more respectful of individual rights, and more devoted to the pursuit of science and profits will do better. There are no other magic development potions. But acceptance of Western liberal (one could say Enlightenment) ideals cannot come overnight. Many religious, political, and philosophical traditions reject them, and, so, the world will continue for a long time to come to be one with both rich societies that are getting richer and poor ones that are falling further behind. At least now we can direct students and friends to a book that explains why this is so.

DANIEL CHIROT

University of Washington
Seattle

OTHER BOOKS

AGH, ATTILA. 1998. *The Politics of Central Europe*. Pp. ix, 244. Thousand Oaks, CA: Sage. Paperbound, $24.95.

ANDERSON, CHRISTOPHER J. and CARSTEN ZELLE. 1998. *Stability and Change in German Elections: How Electorates Merge, Converge, or Collide*. Pp. xii, 361. Westport, CT: Praeger. $69.50.

ARCHIBUGI, DANIELE, DAVID HELD, and MARTIN KOHLER, eds. 1998. *Re-imagining Political Community: Studies in Cosmopolitan Democracy*. Pp. xiii, 352. Stanford, CA: Stanford University Press. $60.00. Paperbound, $22.95.

ARON, RAYMOND. 1999. *Main Currents in Sociological Thought*. Vol. 2, *Durkheim, Pareto, Weber*. Pp. xxi, 346. New Brunswick, NJ: Transaction. Paperbound, no price.

ATHREYA, VENKATESH B. and SHEELA RANI CHUNKATH. 1996. *Literacy and Empowerment*. Pp. 299. New Delhi: Sage. $38.00.

BARDI, LUCIANO and MARTIN RHODES, eds. 1998. *Italian Politics: Mapping the Future*. Pp. 298. Boulder, CO: Westview Press. $65.00.

BAUMAN, ZYGMUNT. 1998. *Globalization: The Human Consequences*. Pp. vi, 136. New York: Columbia University Press. $24.50.

BENNET, TONY. 1998. *Culture: A Reformer's Science*. Pp. ix, 262. Thousand Oaks, CA: Sage. Paperbound, $24.95.

BOURKE, PAUL and DONALD DeBATS. 1995. *Washington County: Politics and Community in Antebellum America*. Pp. xvii, 407. Baltimore, MD: Johns Hopkins University Press. $45.00.

CATTO, HENRY E., JR. 1998. *Ambassadors at Sea: The High and Low Adventures of a Diplomat*. Pp. x, 396. Austin: University of Texas Press. No price.

CHEHABI, H. E. and JUAN J. LINZ, eds. 1998. *Sultanistic Regimes*. Pp. x, 284. Baltimore, MD: Johns Hopkins University Press. $48.00. Paperbound, $16.95.

DALLMAYR, FRED and G. N. DEVY, eds. 1998. *Between Tradition and Modernity: India's Search for Identity* Pp. 374. Walnut Creek, CA: Altamira Press. $49.95. Paperbound, $24.95.

DASIN, JOAN. 1998. *Torture in Brazil: A Shocking Report on the Pervasive Use of Torture by Brazilian Military Governments, 1964-1979*. Pp. xxviii, 238. Austin: University of Texas Press. Paperbound, $15.95.

DIAMOND, LARRY and MARC F. PLATTNER, eds. 1998. *Democracy in East Asia*. Pp. xxvii, 243. Baltimore, MD: Johns Hopkins University Press. $38.50. Paperbound, $14.95.

DOMBROWSKI, PETER. 1996. *Policy Responses to the Globalization of American Banking*. Pp. vii, 247. Pittsburgh, PA: University of Pittsburgh Press. $34.95.

DUBLIN, THOMAS. 1998. *When the Mines Closed: Stories of Struggles in Hard Times*. Pp. xii, 257. Ithaca, NY: Cornell University Press. $55.00. Paperbound, $16.95.

ELAZAR, DANIEL J. 1998. *Constitutionalizing Globalization: The Postmodern Revival of Confederal Arrangements*. Pp. vii, 250. Lanham, MD: Rowman & Littlefield. $63.00. Paperbound, $23.95.

ELLIS, RICHARD J., ed. 1998. *Speaking to the People: The Rhetorical Presidency in Historical Perspective*. Pp. viii, 283. Amherst: University of Massachusetts Press. $45.00. Paperbound, $16.95.

EPP, CHARLES R. 1998. *The Rights of Revolution: Lawyers, Activists, and Supreme Courts in Comparative Perspective*. Pp. xv, 326. Chicago: University of Chicago Press. Paperbound, no price.

FALCOFF, MARK. 1998. *A Culture of Its Own: Taking Latin America Seriously*. Pp. 337. New Brunswick, NJ: Transaction. $32.95.

FEDERSPIEL, HOWARD M. 1998. *Indonesia in Transition: Muslim Intellectuals and National Development*. Pp. 244. Commack, NY: Nova Science. Paperbound, $27.00.

FLOCKHART, TRINE, ed. 1998. *From Vision to Reality: Implementing Europe's New Security Order*. Pp. xiv, 228. Boulder, CO: Westview Press. $65.00.

FORAN, JOHN, ed. 1997. *Theorizing Revolutions*. Pp. x, 300. New York: Routledge. $80.00. Paperbound, $24.99.

FREEDMAN, JEAN R. 1999. *Whistling in the Dark: Memory and Culture in Wartime London*. Pp. xiii, 230. Lexington: University Press of Kentucky. $29.95.

FROST, CHRISTOPHER and REBECCA BELL-METERAU. 1998. *Simone Weil: On Politics, Religion and Society*. Pp. xii, 129. Thousand Oaks, CA: Sage. Paperbound, $24.95.

GAO, GE and STELLA TING-TOOMEY. 1998. *Communicating Effectively with the Chinese*. Pp. ix, 109. Thousand Oaks, CA: Sage. Paperbound, no price.

GAY, PETER. 1998. *My German Question: Growing Up in Nazi Berlin*. Pp. xii, 208. New Haven, CT: Yale University Press. $22.50.

GEORGE, STEPHEN. 1998. *An Awkward Partner: Britain in the European Community*. 3d ed. Pp. x, 298. New York: Oxford University Press. $67.00. Paperbound, $24.95.

GIES, FRANCES and JOSEPH GIES. 1998. *A Medieval Family: The Pastons of Fifteenth-Century England*. Pp. xiii, 392. New York: HarperCollins. $25.00.

GIUGNI, MARCO G., DOUG McADAM, and CHARLES TILLY, eds. 1998. *From Contention to Democracy*. Pp. xxvi, 285. Lanham, MD: Rowman & Littlefield. $60.00. Paperbound, $25.95.

GOLDSTENE, PAUL N. 1998. *The Collapse of Liberal Empire*. 2d ed. Pp. xxi, 138. Novato, CA: Chandler & Sharp. $24.95. Paperbound, $12.95.

GRAY, HERMAN. 1995. *Watching Race: Television and the Struggle for "Blackness."* Pp. xii, 201. Minneapolis: University of Minnesota Press. $22.95.

GRIFFIN, ROGER, ed. 1998. *International Fascism: Theories, Causes and the New Consensus*. Pp. xv, 334. New York: Oxford University Press. $60.00. Paperbound, $19.95.

GULLAN, HAROLD I. 1998. *The Upset That Wasn't: Harry S. Truman and the Crucial Election of 1948*. Pp. xii, 241. Chicago: Ivan R. Dee. $24.95.

HARBOUR, FRANCES V. 1998. *Thinking About International Ethics: Moral Theory and Cases from American Foreign Policy*. Pp. xi, 212. Boulder, CO: Westview Press. $55.00. Paperbound, $18.00.

HEYMAN, JOSIAH McC. 1998. *Finding a Moral Heart for United States Immigration Policy: An Anthropological Perspective*. Pp. vii, 120. Arlington, VA: American Anthropological Association. Paperbound, no price.

HOFFMANN, EDWARD, ed. 1996. *Future Visions: The Unpublished Papers of Abraham Maslow*. Pp. xviii, 220. Thousand Oaks, CA: Sage. $42.00. Paperbound, $19.95.

JAIN, ANRUDH, ed. 1998. *Do Population Policies Matter? Fertility and Politics in Egypt, India, Kenya, and Mexico*. Pp. xix, 202. New York: Population Council. Paperbound, $14.95.

JEFFREYS-JONES, RHODRI. 1998. *The CIA and American Democracy*. Pp. xii, 340. New Haven, CT: Yale University Press. Paperbound, $18.00.

JOPPKE, CHRISTIAN, ed. 1998. *Challenge to the Nation-State: Immigration in Western Europe and the United*

States. Pp. xi, 360. New York: Oxford University Press. $75.00.

KALMAN, LAURA. 1996. *The Strange Career of Legal Liberalism.* Pp. viii, 375. New Haven, CT: Yale University Press. $40.00.

KATZMANN, ROBERT A., ed. 1998. *Daniel Patrick Moynihan: The Intellectual in Public Life.* Pp. xv, 224. Baltimore, MD: Johns Hopkins University Press. $24.95.

KAVANAGH, DENNIS. 1998. *The Reordering of British Politics: Politics After Thatcher.* Pp. viii, 265. New York: Oxford University Press. $65.00. Paperbound, $19.95.

KING, RICHARD H. 1996. *Civil Rights and the Idea of Freedom.* Pp. xvi, 269. Athens: University of Georgia Press. Paperbound, no price.

KUMAR, ANIL. 1998. *Medicine and the Raj: British Medical Policy in India, 1835-1911.* Pp. 246. Walnut Creek, CA: Altamira Press. $39.95.

KURIEN, C. T. 1996. *Rethinking Economics: Reflections Based on a Study of the Indian Economy.* Pp. 272. New Delhi: Sage. $32.00.

KYTLE, CALVIN and JAMES A MACKAY. 1998. *Who Runs Georgia?* Pp. xxvii, 296. Athens: University of Georgia Press. Paperbound, no price.

MAGNAGHI, RUSSELL M. 1998. *Herbert E. Bolton and the Historiography of the Americas.* Pp. xvi, 211. Westport, CT: Greenwood Press. $59.95.

McCUBBIN, HAMILTON I., ELIZABETH A. THOMPSON, ANNE I. THOMPSON, and JULIE E. FROMER, eds. 1998. *Resiliency in Native American and Immigrant Families.* Pp. xviii, 454. Thousand Oaks, CA: Sage. $67.50. Paperbound, $33.95.

MESSING, KAREN. 1998. *One-Eyed Science: Occupational Health and Women Workers.* Pp. xx, 244. Philadelphia: Temple University Press. Paperbound, no price.

MINERS, NORMAN. 1998. *The Government and Politics of Hong Kong.* 5th ed. Pp. xvi, 340. New York: Oxford University Press. Paperbound, $19.95.

MISRA, RAJENDRA K., MEENA K. KHARKWAL, MAURITA A. KILROY, and KOMILLA THAPA. 1996. *Rorschach Test: Theory and Practice.* Pp. 290. New Delhi: Sage. $32.00.

NAJITA, TETSUO, ed. 1998. *Tokugawa Political Writings.* Pp. lxxiii, 156. New York: Cambridge University Press. $59.95. Paperbound, $18.95.

NIPPERT-ENG, CHRISTENA E. 1996. *Home and Work.* Pp. xviii, 325. Chicago: University of Chicago Press. $48.00. Paperbound, $16.95.

OJO, BAMIDELE A., ed. 1998. *Nigeria's Third Republic: The Problems and Prospects of Political Transition to Civil Rule.* Pp. xiii, 174. Commack, NY: Nova Science. $49.00.

PATTATUCCI, ANGELA M., ed. 1998. *Women in Science: Meeting Career Challenges.* Pp. xiv, 304. Thousand Oaks, CA: Sage. Paperbound, $24.50.

PAYNE, JAMES L. 1998. *Overcoming Welfare: Expecting More from the Poor and from Ourselves.* Pp. xii, 243. New York: Basic Books. $26.50.

PURUSHOTHAMAN, SANGEETHA. 1998. *The Empowerment of Women in India: Grassroots Women's Networks and the State.* Pp. 384. New Delhi: Sage. $38.00.

RASOR, EUGENE L. 1998. *Arthur James Balfour, 1848-1930: Historiography and Annotated Bibliography.* Pp. xvi, 121. Westport, CT: Greenwood Press. $65.00.

RICHARDSON, MICHAEL, ed. 1998. *Georges Bataille: Essential Writings.* Pp. xiv, 228. Thousand Oaks, CA: Sage. Paperbound, $26.50.

ROELOFS, H. MARK. 1998. *The Poverty of American Politics: A Theoretical Interpretation.* 2d ed. Pp. xxiv, 310.

Philadelphia: Temple University Press. Paperbound, no price.

SEIDLER, VICTOR JELENIEWSKI. 1997. *Man Enough: Embodying Masculinities.* Pp. xiv, 236. Thousand Oaks, CA: Sage. $79.95. Paperbound, $32.00.

SHERWIN, SUSAN. 1998. *The Politics of Women's Health: Exploring Agency and Autonomy.* Pp. viii, 321. Philadelphia: Temple University Press. Paperbound, no price.

SHOGAN, ROBERT. 1998. *The Double-Edged Sword: How Character Makes and Ruins Presidents, from Washington to Clinton.* Pp. xii, 284. Boulder, CO: Westview Press. $25.00.

SINCLAIR, BARBARA. 1995. *Legislators, Leaders, and Lawmaking: The United States House of Representatives in the Postreform Era.* Pp. xiv, 329. Baltimore, MD: Johns Hopkins University Press. $39.95.

SISK, TIMOTHY D. and ANDREW REYNOLDS, eds. 1998. *Elections and Conflict Management in Africa.* Pp. viii, 224. Washington, DC: United States Institute of Peace. Paperbound, $14.95.

SKRENTNY, JOHN DAVID. 1996. *The Ironies of Affirmative Action: Politics, Culture, and Justice in America.* Pp. xiii, 312. Chicago: University of Chicago Press. Paperbound, $16.95.

STERNBERG, ROBERT J. and LOUISE SPEAR-SWERLING, eds. 1998. *Perspectives on Learning Disabilities: Biological, Cognitive, Contextual.* Pp. xvi, 296. Boulder, CO: Westview Press. $69.00.

SWEENEY, RICHARD J., CLAS G. WIHLBORG, and THOMAS D. WILLETT, eds. 1998. *Exchange-Rate Policies for Emerging Market Economies.* Pp. x, 391. Boulder, CO: Westview Press. $70.00.

TESON, FERNANDO R. 1998. *A Philosophy of International Law.* Pp. viii, 196. Boulder, CO: Westview Press. $52.00. Paperbound, $25.00.

THOMPSON, LAWRENCE. 1998. *Older and Wiser: The Economics of Public Pensions.* Pp. xviii, 175. Lanham, MD: Urban Institute Press. $59.50. Paperbound, $23.95.

UBEROI, PATRICIA, ed. 1996. *Social Reform, Sexuality and the State.* Pp. xxvi, 404. New Delhi: Sage. $45.00.

VAN BEEK, STEPHEN D. 1995. *Post-Passage Politics: Bicameral Resolution in Congress.* Pp. xi, 227. Pittsburgh, PA: University of Pittsburgh Press. $49.95.

VELODY, IRVING and ROBIN WILLIAMS, eds. 1998. *The Politics of Constructionism.* Pp. ix, 241. Thousand Oaks, CA: Sage. Paperbound, $27.95.

VOET, RIAN. 1998. *Feminism and Citizenship.* Pp. ix, 182. Thousand Oaks, CA: Sage. Paperbound, $22.95.

VOSKRESSENSKI, ALEXEI D. 1998. *Russia, China and Eurasia: A Bibliographic Profile of Selected International Literature.* Pp. x, 209. Commack, NY: Nova Science. $59.00.

WELLS, MIRIAM J. 1996. *Strawberry Fields: Politics, Class, and Work in California Agriculture.* Pp. xxv, 339. Ithaca, NY: Cornell University Press. $45.00. Paperbound, $18.95.

WINOCK, MICHEL. 1998. *Nationalism, Anti-Semitism, and Fascism in France.* Pp. vi, 351. Stanford, CA: Stanford University Press. $55.00.

WOODALL, BRIAN. 1996. *Japan Under Construction: Corruption, Politics, and Public Works.* Pp. xiii, 214. Berkeley: University of California Press. No price.

XIN, JIANFEI. 1998. *Mao Zedong's World View: From Youth to Yanan.* Pp. xxi, 220. Lanham, MD: University Press of America. $39.00.

INDEX

Reliable

Confidence in knowing. It's important to feel secure about your insurance coverage. Now you can. AAPSS carefully selects experienced providers with the financial stability to ensure competitive insurance options for its members.

Take advantage of one of your best membership benefits. Affordable coverage. Reliable providers. Portable benefits. **Call 800 424-9883, or in Washington, DC 202 457-6820,** to speak to a customer service representative. Because you want an insurance plan you can count on.

GROUP INSURANCE FOR AAPSS MEMBERS
Cancer Expense • Catastrophe Major Medical Dental Plan • High Limit Accident • Medicare Supplement • Member Assistance • Term Life

Child Maltreatment
Volume 1, Number 2 /
May 1996
Volume 1, Number 3 /
August 1996
Single issue: Individual $19 /
Institution $55

Special Sections of
Child Maltreatment

Child Interviewing, Part I & II

Editors
Kathleen Coulborn Faller, Ph.D.
University of Michigan
Mark D. Everson, Ph.D.
University of North Carolina

The articles in the Special Sections focus on the two targets of controversy in cases in which child interviews are central to establishing the likelihood of sexual abuse: the interviewers of children and the children who are interviewed.

Part 1
Interviewing Children Who May Have Been Abused: A Historical Perspective and Overview of Controversies / Concerning Practices of Interviewers Using Anatomical Dolls in Child Protective Services Investigations / Findings From Research on Children's Suggestibility and Implications for Conducting Child Interviews / Improving Children's Person Identification

Part 2
A Model for Conducting Forensic Interviews With Child Victims of Abuse / Helping Children Tell What Happened / Taint Hearings to Attack Investigative Interviews: A Further Assault on Children's Credibility / Suggestions for Improving Interviews in Child Protection Agencies / Do Investigative Interviewers Follow Guidelines Based on Memory Research?

Order Today!
Phone: 805-499-9774 • Fax: 805-499-0871
E-mail: order@sagepub.com

SAGE PUBLICATIONS, INC.
2455 Teller Road
Thousand Oaks, CA 91320

SAGE PUBLICATIONS LTD
6 Bonhill Street
London EC2A 4PU, England

SAGE PUBLICATIONS INDIA PVT. LTD
M-32 Market, Greater Kailash I
New Delhi 110 048, India

CRIMINAL
JUSTICE
and
BEHAVIOR
An International Journal

Criminal Justice and Behavior
Volume 26, Number 1 /
March 1999
*Single issue rates: Individual
$17 / Institution $62*

A Special Issue of
Criminal Justice and Behavior

Psychological Assessment in Forensic Settings

Editor:
Dr. Curt R. Bartol,
Castleton State College

Contents

ORDER TODAY!
Phone: 805-499-9774 • Fax: 805-499-0871
E-mail: order@sagepub.com

SAGE PUBLICATIONS, INC.
2455 Teller Road
Thousand Oaks, CA 91320

SAGE PUBLICATIONS LTD
6 Bonhill Street
London EC2A 4PU, England

SAGE PUBLICATIONS INDIA PVT. LTD
M-32 Market, Greater Kailash I
New Delhi 110 048, India

A Special Issue of
Crime & Delinquency

Juveniles in Custody

Editors
James C. Howell and Barry Krisberg

"This special issue of Crime & Delinquency reports the end of a chapter: the nationwide collection of individual-linked data on the movement of juveniles through state correctional systems It features several articles that demonstrate the value of reliable data on confinement and for evaluation of policies and programs. . . . Three of the articles in the special issue employ data from the CIC data series—long the only source of national data on confined juveniles. . . . The final article in this volume reports on public attitudes toward pending federal legislation on juvenile justice." —*Editors*

Contents

Robert E. DeComo
Estimating The Prevalence of Juvenile Custody by Race and Gender

Kelly Dedel
National Profile of the Organization of State Juvenile Corrections Systems

Bradford Smith
Children in Custody: 20-Year Trends in Juvenile Detention, Correctional, and Shelter Facilities

Madeline Wordes and Sharon M. Jones
Trends in Juvenile Detention and Steps Toward Reform

Leslie Acoca
Outside/Inside: The Violation of American Girls at Home, on the Streets, and in the Juvenile Justice System

Vincent Schiraldi and Mark Soler
The Will of the People? The Public's Opinion of the Violent and Repeat Juvenile Offender Act of 1997

Crime & Delinquency
Volume 44, Number 4 /
October 1998
Single issue: Individual $19 /
Institution $72

Order Today!
Phone: 805-499-9774 • Fax: 805-499-0871
E-mail: order@sagepub.com

SAGE PUBLICATIONS, INC.
2455 Teller Road
Thousand Oaks, CA 91320

SAGE PUBLICATIONS LTD
6 Bonhill Street
London EC2A 4PU, England

SAGE PUBLICATIONS INDIA PVT. LTD
M-32 Market, Greater Kailash I
New Delhi 110 048, India